THUNDER AND LIGHTNING

THUNDER AND LIGHTNING

The RAF in the Gulf: personal experiences of war

Charles Allen

Foreword by
General Sir Peter de la Billière

WARNER BOOKS

A *Warner* Book

First published in 1991 by HMSO

This edition published by Warner in 1994
Reprinted 1995

Crown copyright © 1991

The moral right of the author has been asserted.

Edited by Charles Allen with Peter Cornish
Designed by: Raymond Mack

A CIP catalogue record for this book
is available from the British Library.

ISBN 0 7515 1130 7

Typeset by Hewer Text Composition Services, Edinburgh
Printed and bound in Great Britain by Clays Ltd, St Ives plc

Warner Books
A Division of
Little, Brown and Company (UK)
Brettenham House
Lancaster Place
London WC2E 7EN

CONTENTS

IN MEMORIAM

Flt Lt Keith Collister, aged 26,
54 Sqn,
killed in training, Oman, 13 November 1990

Flt Lt Kieran Duffy, aged 26,
14 Sqn,
killed in training, Saudi Arabia, 13 January 1991

Flt Lt Norman Dent, aged 28,
14 Sqn,
killed in training, Saudi Arabia, 13 January 1991

Wg Cdr Nigel Elsdon, aged 42,
27 Sqn,
killed in action, Iraq, 18 January 1991

Flt Lt Max Collier, aged 39,
27 Sqn,
killed in action, Iraq, 18 January 1991

Sqn Ldr Garry Lennox, aged 34,
16 Sqn,
killed in action, Iraq, 22 January 1991

Sqn Ldr Kevin Weeks, aged 38,
16 Sqn,
killed in action, Iraq, 22 January 1991

Flt Lt Stephen Hicks, aged 29,
XV Sqn,
killed in action, Iraq, 14 February 1991

'You must be the thunder and lightning of Operation Desert Storm. May God be with you.'

General Norman Schwarzkopf
Supreme Allied Commander Gulf

PREFACE TO THE PAPERBACK EDITION

The 150 interviews that went into the making of *Thunder and Lighting* were recorded within weeks of the ending of the Gulf War. They had all the virtues of immediacy and of fresh experience but they were only first impressions. And of course it really did seem then that Saddam Hussein's deeply unpleasant regime had been given a hammering from which it could not possibly recover. Now we know better.

There were also things left unrecorded – political as well as military – which are still best left unsaid for the time being, at least until the situation in Iraq has resolved itself. But in one respect, we can now fill in some of the gaps.

General Sir Peter de la Billière has revealed the part played by our special forces in denying 'Scud Alley', the central corridor of Western Iraq, to Scud missile launchers – which had major political consequences by making it impossible for the Iraqis to continue to launch missiles on Tel Aviv. Operating from a forward holding base in the desert 900 kilometres north-west of Riyadh, some 300 officers and troopers of A, B and D Sabre Squadrons of 22 Regiment SAS, plus volunteers from reserve R Squadron, joined forces with units of the Special Boat Squadron (SBS) to mount reconnaissance missions and raids that took them deep into Iraqi territory.

They were supported throughout by the RAF's Special Forces Flight, whose Chinooks inserted their patrols together with their Pink Panthers, Dinkies and Unimog vehicles – and returned to lift them out again, as required. The first of these low-level insertions took place on the night of 23 January, when two Chinooks set down an SBS raiding party beside the main road to Basra less than 60 kilometres south of Baghdad. While the pilots kept their engines running, a stretch of the underground communications network linking Baghdad with southern Iraq was uncovered and wired with explosive charges set on timers.

Many other night forays into enemy territory followed, with pilots initially flying 'on the deck' by the light of the moon and then, in the very last stage of the war, with the aid of night-vision goggles. This low-level nightflying often involved the Chinook's Air Loadmasters hanging out of the underside of the aircraft, front and back, and giving the pilot a running commentary on how far off the desert floor they were flying. A further enhancement came with the addition to the Chinook's crew of a gunner on the side door armed with a light machine gun – although in the event his main role turned out to be the guarding of prisoners.

Four members of the SAS died behind enemy lines and four were captured and tortured. Fortunately, there were no casualties among the RAF aircrew who supported them – although one Chinook lost its guidance systems and was lucky to make it back to base after the downdraft of its two rotors set off a landmine as it came in to land.

This is only part of the story of the war in Scud Alley, but it fully deserves to take its place alongside the many acts of courage recounted in these pages.

Charles Allen, December 1994

PREFACE TO THE FIRST EDITION

An author who sought the advice of the Duke of Wellington in writing an account of the battle of Waterloo was told to forget it, for 'you may depend upon it that you will never make it a satisfactory work'.

The same advice applies today. Nothing written at second-hand can hope to capture the atmosphere surrounding a major military campaign – whether it be in the wheatfields of Belgium or the desert wastes of Arabia. Only those who were there know what it was really like.

What follows is an account of the part played in the Gulf War by serving members of the Royal Air Force. It tells only part of the story and it is in no sense an official history – but it has the merit of direct experience. This is the story of that extraordinary war as seen through the eyes of those who were there.

What the planners of the Ministry of Defence named 'Operation Granby' and the Americans termed initially 'Desert Shield' and then 'Desert Storm' involved nearly every one of the 89,000 serving members of the Royal Air Force to some degree, as well as members of the Royal Auxiliary Air Force, the RAF Volunteer Reserve and even RAF Cadets. The total numbers of RAF airmen and airwomen who actually served out in the Gulf, either during the period of tension following Iraq's invasion of Kuwait in August 1990 or through the 43 days of the war itself, probably amounted to about 7,000 personnel. What made their participation so effective was the back-up they received from their colleagues back home based at Strike Command 'flying' stations, Support Command stations and various headquarters posts and offices. Those who stayed behind also did their bit and it is right that their voices should be heard among the more than 150 men and women whose experiences and thoughts are brought together in this book.

These 150 represent a cross-section of the RAF experience of the Gulf War. But there are a number of omissions. The RAF's Special Forces Flight is not represented here for the very good reason that the success of its work rests on surprise and secrecy. What is no secret is that its helicopters and aircrews played a vital role in the support of British and allied special forces operating in hostile territory throughout the period of hostilities. Nor is it possible for reasons of security to go into some details of the strategic air campaign. A third significant omission is due to the fact that large numbers of Chinook, Puma and Hercules aircrews – chiefly from RAF Odiham, RAF Gütersloh and RAF Brize Norton – together with all the 'loadies', 'sooties', 'squippers' and ground crews that support them, continue, at the time of writing, to be heavily involved in Operation Safe Haven along the northern borders of Iraq. For them – as for many RAF personnel still on detachment in the Gulf – the last chapter of Granby has still to be written.

This account of the war could not have been written without the enthusiastic support of many RAF personnel of all ranks, drawn from many stations. Our thanks, firstly, to all those who contributed directly to this book by allowing myself and my colleagues at the Central Office of Information to interview them and who loaned us photographs from their personal albums. They spoke to us freely and frankly – and perhaps not always accurately. In the 'fog of war' assumptions are easily made, misleading impressions inevitable. Although serving members of HM Armed Forces, their views as given here are their own and should not be taken to represent Ministry of Defence thinking.

PREFACE TO THE FIRST EDITION

There were many others who 'volunteered' for interview but whom we were unable to include. Our thanks to them, too, and to all the station personnel who helped us in our researches, arranged our visits and made us welcome on their stations and in their messes. Similarly, our grateful acknowledgement of the kind assistance given by DPR (RAF) and his staff at the Ministry of Defence in allowing us to interview RAF personnel and publish their interviews. Our thanks also go to the families of Nigel Elsdon and Max Collier for allowing us to use their personal photographs.

Secondly, our thanks to General Sir Peter de la Billière for contributing both a soldier's and a commander's view of the Gulf War in the form of a Foreword that puts the RAF's contribution in context.

Our thanks, also, to Maura Hudson, Caroline Egar and their team at Palantype Transcriptions for all their efforts in working round the clock – and to Dr Margaret Brooks and staff in the Sound Records Department at the Imperial War Museum. All those interested in British history will be pleased to know that the hundreds of hours of interviews collected will eventually form the basis of a Gulf War archive at the Imperial War Museum.

Finally, my own thanks as co-ordinator to those on the team who worked to beat the impossible deadline we set ourselves: designer Raymond Mack, editors Pete Cornish, Fiona Hill, and Jony Russell; and Apple Mac operator Mike Edkins. I am also grateful for the contributions of Mike Blake, Chris Davies, Tim Dunmore, Peter Green, Joan Hudson, Cathy Keable-Elliott, Mary Luckhurst, Graham Pike, Sara Sharpe, and Linda Zealey. The privilege was ours.

Charles Allen, August 1991

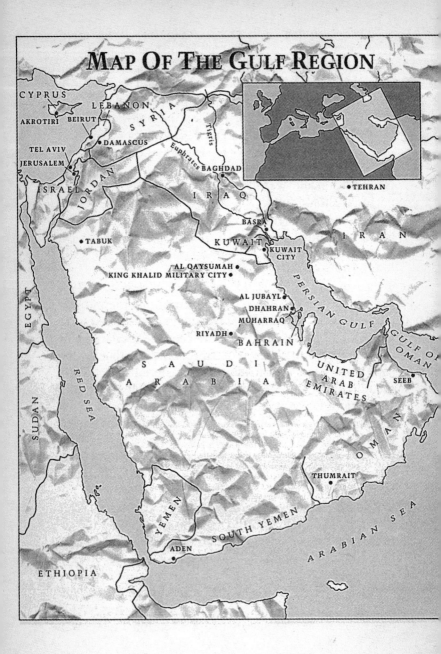

MAP OF THE GULF REGION

FOREWORD

by

General Sir Peter de la Billière, KCB, KBE, DSO, MC and bar

To all of us who had the privilege of serving in Her Majesty's Armed Forces in the Gulf during the autumn and winter of 1990–91 the events that we witnessed were a revelation in all sorts of ways. From the military point of view the Gulf War demonstrated as never before the superiority of air power in modern warfare. It put paid to the old military doctrine which states that a three-to-one superiority in numbers of ground troops is required to launch a successful attack against a well-defended enemy. At the end of the day a ground war still had to be fought – and fought magnificently it was, with enormous dash and determination – but sophisticated precision bombing and interdiction was a decisive factor.

It was here that the Royal Air Force played a vital role. The story told in these pages by aircrew and ground crew, airmen and airwomen is a truly remarkable one. Team effort was what counted. Each person had a part to play in what amounted to an astonishing joint effort involving every RAF station and virtually every member of the service. And, as this account makes clear, the RAF's contribution to the successful prosecution of the war was not confined to air strikes and air defence. It was a well-integrated part of a British tri-services contribution to the alliance that frequently saw elements of one service working for another or in close partnership together.

Just as the three services worked together so, on a much broader canvas, did the combined forces who took to the field to oppose Saddam Hussein's aggression. Those who tell their stories in these pages would be the first to admit that theirs is only part of a much bigger story. It must not be forgotten that this was very much an international alliance in which the major burden was carried by our friends, the Americans. Great credit goes to the Allied Commander General Normal Schwarzkopf, to USAF General Charles Horner and to others in the US high command who saw to it that this alliance, though American-led and American-dominated, was a genuine one.

The fact that so many countries were able to work towards a common cause was in itself astonishing. But, from my own perspective as Commander British Forces Middle East, what was even more remarkable was that so many diverse military formations and units not only took the field together in helping to maintain sanctions against Iraq but were able to fight a war within a united command framework. It showed the immense value of all the multi-national training operations undertaken under the NATO umbrella. In this respect the Gulf War was an extraordinary undertaking which must raise hopes that in the future other aggressor nations or regimes which undertake hostile acts against their neighbours will be met with similarly united fronts by the world community.

Chapter 1

A DEAR PART OF IRAQ

'The Iraqis have destroyed forever the filthy British scissors with which the ancestors of Hurd and old hag Thatcher had cut off a dear part of Iraq . . .'

Iraqi official news agency

'I was pruning my roses, would you believe,' recalls Wing Commander Vaughan Morris, 'when I had a phone call. It asked me how long it would take me to get to RAF Cottesmore. I was there half an hour later, a Tornado from my squadron picked me up and flew me back to Germany and my feet didn't touch the ground for the next three months.'

August is generally as quiet a month for the Royal Air Force as it is for any other section of the British population, a time for holidays and empty workplaces. But August 1990 was different. Within the RAF's 89,000-strong community, mobilisation was to take place on a scale unparalleled since the summer of 1939. When news first broke of Iraq's invasion of Kuwait, on Thursday 2 August, there had seemed little cause for concern. Tornado GR1A navigator Flight Lieutenant Angus Hogg, in Greece on a squadron exchange, was on a beach playing volleyball when he heard: 'It wasn't a big deal. It was a point of interest but no one thought anything about it.' Only a short while before, he and other aircrew from

11 Squadron had been sitting in their crewroom at RAF Laarbruch in Germany discussing the consequences of glasnost: 'We talked about what we were going to do when we were kicked out, because there was no possibility of a war, the RAF as we knew it was about to change drastically and we were all going to be out of a job.'

Corporal Gary Morris from the Tactical Supply Wing (TSW) at RAF Stafford was also in the Mediterranean, completing a hot-weather climate exercise in Cyprus: 'We got called in for a brief by our OC [officer commanding] and he said that Kuwait had been invaded. My first reaction was, "So what? What's it got to do with us?" We were on exercise having a good time.'

'So what?' was also Squadron Leader (Sqn Ldr) Bertie Newton's response. His detachment of Tornado strike attack GR1s drawn from 31 Sqn was on its way from RAF Bruggen in Germany to practise low flying at Goose Bay in Canada. 'I was completely agog with apathy at the news,' he admits. But a week later he flew down to Philadelphia, USA, to take part in an airshow: 'It was incredible – there were about half a million Americans, all of whom had decided they were going to kick Saddam Hussein's arse. It was quite frightening – I thought, "They're not going to think about this. They're going to go in very quickly and get hammered". This bloke Saddam was going to cop it for all the things that had gone wrong for America in the Middle East, starting with the Iran rescue attempt. In fact, I was subsequently proved wrong and I was very impressed with the way the Americans performed.'

Meanwhile, in the UK as well as the USA, the phones had started to ring. On 9 August the Secretary of State for Defence, Tom King, announced that Tornado and Jaguar squadrons were being sent to the Gulf, together with Rapier surface-to-air (SAM) missiles and 1,000 support personnel. The nearest aircraft to Saudi Arabia were the Tornado F3 fighter interceptors of 29 and 5 Sqns on detachment in Cyprus. Flight Lieutenant (Flt Lt) Angus Elliott was a pilot with 29 Sqn: 'We were due to go home on the Tuesday [7 August] and at the last minute we were at the bar when the boss had a signal "for his eyes only". We were then left for about five days really not knowing what was going on. It was a horrible feeling.'

Then came confirmation that 12 aircraft from those squadrons were to fly directly to the Gulf to hold the line, together with any American aircraft that were immediately available, while a stronger air defence force was being assembled. All available intelligence reports seemed to suggest that the Iraqis were preparing to press on through Kuwait into Saudi Arabia. 'The intelligence was completely over the top,' reflects Flt Lt Mark 'Skid' Richardson, also with 29 Sqn, as a navigator. 'It felt as though we were probably going to last two or three days out there and then we'd be overrun. And I think if they *had* carried on pushing past Kuwait and gone down the coast to take the oil refineries, that could have been the case.'

Fellow navigator Flt Lt Mark Robinson shared the general feeling that they were becoming embroiled in a 'nightmare'. The RAF's Tornado F3s were undergoing a major enhancement programme, but at a peacetime pace, 'so we were being deployed out to the Gulf with jets that hadn't been modded up for war. We had no chaff, for example, no flares. We didn't have the good missiles on, we didn't have the good radars and I think a lot of us didn't feel we were going to come back. Everybody went through a day of complete shock, all walking around like zombies. The next day we started practising for real and we started getting our act together.' Gary Morris's little unit on Cyprus was also close at hand: 'They asked for volunteers so I put my name down but, mind you, when I talked to the boss later he told me my name was already on the list of the first 12 to go out anyway, so it was just as well I'd volunteered.'

The TSW unit of 12 spent a lot of time rehearsing nuclear, biological and chemical (NBC) warfare drills: 'The night before we went the boss told us that the chemical threat was really quite high. Then he said, "Well lads, the only thing to do tonight is to go and get yourself a few beers and have a good night". So we did have a good old drink that night but I remember talking to a couple of the lads and the thing that was really worrying us was the NBC, because the next time you put your respirator on, it could be nerve gas and that was you gone.'

Will forms were filled in, last letters written and last phone calls home made. 'It was about four in the morning,' remembers Morris. 'The old man answered the phone and said, "Why are you ringing now?" and I said, "Well, I'm off tomorrow". He said, "Where are you going?" "I can't tell you," I said. "As soon as I get there I'll try and drop you a letter". Then I said, "Right, I'll see you. I've got to go now". And it was sort of weird because my dad *knew* – it was in my voice.'

The unit then went down to Akrotiri airbase to await the arrival of the first Hercules transporters coming through: 'It was a glorious day – on one half of the airfield all the families were coming for summer holidays and on the other were these blokes going to war. These people were off down to the local beach and there's us lot loaded up with about 9,000 rounds and everything we needed. We were saying, "Do they realise what's going on here?"'

As those in Cyprus stood by to leave, an advance party was being assembled at Lyneham, the RAF's movements centre. On the morning of 9 August Group Captain

4

(Gp Capt) Rick Peacock-Edwards, station commander at RAF Leeming, had been informed that he was to be the RAF's Gulf detachment commander – and was to fly out that same night: 'In an hour and a quarter I handed over the station, stuffed a few things into a suitcase and said farewell to my family. Whilst I was changing in my dressing room the doc came round and stuck a needle in my thigh. I left fully armed with a gun, my NBC kit, a towel, toothbrush, a pair of slacks and a shirt. I went straight into the aircraft and sat looking out at Leeming. It was a lovely summer day and we had our country fair coming up that weekend. I thought, "My goodness, my life's changed pretty quickly".'

Peacock-Edwards spent the afternoon at briefings in the Strike Command Headquarters bunker near High Wycombe: 'The Commander-in-Chief [Air Chief Marshal Sir Patrick Hine] came back from London late that afternoon – presumably once a decision had been made by the Cabinet – and I discovered I was going to Dhahran, although I didn't know what the situation was going to be when I got there. At that stage there were about 120 men waiting for me at Lyneham not knowing where they were going – air movements, caterers, operational staff, RAF Regiment, NBC personnel, doctors, admin staff and a team of experts going out with me. At 11.30 that night I finally got to Lyneham, got all the chaps together and briefed them: a squadron of Tornado fighters was going to Dhahran next day and we were to go out there and sort it out. I explained that it was pretty tense. There were four Hercules going out in the first wave and I went in the first aircraft, which took off at about half-past six in the morning. I took the 17 key personnel with me, and some of the caterers, plus two 4-ton lorries. Throughout the journey I was in committee.'

At Akrotiri the force commander met and briefed the

nominated Tornado force commander, Wg Cdr Euan Black, whose 12 aircraft were to follow in two flights the following day. Then it was back onto the Hercules and off to Dhahran, Saudi Arabia's principal military airfield sited on the Gulf coast, arriving shortly before midnight on 10 August after 'a total of 16 bum-numbing and noisy hours'.

Gary Morris left Cyprus on the fourth Hercules: 'The 12 of us were sitting at the back of the aircraft, playing cards and having a laugh between ourselves, just to stop thinking of it.' On one of the other planes was Senior Aircraftman (SAC) Tam McLure, a steward who had been summoned at one and a half hour's notice from RAF Wyton. The most difficult thing for him had been the tension that had built up while they waited at the airfield: 'There were a lot of guys crying at the briefing. Some of these guys thought they might not be coming home. In the back of the Hercules it was quite confined. There was a Land Rover, a trailer for a 4-tonner truck and a few thousand boxes of compo in this trailer. There were 19 of us and the spare crew. There were guys sleeping under the Land Rover, under the trailer, on top of the compo boxes on a plastic tarpaulin.'

They arrived at Dhahran airfield in the early hours of 11 August. 'It was so hot it was unreal,' declares McLure. 'It was 87° at two o'clock in the morning, a dry heat with no breeze or anything'.

Also flying out by Hercules were a number of aircrew and ground crew from the two Tornado squadrons, including Mark Robinson and his flying-partner Angus Elliott. 'Standing on the flight deck I saw a huge number of American C5 Galaxies,' remembers Elliott, 'either going faster than us in the same direction or coming back – we realised then that the Americans weren't fooling around and were going to throw in whatever was necessary to do the job. But at Dhahran itself the pan was virtually empty. The Saudi aeroplanes were all there but covered up and there wasn't a Saudi in sight. The Herc crews, who would normally take forever and a day to unload, kicked us out of the back like there was no tomorrow and the Herc was off taxiing before we'd even put our kit down. At that point I suddenly thought, "My God, this is all getting a little bit tense".'

With the Hercules captain's 'good luck' ringing in their ears, the aircrews took stock of their situation. 'We felt very vulnerable,' Robinson recalls. 'We were having all these briefs about where we were going to live but all I wanted was a respirator and a gun. There were a lot of British Aerospace people working at Dhahran saying, "What's all the rush? Of course they won't invade" – and yet only 150 miles up the road were half a million Iraqis. I couldn't believe it. We had no ground troops – but the American F-15s arrived at the same time as we did.'

The Tornado F3 aircrews immediately began flying round-the-clock combat air patrols (CAPs) with the American F-15 squadron. 'Our first aim was to get them turned round and available to fight,' explains Peacock-Edwards, 'so if the Iraqis had launched their air force at us we had the Tornados and the F-15s, even though those first Tornados were a bit deficient. So we could fight in the air – but we didn't have anything to fight the Iraqi army had they decided to march into Saudi Arabia.' His second priority was to establish good relations with the Saudis: 'I went off to meet the base commander, Prince Turki, and agreed that night that the Brits would sit side by side with the Saudis and the Americans. In the cold light of morning that turned out to be harder to do than we thought, even though the relationship between the three nations was very good indeed. We commandeered the briefing room in the station headquarters. The Saudis weren't keen on that so they gave us a portakabin, one hut to start with, which was totally inadequate. We decided that since we didn't have the buildings we wanted we'd better acquire some. I had a gem of a supplies officer, Don Belmore, who we nicknamed "Del Boy". He produced the goods and within a week we'd built ourselves a headquarters environment.'

The rest of the advance party was also settling in – and learning to take the rough with the very smooth. 'For three nights they put us into this five-star hotel, the Gulf Meridian,' states Gary Morris. 'There were the 12 of us in uniform walking around with weapons, carrying 150 rounds each, in this massive foyer with all these Arabs. Members of the Kuwaiti royal family were staying there and there's us in this hotel which cost £200 a night. It was just unreal. We'd had to hire a vehicle and we came out one morning to find all the tyres slashed. By this time there was talk of a terrorist threat so we turned round to the boss and said, "Look, we don't feel safe here". Then they pulled us into a British Aerospace compound along with all the Tornado ground crew, and we stayed in there for the rest of our tour.'

The small RAF detachment desperately needed support on the ground and in the air. Air support came 48 hours later with the arrival of a squadron of Jaguar fighter-bombers backed up by a flight of VC10 tankers.

Once the backbone of the RAF's ground attack force, the Jaguar had largely been replaced by the Tornado GR1 – but not quite. At RAF Coltishall in Norfolk there remained a reserve force of two squadrons, 6 and 54 Sqns, together with a reconnaissance squadron, 41 Sqn. Despite their age (the first Jaguars had come into RAF service in 1975), they were reckoned by those who flew them to be in better shape than the F3 fighters at Dhahran – and they could offer a vital low-level ground attack capability as 'tank-busters' and 'can-openers' should Saddam's army advance on Saudi Arabia.

As more comprehensive plans started to emerge from HQ RAF's bunker in High Wycombe, RAF Coltishall quickly began generating a composite wing of aircraft from all three squadrons, together with 300 personnel. Flight Sergeant (Flt Sgt) Gil Harding's Aircraft Services Flight supplied 46 men to go out on the 'first push. Not a man in the hangar said, "No". They were on a high. The feeling was that we were going to war right then.'

The euphoria soon evaporated as the practicalities took over. 'We were told to report by sections to the Medical Centre,' recalls Chief Technician (Chf Tech) Bob Selway. 'You joined the back of the queue, worked your way forward. Somebody took your details, then hands on hips, shirt down, a nurse on each arm, none of the niceties, just jab, jab. The queue was trying to get out the door but you were dragged straight off to the dentist'.

Then came kit issues: 'All the squadrons had produced lists of what people required. One of the things I remember was that you had to take a good knife. People were turning up with things like machetes and had to be calmed down.'

At the same time aircraft were being prepared and painted with desert camouflage 'Pink Panther' paint: 'Overnight in eight hours we got 12 aircraft ready, which is a tribute to the painters and finishers we had here. And a lot of other people from all over the unit – clerks, cooks, everybody – appeared on 6 Sqn's line. We were getting ATC [Air Training Corps] cadets down voluntarily to help and they actually flew in a Herc-load of specialist painters from Brize Norton as well.'

The Jaguar wing, led by Wg Cdr Jerry Connolly, and its attendant fleet of transports left Coltishall early on 11 August. After a stopover in Cyprus they proceeded to the Gulf then flew south to Oman – landing at the desert airfield of Thumrait, 40 miles inland of the coastal town of Salalah.

There were good reasons for this move so far south, as 6 Sqn Jaguar pilot Flt Lt Dick McCormac explains: 'The Omani air force had Jaguars as well, we did training missions with them and they were pretty good to us down there. It was of mutual benefit. They used to simulate air threats against us, bouncing us on training missions.' Within a couple of days the detachment had given itself the title of the Desert Cats.

Also sent to Thumrait was one of four teams despatched from the Mobile Servicing Section, based at Brize Norton, whose job it was to refuel aircraft. 'Because we're a mobile section my bags are packed the whole time,' states Sergeant (Sgt) Jim Carr. 'But we didn't know where we were going till we landed. The VC10 captain said, "Welcome to Thumrait. The time is eight o'clock local time" – that was a shock to the system. The Americans were already there and were very helpful in lending us ground refuelling equipment. The next day the Hercs and VC10s started pouring in. We had to refuel them at three different locations, the four of us, working 18 hours on, having a short break, then back to work again.' Spending long periods out on the apron, Carr's main concern was heatstroke: 'I had a problem with the heat when I first started. Working through the night was all right but I was paranoid about the sun. I wore a baseball hat and covered up. But I got used to it after a while.'

Heat also affected the pilots and the aircraft on the ground. 'It's 100° outside and the pilot's sitting in this greenhouse with all his clothes on getting baked – because the pilots were sitting there for hours and hours,' recalls Gil Harding, 'and the canopies were expanding and locking.' "Let's design some sunshades", they said, so here in Coltishall we bought lots of tubing and canvas and came up with one. We made a video to show them it, sent a bloke out there overnight to teach them how to put it up, because it was quite elaborate – about 20ft high. But it didn't work in the desert because we didn't take into account the strong winds out there. Last seen disappearing over the runway.'

As the Thumrait detachment prepared, those left behind at Coltishall also moved into emergency drive, modifying the aircraft to be flown out to replace the first group. This rapid modification was to become one of Operation Granby's most remarkable features as far as the RAF was concerned, though that is not how the ground crew saw it at the time: 'The official programme was named "fast track" mode but on the hangar floor was known as "Operation Goalpost" – because the size kept changing. They started off with four or five modifications to enable the aircraft to operate in a desert environment, so the boffins were saying, "Fit it this way. No, take it off and fit it that way". Basically, we were doing what we were told, working 12-hour shifts. On a good day we have 85 people working in aircraft servicing. We were down to 21 at one stage.'

An immediate requirement out in the Gulf was for airfield defence – which was the role of the RAF Regiment's field and Rapier surface-to-air missile (SAM) squadrons. At RAF Honington in Suffolk the Regiment's 20 (Rapier) Sqn provided short-range air defence for the nearby USAF airbases. Sqn Ldr Bill Lacey was the squadron commander. 'We were put on standby round about 8 August,' he remembers. 'I found a map, looked at Saudi Arabia and thought – knowing my luck – it could be in the middle of the desert. We had to be self-contained, I decided, for 10 days. That meant extra food, water, extra jerry cans for waterbottles and desert cam nets for camouflage. For the next six days vehicles from Honington were going all over the country picking up equipment. My big RAF hangar was absolutely full and in the end it took 36 Hercules to take my whole squadron out. I took an awful lot of missiles – we didn't know whether we were going straight into a shooting match. Everyone was telling us that the Iraqi air force was 700–800 aircraft strong. It had fought an eight-year war, it was good, it had modern aircraft – the boys had to refresh quickly on aircraft recognition.'

Inevitably there were delays as negotiations took place to decide where a Rapier squadron was needed – and where it was politically acceptable. Orders changed daily: 'This lasted for about eight to ten days. We kept the men going on 24-hour then six-hour standby, and that really started to drain them, because they'd kiss their wives or girlfriends goodbye in the morning, put on the kit and come in to leave.' But in all the excitement Lacey neglected his own farewells: 'I have two children at boarding school and I actually forgot to ring them to tell them what was going on.' It was only when his daughter rang him, having seen him on television, that he realised, 'I'd completely forgotten about the girls.'

Arriving in Akrotiri, 20 Sqn immediately deployed its eight Rapier fire units to defend what was to become Granby's key staging post. Ten days later they were ordered forward again: 'At one stage it was Tabuk, on the west coast of Saudi Arabia. Then we were going to Dhahran. Someone then said Bahrain. I got out the map and said, "No, that looks quite civilised". But Bahrain – an oil-rich island state just off the coast from Dhahran – it was. 'We flew during the night and arrived on 31 August. We got off, armed up ready to go, and the detachment commander, Group Captain Rocky Goodall, grabbed hold of me and said, "How many missiles have you brought?". He said we probably had no more than nine days to get our act together'.

Behind all the deployments lay the vast task of training

and equipping. At RAF Innsworth in Gloucestershire, Sgt Mick Kelly was in charge of clothing and overseas kitting: 'We got information at about 10.30 on the morning of the 10th that we would be getting up to 110 draftees coming through that day. They started arriving at about two o'clock and were given NBC suits, overboots, everything. The bulk they had to carry with all the webbing, sleeping bags and everything meant there was no way they could walk to the armoury and back so we had to issue the weapons out of the main accounts building. At about eleven o'clock all the lights failed so for the best part of the night we were issuing kit under lamplight. By three o'clock the sense of humour had totally gone. I remember one guy said to me, "These trousers don't fit me at all", and I said, "What the bloody hell do you think we are, Burtons?". Then there was a girl who dropped her jeans to try on a pair of trousers. I said, "The cubicles are over there, love". "Bloody hell, I don't care," she said. "I want to get out of here."'

Another difficult customer was a heavyweight RAF Policeman 'about 6 foot 10 tall. When he came through the door he blocked out any light there was. I turned round to one of my corporals and said "no way." But we kitted him out.'

Working with the RAF's NBC specialists from Winterbourne Gunner, instructors from the RAF Regiment were to show all draftees how to use their vital equipment. Sgt Mac McGlinchey, one of five NBC instructors at Brize Norton, found himself teaching journalists. Though many had been in war zones before they had never had to face the threat of nerve agents or mustard gas: 'We had to instil into them that they had the best equipment in the world but if they didn't use it correctly they'd be dead. Once they saw it was for real, that they could use it to save their lives, their attitudes changed completely.'

The NBC kits issued included anti-nerve-gas injections which Flt Lt Peter Jerrard, an administration officer passing through RAF Innsworth on his way to Muharraq on Bahrain, found particularly unnerving: 'At Innsworth, they gave us yet another lecture on how to use your atropine autojet, a device which you stick in your thigh if you feel you've been hit with nerve gas. People are more frightened of the autojet than they are of the nerve gas. If you fired it across the room the needle would hit the far corner of the ceiling. The first thing they say is, "Sit down when you do it", because otherwise you'll fall down.'

Like everyone else, Jerrard was required to fill out a will form and detail his next-of-kin: 'I thought then, "OK, they're really going about this as if they expect lots of casualties." That was the first insight we had that perhaps this was a one-way job.'

But perhaps nothing underscored the seriousness of the undertaking as clearly as the RAF's early commitment of large numbers of medical personnel, drawn from their hospitals at Wroughton, Ely and Halton. Among the first to go was a ward nursing officer from Wroughton, Flt Lt Colin McMillan: 'At about a quarter past four on the 15th, matron rang me: "You've been nominated from a cast of thousands to represent the PMs [Princess Mary's RAF Nursing Service] and go off with an army unit," she said. Three of us from Wroughton went on that first team.' A full field hospital unit, 22 Field Hospital, followed, taking with it three women officers – 'as they were the first into the Gulf theatre they became something like celebrities'.

Dhahran, where the medical team was to be based, was beginning to buzz: 'Going along the flight line was like the Farnborough Air Show five times over, with aircraft landing every 10 minutes – Mirages, F-16s, all our Tornado aircraft, our beloved Hercs, and the old

"10" – my favourite. It was really exciting, Boys' Own stuff.' Also very evident in the heat – 'like walking into a bakery when the furnace door is open' – was the smell of the East: 'I'll never forget that smell. It was the spices they use and the incense. You could buy stuff that was around in the time of the Bible. Frankincense was freely on sale. It was a mixture of incense, perspiration and spices.'

But finding space to work and sleep was a major problem: 'There were 26 of us in one very small house, but it was air-conditioned, we had access to water and we weren't stuck in the heat. The catering was provided by Philippines Airlines. They were lovely chaps but the cuisine was very limited.' The intention was for the field and US hospitals to 'combine resources to offer a bigger facility to the allies, but the Saudis couldn't let us have the site we wanted. After much negotiation we ended up stuck between a fuel dump and a power station, which made it a wonderful target.'

By the third week of August Operation Granby was in full swing; all the machinery of Support Command was generating the personnel, the equipment and the organisation required to enable Strike Command to get a second wave of aircraft to the Gulf and bring a third wave to combat readiness. A Nimrod detachment had already been despatched to Oman to support the United Nations (UN) naval blockade on Iraq, and on 23 August it was announced that upgraded Tornado F3s were being sent from RAF Leeming to replace those already in Dhahran – as well as a first squadron of Tornado GR1 ground attack bombers from RAF Bruggen in Germany.

RAF Leeming in Yorkshire was where the RAF's modernised F3s were concentrated. Wg Cdr David Hamilton, 11 Sqn's commander, had been furious when told by 11 Group Headquarters that the two F3 squadrons at Akrotiri had been chosen in preference to his own 'deployment' squadron. He was told to reinforce them with five of his best aircrews: 'Twenty-four hours later they said, "We want 10 crews. Cyprus. Two days". I said, "I haven't got 10 combat-ready crews. You've already taken five of mine". I was blazing over it. That was the low point.' Hamilton picked three crews from 25 Sqn and the remainder from his own. 'The high point was getting the new planes worked up and out.'

Arriving in Cyprus, Hamilton collected another eight F3s from 29 and 5 Sqns with their remaining eight crews: 'I told the troops that we were from 5, 29, 25 and 11 Sqns, "So go away and come up with some sort of title". They came back with Combined United Nations Tornado Squadron, which was the shortest lived unit in history.' When further reinforced at Dhahran the composite squadron became the Desert Eagles.

At RAF Bruggen Vaughan Morris, recalled from pruning his roses, was chosen to assemble a composite squadron of Tornado GR1s: 'We have four independent squadrons – 9, 14, 17 and 31 – on a day-to-day basis we each run our own business. But as it was August, the favourite time of year for people to go on holiday, we didn't have the luxury of sending away a single squadron.' A composite Bruggen detachment was assembled and on 27 August 12 GR1s flew out bound for Bahrain's Muharraq airbase. Three weeks later another 12 followed, drawn from RAF Laarbruch, the other Tornado GR1 front line base in Germany.

The Tornado GR1s' official role in the Gulf was, in the words of the Secretary of State for Defence, 'to deal with armoured thrusts'. But, as Morris explains: 'The primary capability of a Tornado is offensive, attacking airfields, denying the opposition the ability to get their aircraft airborne. However, we also took weapons down there such as anti-armour weapons, which could be used to counter an armoured thrust. I always came out with the line that we could do anything. In order to keep the opposition guessing and in the interests of my crews I would suggest in press interviews that the primary threat was an armoured thrust and we would counter the armoured thrust if necessary. But we always went down there with the aim in our minds that we would be doing "airfield bashing", as we call it.'

For other, very different, RAF units, the Gulf crisis meant a change of roles. Brize Norton's Personnel Management Squadron – 'in peacetime we look after pay, personnel, welfare, careers, leave, discipline' – took on the task of putting together an evacuation plan to bring out the several thousand British citizens stranded in Kuwait – Saddam's 'hostages': 'We had to have a reception plan, a way of documenting, organising immigration, finding them homes, money, travel warrants. We had to have a set-up that would work, so we could swing into action at relatively short notice. Then as time went on, we appreciated that the Kuwaiti families were obviously not going to get out. But we kept that particular operation order around so that we could use it at a later stage.'

Brize Norton was also the base of the RAF's VC10 fleet, with 10 Sqn acting as the RAF airline. 'In peacetime that's our prime job,' explains VC10 captain, Sqn Ldr Derek Sharp. 'When war comes our job is carrying bombs. So we took off our nice shiny uniforms and put on our not so shiny green bags and went to war. We didn't live in nice hotels. We became soldiers. Some of our airheads were close to the front line and I remember talking to one chap who spent three months in a hole in the sand with a poncho over the top. In the first 21 days of Granby we moved something like 4 million lbs of bombs.'

Akrotiri was 10 Sqn's main staging post for air movements to and from the Gulf: 'In Akrotiri they had a crew sheet telling you where you would be accommodated and so forth. It had a crew number at the top and towards the end the crew numbers were in the thousands. I think about 5,000 crews had landed in Cyprus, taken overnight rests and then gone on. So 5,000 plane loads had stopped there for the night, although many more overflew and went direct to the Gulf.'

As August drew to a close, so the first, reactive, phase of Granby ended. Quick and decisive action had reduced Saddam Hussein's chances of success if he attempted to take Saudi Arabia's northern oilfields. But the overall problem remained. The Iraqi occupation of Kuwait had been secured, thousands of hostages in Kuwait seized and Iraq's long-term ambitions coupled with its massive military strength remained a major threat. The 'desert shield' had arrived but it had still to be set up and strengthened. Along with its allied counterparts, the RAF began to dig in. Granby Stage Two was about to begin.

Chapter 2

OUT WITH THE FLICK-KNIVES

'Better they do it imperfectly than you do it perfectly, for it is their country, their war and your time is limited . . .'

T. E. Lawrence (Lawrence of Arabia)

In mid-August the British forces in the Gulf gained a commander described by his subordinates as a 'bulldozer' and a 'whirling dervish' on account of the speed of his thoughts and directives. This was Air Vice Marshal (AVM) 'Sandy' Wilson, who flew out to the Gulf in his own HS125 communications aircraft and was to clock up some 67,000 miles over the next three months. 'People forget how big that region is,' he stresses. 'The distances were enormous. For instance, it took me two hours flying in the 125 from Riyadh to Tabuk, right up on the Jordanian border. And it's as far from Riyadh to Thumrait in Oman as it is from London to Rome.'

Sandy Wilson's first problem was a diplomatic one – getting the Saudi commanders to accept the realities of a crisis (and of an allied response) totally outside their experience: 'I found the Saudi air force bemused by the speed, pace and numbers of the reinforcement that was going on. Their country was being literally overturned and yet I felt they were very patient and understanding. Unless you've dealt with Arabs before you do find they have a very special way of working, they have more bureaucracy than we do and you have to put lots of things in writing. But once they agree your point it's done and I have nothing but praise for the way they received me and my staff.'

A key member of this staff was Wg Cdr Oli Delany, who saw the two sides of Sandy Wilson at work: 'He was tough with his own staff. He drove us hard and he worked bloody hard but there was a need for it. Saddam had this enormous offensive potential, the prospect of war was imminent and we needed to get a grip on things fast to establish a defensive position. He took an entirely different approach with the Arabs, where it was a question of, "be sensitive, cultivate, encourage". His particular strength here was his body language and his ability to get on with the Arabs. The Arabs read a lot from the way you approach them. Facial gestures must be very positive, the way you move, the physical contact. When you shake the hand of an Arab it's not a fleeting shake of the hand but one hand on top of another. You're saying in your approach, "I'm telling you with my entire being that I like you, I'm on your side and want to work with you". That's why you spend time talking about wives, daughters, the weather and background matters – you don't address the main issue for some time. He went in for that. He was very conscious of Arab culture and the importance of face, of presenting it as an Arab fight to which we were contributing. He was very fond of the Lawrence quote about it being their country which we were only passing through'.

Tact and diplomacy were qualities that every serviceman and servicewoman had to acquire. 'Drinking coffee or the cinnamon coffee that we drank out of these tiny little cups was very much a feature,' Oli Delany explains. 'Meetings always went on longer because of these formalities. Probably the most successful business

I ever conducted was when I spent half an hour talking about nothing in particular. Then I said, "I must go now", and the guy I was dealing with said, "My friend, can I do anything for you?" And I said, "Perhaps there is one small thing", which had been my prime purpose in going there – and he understood that.'

Inevitably, however, there were incidents that arose from the cultural differences between the allies – particularly from the presence of so many women soldiers within the American contingent. From the British point of view it appeared that the Americans 'weren't terribly discreet about the way they introduced women into the Saudi culture'. And the more conservative elements in Saudi society, such as the religious police, did not take kindly to gun-toting American women driving 10-tonners through their streets. But an accommodation of cultures was arrived at, as Rick Peacock-Edwards explains: 'The Saudi Arabians were very reserved not because they thought they were superior, but because they were a little scared we were going to change their whole way of life. So one has to respect that. Nevertheless, I found the Saudi Arabians in general very, very nice.'

Every airbase had its share of problems that needed to be sorted out. At Riyadh, the Saudi Arabian capital, Wilson had to begin with a week of shuttle diplomacy where it was 'a matter of going round and talking to people and talking back to England from the Embassy, because for the first week we didn't even have a phone. I persuaded General Al Buhari (the Saudi Chief of Air Staff) to give us two little offices in his own magnificent headquarters building, which was already overcrowded because the Americans were piling in. In the end I persuaded him that we could build something in the car park. So we built in two days the "Sandy House", which later became the "White House" and from which my successor Bill Wratten ran the war.'

This was RAF Air Headquarters, 'a bit reminiscent of a tube train, very narrow and very long', where 40 staff officers worked within two portakabins. Close by was the huge 'bubble' where the Americans had their HQ, with 'a reverse pyramid all pointing down to this one room in the basement, the war control room, where the senior air commander and all the generals had seats round a table and conducted twice-daily briefings.'

Good relations with the Americans were just as important. In many cases, because of extended RAF-USAF contacts and joint exercises, it was a matter of meeting friends and acquaintances and following shared working methods. 'That was the whole thing about an alliance. NATO works. It's no magic thing. We're flying with Americans every flipping day. If the Belgians had pitched up or the Germans or the Dutch we'd have flown with them because we have standard operating procedures.'

It was quite clear to Wilson from the start that in General Norman Schwarzkopf the allies had a formidable commander: 'He struck me immediately as a large man in every sense, with tremendous presence. American troops like their generals to be gung-ho but Schwarzkopf was a very different man underneath. He had a lovely touch with his senior staff and he was extremely kind to me, never failing to find time to talk to me. He also handled the Saudis brilliantly. General Khaled, who was the Saudi Commander-in-Chief was an awfully nice man, very young and without much experience in these things, and General Schwarzkopf gave him every support. Never once did he seek to pull one over him. He had a deep understanding of the Arab mind and Arab way of life and the courtesies and therefore was able to command their respect right from the start.'

A crucial question concerned the command and control of allied forces. 'At times it looked almost impossible that we could get agreement but in the end what was put together was quite brilliant. It allowed General Schwarzkopf to command the operation in war whilst leaving General Khaled as Commander-in-Chief of the coalition forces in a defensive posture. That put most of the Arab forces together and Arab face was maintained – and General Schwarzkopf was the guy who convinced them.'

Riyadh itself was a 'city of contrasts, with space-age buildings, marvellous technological facilities and outside there'd be this Bedouin with his tent and his camel, or a four-wheeled tracked vehicle as a substitute.' The greatest hazard to the forces was the traffic. 'It was lethal,' recalls Delany. 'I didn't go a day without seeing a traffic accident. There isn't a highway code or a driving law because if you strike another vehicle it's God's will and has nothing to do with you. To get to HQ everyone had to negotiate Suicide Roundabout, which was really a total lottery because no one gave way and whatever happened was God's will.'

It also made a deep impression on Hercules navigator Flt Lt John Ayers: 'The sound of car horns drowned the call of the muezzin. At the traffic lights the cars lined up like a Le Mans start and as soon as the lights changed the car horns would sound. We always said the definition of a nanosecond was the time it takes for the first car horn to sound after the traffic lights turn green.'

King Khalid International Airport became the RAF's main trooping centre: 'The Saudis had built an airfield with far more runway space and parking space than they needed and extensive terminals. This redundancy was a feature all round the country – and was fundamental to our ability to reinforce Saudi Arabia.' In November KK International became the hub of allied air movement as 'everything was brought to Riyadh and then distributed.' It became a base for a Hercules detachment and for the tankers, whose crews and ground support teams had their own RAF field kitchen.

Flying Officer (Fg Off) Cliff Foggo and others from 101 Sqn were astonished by the standard of catering: 'They started from a concrete floor and a couple of little stoves and all they could do was heat things up. "We don't want this", we thought. But in a few weeks the cafeteria was out of this world. We could go in for lunch and have four choices of main meal and a couple of choices of dessert and an enormous round of Stilton. There are two branches that I personally hold in higher esteem now: the catering branch and the supply branch – the blanket stackers – because they also did a brilliant job.'

One supply branch effort was to provide comfy chairs for the transit lounge, set up by Sqn Ldr Chris Hewat's Mobile Air Movements (MAMS) team. After a while they began to disappear – just as the hospital on the floor below was being set up: 'Raiding parties were moving these chairs into the hospital area. Eventually I tracked down this lieutenant-colonel and accosted him. His attitude was, "We found them, we've got them, they're ours now. You go and get some more". Fortunately, there weren't many of that sort of character around.'

If KK International was big, Dhahran military airbase was bigger. 'This was very much Prince Turki's fiefdom,' explains Delany. 'It was well ahead of anything we've got in Europe. Seven runways, the most modern hardened shelters, underground bases, all mod cons, a very impressive set-up indeed.' It was where the initial deployments concentrated, and Gary Morris of Tactical Supply Wing was stunned by what he saw when he arrived: 'The first day we saw 550 helicopters all lined up. All the Americans – the US Marines, the Army, the 82nd Airborne – were coming through.'

Understandably, the Americans dominated what space

was available – as well as inflating local prices with their spending habits. 'A fair bit of bartering went on,' explains Morris. 'We had to procure everything from mugs to computers. Virtually everything that was needed on an RAF station we bought or hired. Whatever price they asked we halved and just haggled. For example, when we bought a photocopier the starting price was 17,000 riyals, about £2,500, and we actually paid 9,000 riyals. They were happy to do that, but whatever price the Saudis asked the Americans said, "OK, we'll take it" – so they were making a bomb out of them.'

This was where the NCOs came into their own. 'They're the Mr Fixits,' states Wilson. 'They just get on and do it and you just don't ask any questions. At Dhahran where we started to build sandbag emplacements and air raid shelters, they went out to the market and came back with whole portakabins on trailers after an afternoon foray. They found hessian nets, they mixed concrete and fixed it all. It was a great team effort with the Royal Engineers – and wonderful to see.'

As the squadrons settled in so their demands grew – 'everything from toilet paper to an engine for a Tornado.' To Morris and his colleagues in TSW some requests seemed a little excessive: 'I remember a group captain who didn't like his sleeping bag so we went out and bought him a duvet with matching pillows, but what really used to make us laugh was the aircrew. For some reason they all wanted a laptop computer. Then they wanted coffee percolators. Then there was a pilot who came in about five o'clock one morning and asked for *The Times*. I said that all we had was *Today* and the *Daily Telegraph*. "Who gets these papers?" he said. "Well," I said, "they're flown out free from the UK. Whichever ones come out, that's what we get". He said, "Well, I normally read *The Times*. Why can't you get me a copy?" Here we were with half a million Iraqis up on the border about 100 miles away and he was worried about not getting his copy of *The Times*.'

The ground crews also made demands: 'They couldn't service Tornados unless they had aircrew sunglasses. We all bought our own but they had to have RAF issue aircrew sunglasses.'

The 800-strong RAF detachment lived off base in compounds, many belonging to British Aerospace. Because of a possible terrorist threat, off-duty visits to the town were limited: 'After we'd been round there twice we'd virtually seen everything we could, so we didn't get out and about a lot. We used to go for a run about eight or nine o'clock in the evening, but you're talking about 50° centigrade and 98% humidity – as soon as you walked outside you were instantly drenched.'

For those unfamiliar with the Islamic culture of Saudi Arabia it took time to adjust to local customs, such as the absolute ban on drinking alcohol. To some the sight of Arab women veiled from head to toe was a disconcerting one. A popular comment was that these figures, dressed in black, brought to mind the image of 'Darth Vader'. Arab male regalia also attracted comment. The full robe and headgear became known as the 'full Lawrence' and the headgear worn alone as the 'half-Lawrence'.

Working with the Saudis in Dhahran and Riyadh may not always have been easy but there were plenty of creature comforts. Not so in Tabuk. For all the bridge-building going on in Riyadh, when the first Tornado squadrons arrived in this very conservative corner of Saudi Arabia they found a marked absence of the co-operative spirit. One of those who took part in the move from Dhahran was Sgt Mick Johnson: 'There was all this kit coming in and 50 guys sat on the pad. A group captain was sat in the back of the car. That was his office because at the start we couldn't get our hands on a building or a phone.'

It needed intervention at the highest level to smooth things out. 'We had to build from scratch every bit of accommodation we wanted, both domestic and technical,' admits Sandy Wilson. 'Having said that, the speed with which the Saudis reacted to our request for buildings and infrastructure was absolutely breathtaking.'

Tabuk's lack of facilities meant that those who went there showed the greatest enterprise in making up the shortfalls: 'They got what are called ISO containers, which look like those on the back of a container lorry. The engineers dug a hole, dropped these things in, and cut and welded and covered it all so that they had an underground shelter for an operations centre from which the war was fought. It amazed the Saudis and the Americans there, too.'

Nevertheless, with overcrowded quarters and no recreational facilities, Tabuk was not popular with either ground crew or aircrew. 'It was just desert for hundreds of miles around,' explains Flt Lt Neil Cobb. 'The base was very tightly controlled and they were very wary of foreigners. Outwardly they were very friendly but there was this sense that this was their country and we were strangers. But the flying out there was absolutely fantastic, the best flying I've ever done in the Air Force. Most of the Saudi desert is absolutely flat but here there were fantastic valleys, mountains, volcanoes and standing stones in the middle of the desert – and we were told we could fly as low and as fast as we needed to go. But I felt sorry for the ground crew.'

They also flew mock combat sorties against F-15s of the Royal Saudi Air Force: 'They were very, very good, which was a bit of an eye-opener.' "Maybe the Iraqis are just as good", we thought.'

Neil Cobb's squadron had come to Tabuk from the delights of Bahrain. Here the RAF detachment was concentrated on the airfield at Muharraq, which is on a small peninsula on the eastern side of the island – but accommodated for the most part in some of the finest hotels in the world, with the Bahrain Sheraton becoming a sort of unofficial officers' mess. 'There was a feeling of Benidorm about Bahrain,' says Cobb. 'We could go horse-riding, wind-surfing, sailing, stuff like that. The Muslim influence wasn't that strong so we could walk around with bare legs and arms and it was free in terms of alcohol. When we had time off we could lie around the hotel pool getting a sun tan, with the clink of gin and tonics, and imagine Alan Whicker walking around. We had five-star comfort – but we had to pay five-star prices'.

Admin officer Peter Jerrard found the atmosphere a little strange: 'I kept on thinking of Nero fiddling while Rome burned. We could buy tapes very cheaply and one of the tapes I bought was the Warsaw Concerto and I remember sitting by the pool with this feeling in the air that something was about to happen.'

Jerrard's job was 'running the shop. We had a squadron leader who looked after bogs and drains and getting new accommodation built and looking for compounds that could be hired, because hotels were expensive. Another officer dealt with the money side. He'd go into town with a great bag and come back with notes, because in Bahrain people don't believe in cheques. He'd distribute everybody's weekly allowance, 24 dinars a day, which is about £30. That was for two meals a day. I did everything else, including dealing with compassionate cases, because we had a lot of people who for one reason or another wanted not to be where they were. Ninety-nine per cent of people just got on with it but there were a few who got wound up. I remember a guy whose wife was having a baby in Cyprus. It wasn't the biggest thing in the world but it was no skin off my nose just to bung him home and tell him to come back in 48 hours.'

Admin also dealt with standing orders. 'These were to tell people things they ought to know like "Don't walk around town wearing T-shirts saying things like Saddam Busters or Sod Off Saddam", or "Don't walk around in uniform". You don't pick up these things unless somebody tells you, so the first orders tended to be how to behave – to drink water regularly or to always carry NBC kit round with you.' The servicemen were also given strict guidelines on how to avoid offending the local women and their husbands. 'For the first three or four weeks we were walking around with our eyes on the ground,' recalls Cpl Eoin Selfridge, 'we were scared to look at anybody.'

Problems with the locals were few. It was generally agreed that the Bahrainis were a 'really nice bunch' and mostly very pro-British, although there was no escaping the cultural differences: 'The worst thing was the Bahrainis wailing from towers. I heard it in my dreams.'

Because of its more liberal atmosphere, Bahrain soon became the regional 'Rest and Recreation' centre for 48-hour local leaves. 'The Saudi Arabians have a different set of rules and standards and we had to respect that', observes Peacock-Edwards. 'So the troops really enjoyed going to Bahrain. They went to hotels, swam in pools, went shopping, just to get a break.'

But not every airman or airwoman in Bahrain lived in luxury. The gunners of Bill Lacey's Rapier squadron ended up living amongst the local fishing villages in portakabins: 'The principle of air defence is that you put a ring around the airfield but at some distance. So we needed to deploy the Rapier off the base. Eight men are on each Rapier kit and they live, eat and everything else off there. We were really worried about the northern side of the island but there was an old causeway, just a little track into the water that the fishermen used, which we could build out into the water. I happened to bump into an Arab one day whom I nicknamed Arthur Daley and his driver Del Boy. I took him to the causeway and explained that I needed to extend it into the sea. We signed a contract on the back of a cigarette packet and he started work about an hour later with truck upon truck – and about three days later they'd built this causeway. We then built defensive positions round it and then portakabins with air-conditioning. Fantastic! It was quite funny because on all the radios it was "Arthur is after you" or "Del Boy is after you". After that we became the Mr Fixits of the station and could fix anything for anyone.'

Some of the Rapier teams had problems settling in: 'At one place I heard a scream from the boys and found they were being attacked by rats. A sentry was in his bunker and got visited by three rats the size of dogs. In the end he bayonetted them. Only the British could have built a missile system where the fishermen gut their fish!'

There was also the occasional cultural misunderstanding, as when a group of Regiment gunners saw lines of shoes lined up against a wall in the local souk and began trying them on for size: 'They were surprised when a load of irate Arabs started chasing them. It transpired that they'd been trying on the shoes of the lads in the local mosque.'

For those who did live out in the field in their own units, there was undoubtedly a stronger sense of team spirit. This was something that Flt Lt Steve Moull regretted losing when his TSW group from Thumrait in Oman moved up to Bahrain: 'We had a much stronger camaraderie in the harsh desert conditions in the tents that we lived in, with all the dust and heat, than we did in the Sheraton, because in the hotel we'd go to our anonymous rooms on an anonymous floor, shut the door and no one would bother us, so we lost that team identity.' However, the discomforts of the outdoor life were considerable: 'The sand got everywhere. In pictures from this conflict you'll see that people have had their heads shaved or had close-cropped hair. Not only was that cooler, but when it gets sweaty long hair picks up sand and you end up with a sort of concrete set on your head. It's so uncomfortable you wouldn't believe it. Only one of my blokes couldn't stand the heat and he had to be returned. But I had another one whose eyes were continuously inflamed by the dust and sand. Most people's were irritated but this guy's eyes were almost closed – so I had to send him back as well.'

The desert airfield of Thumrait, where the Jaguars were briefly based before being brought forward to Bahrain, was to become known as 'Bumrate' – largely on account of the allowances that caused much upset among British servicemen and servicewomen: 'The principle was that if we were in Riyadh, for instance, where there were no military barracks, we were given an allowance to pay for our food and accommodation. That meant people in Riyadh and Bahrain got a decent allowance but people in Thumrait, accommodated on a military base and fed from military resources, got nothing other than a water allowance. Hence bum rate, because there were these guys in horrendous heat living in thick northwest Europe canvas tents.'

In Thumrait, trading with the Americans became the norm. 'There were a lot of schemes going on,' remembers Steve Moull. 'A bloke would pitch up with cases of Pepsi and say, "Boss, have we got a spare jungle hat?" He'd come back later with American uniforms. In a situation like that where resources and material were hard to come by, the only way was to barter your way out. But the Americans were very, very kind to us. If we sat there arguing over who should have five camp beds, say, very often we'd get them, out of a sense of sympathy because "it was good to have the Brits along". And we enjoyed having them along, too.'

The scale of the US presence in the Gulf was now awesome – 'they were out there to win. If it had taken another 100,000 troops they would have sent them. They would have kept putting pieces on the chessboard until there was room for no other colour' – and put the British contribution into its true perspective. Even the F3 aircrew in their swingwing 'flick-knives' couldn't help but be impressed. 'Every time I saw an F-15 taxi past the front of the line I felt a measure of jealousy,' admits Mark Richardson. 'These blokes were sitting probably about ten foot higher than you and, psychologically, when someone looks down at you and waves, you feel very inferior.'

His colleague Angus Elliott was envious of the American fliers for another reason: 'The Brits were very keen about the chemical threat, so we were still wearing all the kit, which wasn't good news in all that heat. We sat there in our jets with our chemical suits on, our thermal underwear, our flying suits, our LSJ and our rigging lines all over the place, with our gloves on and our sleeves rolled right down, all tied up quite tightly and cramped – and we'd see an F-15 drive by. He'd be sat up there – we could see him from the waist up because of the big canopies they've got – and he'd be shirt-sleeves rolled up, no gloves and waving, "Hi guys!". And we'd think, "What are we doing?"' A compromise was quickly arrived at; the Interim NBC kit, which gave aircrew some degree of protection from chemical attack without putting them through such discomfort.

In the air it was a different matter. The F3s often flew against the US Marine Corps F-18s and surprised both parties, as David Hamilton recalls: 'Because the F-18 is very similar to the Iraqis' MiG-29 we asked them to fly Iraqi tactics on certain sorties and the

American commander couldn't believe how good the F3 was. We were shooting them down, as it were, with the long-range Skyflash before they got near us. In one versus one the Tornado didn't do terribly well but once we got into a fight with lots of aircraft their air picture broke down and that's where the two-seater Tornado had a big advantage.'

What had to be established very early on among the allies were the Rules of Engagement – a very sensitive issue, as Sandy Wilson confirms: 'The thing we feared most was that we might accidentally shoot down an Iraqi aircraft, because the last thing we wanted was to start a conflict at that stage – and there were a number of times when they tried us on, definitely.' Hamilton recalls just such an incident in late September when an F-15 got very close to shooting an Iraqi plane down. 'Air Vice Marshal Wilson was quite adamant. "David", he said. "Your squadron will not shoot an aeroplane down unless that wreckage is well this side of the border". That was quite a responsibility. You're talking about split-second decisions here, when a very small error of judgement could have started the war before the allies were ready. So we eventually put down a buffer zone and most combat air patrols (CAPs) were done 40–50 miles south of either the Iraqi or Kuwaiti border, depending on where they wanted us to CAP. We'd have two CAPs up at any one time. We flew four aircraft on CAP, flying in two pairs and halfway through our time maybe the Americans would relieve the other CAP and the Saudis would relieve ours. We always had two radars pointing at where the enemy might come from, while the other two were going away. The tankers were generally out 100 miles south of us and two aircraft would be sent down to refuel. It was all done silently. The tanker was on a set geographical position turning on its racetrack at a set time. We'd just fly along, pick him up on radar, roll in behind him, take the fuel and go away, all completely silently.'

While the F3s, F-15s and F-18s guarded the skies, the ground attack aircraft refined their night-time low-flying skills to make the best use of the desert terrain – not without problems. 'As you fly along, the radar looks ahead for the ground and the aircraft flies itself over the top,' explains Neil Cobb of 617 Sqn. 'We had the hard deck of the desert, then all the sand dunes going up to about 150–180ft, and flying at 200ft the radar didn't always see them. One night we were flying along when the radar altimeter suddenly shot down to 50ft and up again, the aircraft jerked. "I wonder what happened there?" I thought. It did the same thing again about three or four times – to everybody in the formation. We thought that was a bit strange, so we went back in the daytime and found that some sand-dunes weren't being seen by the radar, because the sand was very fine. We'd been very lucky and we thought, "Four aircraft could have flown into the ground and no one would have known why". We had a few Bacardi and Cokes that night and went to bed at about four in the morning. There was some scratching of heads and bottoms and they came up with a tweaked-up radar that could see the sand-dunes.'

But the high risks that low flying entailed remained. On 13 November a Jaguar of 54 Sqn hit the crest of a sand dune in Saudi Arabia and crashed. The pilot, 26-year old Flt Lt Keith Collister, was killed instantly. He became Operation Granby's first casualty.

On 1 October Lt-Gen Sir Peter de la Billière was appointed British Forces Commander Middle East, signalling the commitment of British ground forces to the Gulf in the form of the 7th Armoured Brigade. The last of the RAF's main airbases was now established outside the port of Al Jubayl, 55 miles up the coast from Dhahran, which became the headquarters of the Support Helicopter Force (Middle East). Here the initial RAF contingent of 15 Pumas and a flight of Chinooks was joined by more Pumas and Chinooks, as well as two squadrons of Royal Navy Sea Kings. But, again, it was the American contingent that dominated the scene. 'They had more helicopters at Jubayl than we've got in the British forces,' declares Flt Lt Andy Bell. 'Sea Stallions, Short Chinooks, Apaches, Cobras, Jolly Green Giants – hundreds of them. The Navy guy I sat next to looked at all these helicopters on that pan and said, "Twelve Sea Kings are really going to make a big difference to this lot, aren't they!"'

All the helicopters received operational enhancements in the form of sand filters, improved communications and comprehensive defence aid suites. The Chinooks gained the latest tactical air navigation and position fixing systems, as well as door guns and night vision goggles for the aircrew. Infra-red night sights issued to those on guard turned the desert night into day. 'We watched this army major coming along,' recalls Sgt Mick Johnson. 'He walked straight into this gunpit and there was a burst of laughter. He did see the funny side of it afterwards, but not at the time.'

By the end of October the night temperature often dropped below freezing, and those sleeping in tents were grateful for the warmth of their sleeping bags. Darkness fell swiftly, as Steve Moull recalls: 'The nicest thing was the sunsets. Because the horizon is so low you can see the sun until it sinks and the sky goes through beautiful colour changes. There was something magical about it. And, believe it or not, aircraft noise was also very comforting, especially jet noise, because you felt protected. We knew the aircraft were flying and everything was OK.'

Chapter 3

ON THE MAGIC ROUNDABOUT

Call sign Dylan 45 in 255.
No problems with transit. Very good comms with
Strike, Red Crown and ACE. Good secure comms
throughout.
On task. Task to concentrate search around Bubiyan
Island, looking for two OSA patrol boats.
17.30 reported our locating six. SUCAP despatched
by PB to investigate. Contacts identified as military
by A-6.
At 18.18 PB informed us that SUCAP was engaging
targets. Control and co-operation with PB throughout.
Passed sitrep to Dylan 46.
Return transit uneventful. One up for the good
guys.

Captain's log, Crew 6, 206 Sqn, 6 Feb 1991

One unit that was to pursue its own dogged course
throughout Granby was the Nimrod detachment from
RAF Kinloss. At the outset, its role was peripheral but
– as this chapter relates – the 'Mighty Hunter' had its
own part to play. Tucked away in the sand-dunes of the
Moray Firth, RAF Kinloss is one of those old-fashioned
flying stations that harks back to earlier days. It lacks
the hustle of the bigger fast-jet bases, concentrating its
efforts on one task. 'Everything we do is about flying
the Nimrod,' explains station commander Gp Capt Brian

Burridge. 'We're out there tracking hostile submarines and on search-and rescue. So we're all pulling in the same direction.'

Kinloss is home to three flying squadrons – 120, 201 and 206 Sqns – which share the task with 42 Sqn at St Mawgan in Cornwall of keeping watch over the North Sea and the Atlantic as far south as the Azores. They fly the Nimrod MR2P – a flying weapons platform devoted to tracking and, if needs be, destroying enemy submarines.

The Nimrod has its origins in the de Havilland Comet, first and most elegant of the four-engined passenger jets. The underbelly of the Comet airframe was opened up to accommodate a mass of electronic gadgetry and in 1969 the Nimrod MR1 went into service as the RAF's submarine hunter-killer. Each aircraft flies with 12 or 13 aircrew aboard: a pilot, navigator and engineer together with a team of Air Electronics Operators (AEOps) who handle the listening and detecting gear in the main cabin. These AEOps divide into 'wet' and 'dry' operators. 'There are four dry men like myself,' explains Sgt Steve Wyatt of 206 Sqn. 'We operate the radios, the radar and the electronic support measures (ESM) equipment. The wet operators do the acoustics equipment. They listen to submarines under the surface, while the dry sensors detect submarines when they're above the surface.'

The invasion of Iraq caused few ripples on this remote Scottish outpost. 'In all honesty, I couldn't see an obvious role for the Nimrod,' admits Wg Cdr Andy Wight-Boycott, OC 201 Sqn. Since Iraq possessed no submarines and the Persian Gulf was too shallow for submarines to hide in, there seemed to be no likelihood that they would take part. Nevertheless, 'there were sea areas involved and in my bones I felt that we would be there in one form or another.'

For the officer in charge of the Nimrod line, Sqn Ldr

Seán McCourt, it was a case of having seen it all before: 'I go back a fair time in the Air Force. When I first joined as a young airman in 1960 I was involved in a similar operation when British troops actually went into Kuwait in Britannias and Comets. They went in and prevented an invasion by Iraq. So I was only surprised that we didn't get involved more quickly.'

Seán McCourt, Steve Wyatt and Andy Wight-Boycott were all on leave when the August invasion took place. 'At the morning brief on my first day back we were told that there were no plans and we wouldn't be involved,' remembers Wight-Boycott. 'The day ran its course until six o'clock that evening when the station commander summoned all the wing commanders to Ops – and we discovered that there was indeed a plan to send the Nimrods to the Gulf.'

In fact, the Nimrod was no stranger to the area: 'For the previous eight years we'd been sending Nimrods to Oman as part of a deployment known as the Magic Roundabout. Its primary role was to have a British presence there to support the Omanis.' In fact, Wyatt had only recently returned from the Gulf: 'I'd just come back from a 10-day detachment, my first since joining the squadron at the end of June. It's a bit daunting when you first come up off a training unit. But all the crew help you as a new boy and you get stuck into the job – which was surface surveillance with tankers and ships, in support of the Omani armed forces.' These Gulf detachments proved invaluable as rehearsals for what was to follow.

The first question was who to send out, as Wight-Boycott remembers: 'The decision was to send two crews from 120 and 201 Sqns. But who should command? Andrew Neal, OC 120 Sqn, and I were both keen to do the job so we tossed a coin to determine who should do it. I can't remember who called but I know I lost the toss.'

It was a bitter moment for a man whose grandfather had flown with the Royal Flying Corps in the First World War and had been stationed in Iraq in the inter-war years – 'he thought the Iraqis were very nice and pleasant people' – and whose parents had both served in the RAF throughout the Second World War – 'my mother joined the WAAFs as an MT driver and met my father at an officers' mess dance somewhere outside Cambridge'. During his own career he had 'missed out' on a tour in Northern Ireland and the Falklands conflict 'and it looked to me as though this was the third occasion on which I would miss out on some form of action'.

While the Nimrod lines got the first three aircraft readied for departure – unlike other Gulfbound aircraft they required no desert camouflage, since their drab marine overcoat was considered sufficiently protective – the aircrews and accompanying ground crews were assembled. 'Everyone wanted to go,' insists McCourt. 'We chose people very carefully, to get the best ground technicians down there to begin with, in case hostilities started very quickly – but everyone wanted to go.' Flt Lt Drew Steel remembers the atmosphere as being 'frantic but controlled. We had no concept of the scale of the whole thing at this stage. We were very much a small Nimrod detachment going out, potentially the first Brits out there. But we were used to sending aircraft away to all sorts of strange places so there was no confusion.'

Soon they were given their task: 'We were going to be enforcing sanctions in line with UN policy – and once it was decided that we would go to sea all the bits fell into place. The fit of the aircraft was sorted out.'

Steel flew out on the first aircraft, to take on the role of air operations controller at their base, the Omani airfield of Seeb: 'It was 12 August, the Glorious Twelfth. As we were taxiing onto the runway at Kinloss all the linies were out with a huge notice – "Baghdad or bust". A big laugh went round the plane at that, but once we were actually airborne we were thinking, "What do we do now? What's going to be out there?" So there was a lot of sitting quietly and thinking. Going out that first time was a lot scarier than going out the second time when the war had started, because we didn't know what we were going into. Then halfway through the transit, everybody had done their bit of personal thinking and we started getting maps out and making lists of things to do as soon as we landed.'

Seeb was a shared civil and military airfield on the coast of Oman under the command of the Sultan of Oman's Air Force – a place that they knew well from previous visits on detachment. 'Everything was so normal,' Steel remembers. 'As we pulled off the runway a Saudi Airways jumbo jet landed. The civilian aircrews were coming in, there were tourists and expats working there – everything seemed absolutely normal. We felt a bit odd to be there worrying about missile ranges and all the rest of it.'

Within a week the detachment had swollen to four aircraft and about 100 people, all of whom were housed in Muscat's Inter-Continental, an 'exceptional hotel with all the facilities – swimming pool, beach, multi-gym – and the social centre of most expat activity in Muscat. Its other advantage was that we were all co-located – aircrew, ground crew, administrators'.

However, Steel found conditions at Seeb airfield itself less than ideal: 'There was a breezeblock outhouse, a very basic building situated in the middle of the "forgotten quarter" of the airfield between the tailor's shop and the sickbay. That was where we always operated from when we went out there in peacetime. It had a telephone and a coffee-bar and this was where we had to run things from. Having one electric socket with several computers and lots of hot wiring, I thought I'd need to do something about this. So we got the local Omani electrician to come in, and we were sitting there with the local Arab and his Pakistani apprentice installing all these wires and sockets, with drills going and Arabs shouting at one another. It was all very Heath Robinson. We had to talk quietly about anything secret because just in front of us was the sickbay and there were queues and queues of Arabs waiting to get their medicines. In fact, I remember rushing to the Arab toilet one evening, having had a bit of a reaction to the local food, and tripping over an Omani who was praying in the dark.

'I also remember I was on the phone typing at the computer like a one-armed paperhanger, with lots of secret papers around me and this Pakistani tailor walked in and asked if he could see a flying suit because he was going to try and make some. This wee man wanted to see where all the pockets were, he was measuring me and he wouldn't go away until I'd described a flying suit.'

Their initial task was to 'gather data for the UN embargo which was inevitably going to come. Within a few days we got the first aircraft out and were finding, reporting and talking to all the merchant shipping, asking them where they'd come from, where they were going to, what they had on board – and reporting any suspicious ones to the naval units that were around, which at that stage was the US Navy.'

Though their role was to expand considerably with the outbreak of hostilities, the Seeb detachment was always to remain on the periphery of the great events happening in the Gulf. They lived very much in a world of their own. There was virtually no press coverage of their activities, principally because Oman did not encourage news facilities. 'Their overall philosophy was that when we were gone they'd still be here – and they had to balance the Iranians and the Iraqis and their various neighbours. They didn't wish – not unreasonably – to have the support they gave the allies distributed round the world.'

41

However, the almost daily delivery by Hercules of 'blueys' – many addressed to 'an airman in the Gulf' – as well as gift parcels, was a major morale booster for all, 'because it proved conclusively that the great British public cared about us. It got to be a bit of a joke in the end – "Does anyone else want some talcum powder?" – but never let it be said that the art of letter-writing is dead. The guys wrote a hell of a lot of letters.'

Flying low over warm seas in aircraft designed to operate in colder latitudes also presented problems: 'The biggest was humidity. From about five feet upwards in the fuselage there seemed constantly to be a fog. The air conditioning was simply not up to it so we built little gutters, particularly over the navigators, to channel the condensation away. A gutter failure would invariably result in drips onto bits of electronic equipment – which would then fail.'

By degrees the Nimrod sorties became progressively more adventurous. By the end of August their area of operations had extended into the Persian Gulf, but keeping well south of the Kuwaiti border and well clear of Iran: 'The islands as one enters the Straits of Hormuz belong to Iran so we actually ended up in an extremely narrow corridor. In the Straits we could well find a British Nimrod, a Russian helicopter, an Iranian P-3 and perhaps one or two American planes. The Iranian P-3 was a recce aircraft which was usually trying to find the American carrier. We talked to him on the guard channel. He always told us he was at 1,000ft but he never was. The area to the east of Hormuz was where the Soviets had their viewing point. They usually had a large cruiser plus a couple of supply ships. As the days went on they became increasingly friendly – but then a new ship would come in and be highly suspicious of talking to a Brit.'

The patrolling of the Gulf was honed down to a 'fine

art. We would work our way up the west side where there were a lot of oil rigs and very shallow water. We stayed outside Iranian territorial waters, 12 miles, plus three miles for a buffer zone. Then we would work our way down the west coast. Most crews divided the area up into squares and searched each square before moving on to the next.'

Meanwhile, back in Kinloss Seán McCourt and many others were involved in keeping the Seeb detachment at full strength, with virtually every flight on the station involved in one way or another: 'The push here to support them was incredible. We knew that we had a tremendous role to play in the line because aircraft need servicing just like your car.' The only way to get the work done was to go onto 'a very strict regime of three 12-hour days, three 12-hour nights, then three days off – which was pretty tiring'.

Some major modifications involved civilians from the manufacturers, others were carried out by the Aircraft Engineering Installation Team. New aircrews then had to be trained to use the modified equipment before flying the aircraft out and relieving the crews already there. It was this rotation of personnel that eventually brought Andy Wight-Boycott out to Seeb as the new detachment commander on 13 December: 'I remember saying goodbye to two of my children at boarding school and the youngest one standing on the steps as the car receded, with the world's longest face. Clearly, in his mind this was the last farewell.'

Also among those who arrived at Seeb at this time were Steve Wyatt and Andrew Steel – for whom this was his second Granby tour: 'The wife was a little less enthusiastic this time – "you've done your bit. Why can't they send some other bugger?" – but I felt quite chuffed that somebody had decided I was worthy of going out, although I was petrified of making a Horlicks of it.' Fear of failure was his chief concern. 'It overdramatises the situation to think that we ever felt in danger,' he insists. 'We were in a very different position from the 17-year-olds in the tanks, the young pongos, very different indeed.'

Coming through Riyadh airport on his way down to Oman, Wight-Boycott was astonished by what he saw – 'the air war at that stage, so it seemed to me, was being organised from the car park with the British element in two portakabins and the Americans in an enormous higgledy-piggledy tented headquarters so reminiscent of MASH that I almost fell about laughing' – but reassured by what he found at Seeb: 'The airfield has a single long runway, very long because of the high temperatures. The Omani air force were our hosts and next door to us was the Sultan's Royal Flight, centred on a magnificent 747 lined with marble, and the Omani police.'

Irritations at this stage were few: 'The worst was my blasted telephone. It had Arabic numbers on it which worked from bottom to top. Someone did put tape over the numbers with European Arabic numbers but it kept falling off, so the first move I made was to get a new phone with memory facilities with which I could communicate with some confidence.' By Christmas it seemed inevitable that a conflict of some sort would have to be fought: 'Waiting for the war to start was very difficult. As more and more ships came into the Gulf we were challenging ships that had already been challenged several times by other warships and indeed other aircraft. It was obvious that the war was going to happen, but it wasn't obvious what we were going to do in it. We had our search-and-rescue role – the bomb bay was always loaded with air-sea rescue kit including liferafts – but that wasn't really what I wanted to do.'

A meeting on 9 January with a US Navy lieutenant commander gave the Nimrods the war role they had been looking for: 'They had a task which they couldn't do on their own: providing surveillance at the north end of the Gulf. Although their natural inclination was to make it an all-US Navy operation, they realised they couldn't do it and so they asked us if we would assist them. That was exactly what we were dying to do! So we worked out a very simple plan – that we would take the eight hours from the afternoon until past midnight and they would do the rest. This was entirely to do with the sea war. We were to look for patrol boats, kamikaze launches, mine-layers, anything that moved on the sea along the Iraqi and Kuwaiti coastline and the oil rigs in the northern Gulf.'

On the same day the unit received a visit from the UK's new Prime Minister, John Major: 'He listened to my presentation then talked to about 80 of us without notes for about 10 to 15 minutes. It came across extremely fluently and with terrific conviction. Then he dived into the mass of the detachment and there was a terrific amount of banter and chatting and signing of autographs. He went down extremely well. If I had any doubts, when the Prime Minister left they were gone. I knew we were going in.'

The detachment commander's first response was to call a 'captains and leaders' meeting: 'We discussed what was an acceptable standard of aircraft. In peacetime we would have wanted the radar, the ESM, the decoys, this and that. But we decided at this meeting that as long as we had four engines, a radar and a means of being identified by friendly units, that was enough – and I was overjoyed when the other four captains [of crews] came round to that viewpoint. I knew then that we had a team which would make a go of it, come what may.'

For operational reasons the detachment was now moved. The officers and aircrews were put into a nearby Omani air force officers' mess and the ground crews were moved into quarters – which quickly became known as 'Tenko' – on a naval base an hour's drive away. 'We were in the process of moving out of the hotel on the night of the 16th when I was asked to go to Ops to receive a phone call,' remembers Wight-Boycott. 'After I'd sat around for about an hour a Top Secret signal arrived from AHQ saying that the attack would start at 0400 local time. Everyone else was watching as I read it. They knew it was the start, so I told them what was in the signal and stressed that no one was to utter a word about it. The signal told me to ring the air commander. He asked me whether I had any aircraft flying and I told him I had two, one of which would be on the ground by the time the attack went in and the other on the way home. A recall sign might well have indicated something to the enemy so we decided to leave it as it was. That was it, so I went home and went to bed. Up until then there had been frustration and exasperation, but from the morning of the 17th it was downhill work. We effectively changed from doing low-level flying by day to relatively medium- and high-level flying at night. It was a complete reversal of everything we'd done but we all knew what we had to do and it was very easy.'

Wyatt flew on the first sortie after the air war had started: 'Obviously we were a bit anxious about how it was evolving because we hadn't had a lot of news – although we heard on the BBC World Service about the first air raids [on Baghdad]. It was very clinical really – calling somebody by their position. It was "first pilot", "co-pilot", "engineer" and you were referred to as "radar", "ESM" or "radios". So no first-name terms or anything like that. We flew up to about 28° north to start with, in support of the American carriers east of Qatar and 30 miles south of the border with Kuwait. We had to make sure we were identified by the British or the Americans, for starters, then work up into the Gulf and go into a holding pattern so that we were safe. We'd go up there and say, "What task have you got for us today?" and normally it was looking for fast patrol boats which the Iraqis had captured from the Kuwaitis and were a possible threat to the fleet. So we were looking for these coming out of Kuwait harbour or round the coastline.'

It quickly became apparent that the greatest risk came not from the Iraqis but from the sheer numbers of Allied forces involved. 'The risk of being shot at by an Iraqi fighter was minimal,' asserts Andy Wight-Boycott. 'So, the threats were "blue on blue" – either being shot at by ships or our own fighters. The hazard I started off considering to be minimal, but which by the end of the war was the one that worried me most, was mid-air collision. On night one someone had a major scare when a large formation of planes went past and we knew nothing about it. And talking to the tanker boys, there was more than one occasion on which they found themselves heading into a formation at a similar height about which they knew nothing. So for that reason after the first day of the war we always kept our navigation lights and our anti-collision lights on. It was fascinating in the part of the Gulf we were flying over. It really was like Piccadilly Circus, lights everywhere.'

Rules were simplified 'almost beyond recognition' in order to lessen the risk of accidents: 'The only way we could fight out there and be safe was to keep it simple – the good old KISS principle: Keep It Simple, Stupid! All the old rules about changing your call signs so no-one could identify you went out the window. We kept to the same call sign, "Dylan", day in and day out because everyone knew that was the Nimrod.'

The Nimrods' peacetime deployment to Oman had been codenamed Magic Roundabout, from the BBC children's TV series of the same name, reputedly because of the huge roundabout and clocktower in Muscat. So it followed that the Nimrods should be given codenames from the TV series: '"Zebedee" turned out to be a disaster. It caused great chaos and was only recognised by the Brits. The crews refused to use "Florence" which they thought effeminate, so we ended up as "Dylan", because the Americans could recognise and pronounce that. Our aircraft were "Dylan 45" and "Dylan 46" and we usually relieved an American P-3 whose call sign was "Elk Lodge".'

Within a few days of the air war starting the Nimrods' surveillance area had been extended up to the Kuwaiti border. 'But it was still not far enough,' declares Wight-Boycott. 'The Americans were about to go all the way up and we were being held back. I had to convince my Air Marshal that it was really safe, because obviously, losing a Nimrod with 13 men would have doubled our casualties overnight.' In early February permission was given and 'life was much easier once we could do that!'

Freedom to operate in the northern Gulf allowed the Nimrods to take up a patrolling position about 30 miles off the coast opposite Kuwait's Faylakah Island. Here they generally circled in a figure of eight pattern because 'if you fly in a figure of eight and always turn towards the area you're interested in you keep the area illuminated the whole time. Supply boats used to go from Faylakah Island to the coast and whilst they were doing that chicken run we were reporting on them, visually identifying them so that they could be picked off.'

Steve Wyatt's first contact came on the evening of 6 February: 'We were doing a surveillance sortie as normal, looking for patrol boats, I was on radar. There were very small contacts around the well-heads and I noticed one come round from one of the channels doing about 20–30 knots. We told the control ship. There's a combat air patrol out all the time called the SUCAP – surface combat air patrol, normally American carrier-borne bombers – and they were directed onto this small contact of ours. We kept reporting, updating the control ship and everyone was coming up to make sure I wasn't making any mistakes and making a fool of myself. I didn't feel under pressure at all but I was very excited with this first one when it was being attacked. I think it was two A-6 Intruders went in. First they did a run-by and identified it as military, then came round again, dropped some bombs on it and killed it. They said, "Yes, good call" and that was our first assisted call.'

Before the war was over Wyatt's crew had been accredited with six 'calls'. 'I found another two,' he recalls. 'The second one was at Faylakah Island, which was still an Iraqi stronghold. The SUCAP couldn't get there quick enough so that one got away, but the third one was a boat going towards Faylakah which for some reason turned round. The first A-6 Intruder dropped three bombs which didn't explode at all and the second dropped two, one of which exploded. The boat trundled off to Kuwait at reduced speed, so obviously it was hurt in some way.'

These successes were shared by everyone in the detachment. One of Andrew Steel's tasks was to debrief the crews on their return: 'I remember the delight and the argy-bargying that went on when one Nimrod crew handed over to another. The first crew would come back and say, "We got it," then the second would come back and say, "We got it!". You had to be the diplomat and say, "Well, you probably both got it".' There was no time at this stage for reflection. That came later: 'It wasn't until the transit back you were thinking, "I wonder how many blokes were on there. I wonder if they wanted to be there – those poor, sorry blokes who didn't know what they were getting into". Then you felt quite sad.'

By this stage the aircraft were equipped with a number of new systems and modifications whose production had been rushed through: 'In week two of the war we received our first aircraft with a MAWS [missile approach warning system] defence which automatically initiated the dispensing of chaff and infra-red flares. One of the aircraft also had a towed radar decoy, known as the turd, that was streamed behind the aircraft. We ordered an infra-red turret which gave us 360° vision beneath the aircraft. That was put onto the aircraft about two or three weeks into the war – in practice, it wasn't actually needed. But it did give us a scare, because the crew which had just been fitted with the infra-red turret also had the only plane with the towed radar decoy. The inevitable happened – they were looking through their infra-red and became convinced they had a fighter on their tail. They actually called up the ship before the penny dropped that it was their own decoy that they were trying to evade!'

However, what did arrive in time to make its mark was the Link 11 System, as carried on American AWACS and air control ships, which portrays on screen not only the positions of other aircraft but also identifies them, together with their speed and height: 'That also arrived about two weeks into the war and it was dramatic. Suddenly we realised that we were one of 200 aircraft in the Northern Arabian Gulf. If we'd been worried before about mid-air collisions, we now realised that our concerns were justified.'

Every modification and installation created more work for the ground crews who had to service every aircraft before and after each flight. 'With an aircraft as complex as this and as old as this we had lots and lots of faults,' admits Sean McCourt – who was able to join the Seeb detachment for a second tour just after hostilities had started. 'But we kept the planes going. We lost only one sortie during the hostilities, one aircraft which had to turn back because of a fault. That was all. And the boys loved it because they loved being involved. But to see these young men getting into their aircraft and know where they were going – that was worrying. We were always very glad to see them back again – and the repartee between ground crew and aircrew was tremendous.'

As the war proceeded to its inevitable conclusion the Nimrod crews found themselves with ringside seats for the gathering assault. 'You could have walked up the Gulf on friendly ships,' was Steel's impression of the scene as US Navy vessels gathered for what they thought would be a massive amphibious assault. 'We laid bets on when it was going to happen,' remembers Wyatt. 'We could see the guns of the US battleship Iowa firing and see explosions on Kuwait City and that brought it home that there was a war going on.'

As detachment commander, Wight-Boycott was mostly stuck on the ground: 'I always rather hoped we'd have more sickness which would enable me to have a seat in the aeroplane and perhaps fly as captain myself, but in the event, I've never known a bunch of guys stay so healthy for so long!' However, he was able to observe the effects of the war: 'I never really thought a Nimrod would be in a position to see triple A. I watched it fascinated – I was frightened to watch in case I saw a bigger burst which would be one of our own aircraft being shot down. Every so often I'd see something like a missile going up – a surface-to-air missile. That was a sight which will stay with me.

'After the ceasefire, flying up the Kuwaiti coast, looking at those terrific smoke stacks, was like something out of a Lowry painting of the Midlands, so many columns of smoke. I also looked at Faylakah Island which we had sat off so many times trying to intercept boats, and I saw to my amazement that it was little more than an enormous sandbank – a totally insignificant island. And yet for three weeks we had watched it as if our lives depended on it.'

With the ceasefire, air patrols were stepped down but not discontinued – 'there might still have been a threat that some Iraqi would get away and have a last pop – a suicide bid'. However, with the arrival of newly-serviced aircraft from Kinloss and St Mawgan, with fresh aircrews and ground crews, it was possible for the first Gulf War veterans to start to go home.

Until this point the painting of female mascots on the aircraft had been forbidden, for fear of upsetting their hosts. Now two examples of ground crew nose art appeared overnight. 'I won't say I sanctioned it,' declares McCourt, 'I didn't know it was there till the morning. That was Muscat Belle, and the other one was called Guernsey Lil.' The former was said to be based – with very considerable licence – on the daughter of the British ambassador in Oman.

Andy Wight-Boycott was able to travel home the way he wanted: 'I flew myself back to Kinloss in a Nimrod and, for me, that was a very fitting finale to my flying career.' He found his three sons 'rather disappointed that for most of the war we weren't even within Scud range. Nonetheless, I think they were very proud that their dad was there.'

Andrew Steel came home 'proud to have been able to play a part, frustrated that I couldn't have done more' and saddened to find that the three Nimrod squadrons' long service in the Gulf – 'we were probably there longer than anybody else, we're still there, in fact, as we speak' – had received very little public recognition. Waiting for him on station were his wife and his dog – 'a big, two-year-old yellow Labrador named Loonie because he's got no brain. I was expecting a nice greeting from my wife and I expected Loonie at least to jump up on me. But he got fed up while they were waiting and fell asleep, and I had to step over him to get to my wife and say hello.'

Chapter 4

CONFRONTING A BULLY

> 'We are confronting a bully who thinks he can get away with kicking sand in the face of the world. We will not pull our punches . . .'
>
> *President George Bush*

'I lost one and a half stone and felt much better for it, too.' Sandy Wilson's experience was shared by the vast majority of those under his command. Massive weight loss in the heat and stress of August was common. As regular patterns were established and as the days became cooler, the physical rigours of life in the Gulf lessened, but inevitably tiredness set in. 'It was immensely challenging and there was great job satisfaction,' Wilson declares, 'but it made sense to rotate the crews. So, of course, another team fought the war.' On 17 November he handed over command to AVM Bill Wratten, with the knowledge that 'the scene had been set and the machinery was up and running'.

Such sentiments were voiced by aircrew and ground crews alike. 'When people are operating under pressure, they begin to go off the boil,' suggests Wg Cdr Vaughan Morris. A decision had to be made about whether or not to stay longer 'but the war might be next week, it might be next month, or it might be in six months. We'd done nothing but live and breathe the war effort. When we first went out there it was seven weeks before I was able to give the ground crew a day off. They worked a minimum of 12-hour shifts – most were 14-hour shifts – seven days a week for seven weeks. That was hard. I certainly felt very drained and ready for a rest at the end of three months.'

The first wave of handovers took place in November. 'I felt great sadness at actually leaving the place and handing over to someone else,' Morris admits. But there was the feeling that they had given their successors time to prepare: 'They'd had three months of sitting back, listening, watching, adjusting themselves and their emotions to cope with what was inevitable – that they would be going down to the Gulf themselves.'

For David Hamilton, commanding the Tornado F3 detachment at Dhahran, the last weeks before the handover were particularly hard: 'As it got closer to the end I got more and more worried. We were doing all this training, and the flying was so demanding that by the law of averages we might lose somebody – and I wanted to take everybody home. I kept telling the guys, "Don't let your guard down now. This is the dangerous part. You've got to concentrate". We kept doing that, talking to the guys all the time – and then our time came to go home. Some people were desperate to go home in time for Christmas and some said, "I want to stay and finish the fight".'

'I was ready to go home,' admits Tornado GR1 pilot Flt Lt John Hogg. 'I didn't want to think about anything else. I'd never been away from my wife for three months before and it was a long, long time. I thought, "Hurrah, I'm going home" – and, naively, I didn't think the conflict was going to start.'

Among the RAF Regiment Rapier gunners around Muharraq, there was widespread resentment at having to leave. 'About 80% of the guys were really a bit cheesed off,' reports Bill Lacey. 'We'd done all the work through the heat and we were prepared to stay on. And for me, to have to hand over the kit that we'd cared for and my sites to another squadron just to take over, that was quite a bitter pill.'

His successor was Sqn Ldr John Page, OC 66 Sqn, who was presented with 'a going concern' with sites that resembled 'French Foreign Legion castles coming out of the sea, quite spectacular' – and inherited a lot of local goodwill, both from the British expatriate community and the Bahrainis. 'I can't praise them enough for their friendliness,' he declares. 'Everything we'd asked for suddenly fell into place. That experience taught me not to consider races as a whole. We began to understand their customs, and the troops began to appreciate that the benign paternalism of the Emir of Kuwait actually worked quite well.'

Captain Brian O'Connor, an American exchange pilot flying with 43 Sqn from RAF Leuchars, was conscious too that he and the other newcomers had much to be grateful for: 'Those going home had goinghomeitis. They did all the work without the final reward. But we reaped the benefits of their efforts and that was very good. They'd broken a lot of ground and bashed their heads against a lot of brick walls, so that we didn't have to.'

Sqn Ldr Phil Goodall, coming out to Muharraq to take over as the Jaguar SENGO at the end of November, had the same feelings. 'But our comrades looked very tired and we were glad they were going home. They'd done a superb job, living in very bad conditions in Thumrait, and then in a five-star hotel, but always with the fear of going to war at any minute.'

Before the handover was complete, Saddam Hussein once again changed the whole tone of the crisis. 'It was Sunday 2 December,' Goodall remembers. 'I was with my namesake, Group Captain Rocky Goodall, at the morning brief when someone put their head round the door and said the Iraqis had just launched a Scud. Then about five minutes later, a second Scud was launched and we thought, "Crikey, it's happening. This is the beginning of the war and we've only just arrived in theatre". I looked at the Group Captain, he looked at me, and I said, "Shall we load?" We knew the targets and what weapons to use, so I went off and told my guys, "This is no duff. They've launched Scud missiles and we're to arm the aircraft". In fact, it was just Saddam test-launching his missiles, but we thought they were firing on Israel and there'd be a chain of events that would start the war.'

It soon became clear that there was no threat, 'but we kept the scenario running and it eventually turned into just an exercise'. For David Hamilton, too, the alarm proved most valuable: 'The way we reacted was a high point for me as commander – because the system worked. I was so pleased that as I drove back to the troops I was beating the steering wheel of the car, shouting.'

But Peter Jerrard, preparing to go home, was far from pleased by what later became known as 'Scud Sunday'. 'On the day I was leaving my boss said, "You haven't had much of a chance to see Bahrain because you've been holed up". So he took me for a drive, and when we got back we had the "Red" air raid alert, which meant inbound Scud. "Bloody typical", I thought, "the day I'm going back, World War Three starts!"'

Returning to the UK, Jerrard assumed that he was now 'at the bottom of the list'. However, no sooner had he returned to RAF Hereford from his disembarkation leave than he was summoned to the OC's office: 'He said, "Guess what, Pete! You're on warning to go back to the Gulf as a replacement for casualties!"'

Tornado F3 navigator Flt Lt Mark Robinson, who had gone out with 29 Sqn in the first phase of Granby, also found himself having to prepare for a second Gulf tour: 'We'd been there, we'd got the poseur T-shirt, but we'd have had to be pretty dumb not to realise that we'd probably be going back'. And in late November he got the news that he would indeed be going back – to what now appeared to be certain war: 'This time I did a huge circuit of Britain and saw everybody that I knew, because I had to assume that I wasn't coming back. That sounds really macabre and melodramatic, but it isn't really. I said hello to everybody, had a good night out with a lot of people and then went, thinking, "Well, at least if I'm going to die I've seen everybody before I go".'

Angus Hogg, too, had already been out in the Gulf with 31 Sqn, and he also left with a heart full of foreboding: 'Saying goodbye to my children and to my wife was one of the worst moments of my life. It was the finality of it. I told my little girl, "Remember I love you". I remember taking her to school, and her not really being interested and wanting to run off and be with her pals. But for me it meant everything.'

In December more British ground troops were ordered to join the massive allied build-up. In anticipation of casualties on a large scale, the RAF was asked to provide large numbers of medical personnel. Under Wg Cdr Geoff Davies, 250 RAF medics and support staff drawn from 31 different units trained together for 10 days before flying out to Muharraq to set up the RAF War Hospital. 'The hardest thing,' recalls Davies, 'was to get all these people to trust each other and to trust me. The way to minimise battle shock is to have good cohesion. Then everyone feels more secure and they look after each other better.' By a stroke of luck the entire unit could be housed together in one complex, which was 'the best thing that happened to us'.

Other medical units were also being formed. Brize Norton expanded its peacetime Aeromed Evacuation

Sqn into six teams to staff converted VC10s: 'Each had a doctor, anaesthetist, nurses, nursing attendants and so on. An initial setback was the lack of kit but eventually we had complete standardisation. So if we opened a locker at the back there would be a sphygmomanometer or in that cupboard a syringe pump, while at the front was the intensive care set-up capable of flying five ventilated patients on each aircraft.'

Complex back-up arrangements were prepared, synchronised with local hospitals, so that quick turnarounds and resupplies would allow the planes to keep a constant shuttle going if need be. In the event, of course, the system was never put to the full test: 'Prior to the war starting we were bringing back something like 30-plus casualties a week. We'd get the chap who fell off a tank, the chap who fell off the wing of an aircraft, someone who suffered appendicitis or had an abscess on a wisdom tooth. Then a few weeks into the Gulf War we were bringing back 50-plus and some weeks 70-plus. So it worked. Everybody pulled together and we did it.'

As well as medics, attendants and aircrew needed immediately for casevacs (casualty evacuations) from the battlefield and field hospitals, in anticipation of large numbers of casualties auxiliaries and reservists were also called up and put on standby. Among them was SAC Richard Gregorczyk from 4626 Aeromed Evacuation Sqn, made up mostly of TA part-timers. 'We heard on the One O'Clock News that our squadron was going,' remembers Gregorczyk, who is a stonemason in civilian life. 'The official call-up papers arrived just before Christmas and that was the first time since Suez that a whole auxiliary squadron was called up'. Cpl Jacquie Owen, a full-time auxiliary, was just as surprised and shocked: 'I wanted to go, but on the aircraft we were all thinking the same thing – that this could be a one-way journey.'

They arrived at Al Jubayl as the worst weather for years was setting in. Accommodation was found for them at the appropriately named Baldrick Lines which Owen describes as 'horrific'. 'The tents weren't waterproof and often collapsed and the washing facilities consisted of a big bench outside and bowls of water.' The toilets, adds Gregorczyk, were 'disgusting'.

However, this was to be only a temporary staging post for most of the medics. Senior Aircraftwoman (SACW) Connie Dale, an RAF regular who had worked on a burns unit dealing with injured soldiers from the Sir Galahad disaster in the Falklands, ended up as part of a 10-strong aeromed team at Dhahran airbase, where the mostly female unit's first task was to dig themselves air-raid shelters. 'With the help of the Royal Engineers we filled about 17,000 sandbags in three days. They said they'd never seen women work so hard, but we were doing one sandbag to their one sandbag because we didn't want to let ourselves down. Once that was set up and sorted out, it was Christmas time.'

If the reservists and medics were shaken to find themselves in the Gulf, so too were numerous RAF musicians. Traditionally they had always acted as stretcher-bearers in times of war, but it was not what they had joined the RAF for. Flt Sgt John Williams had just returned from touring the Gulf with an RAF dance band called the Squadronaires. Now, he and other musicians found themselves doing a quick medical training course before returning to Saudi Arabia. They joined the evacuation teams – whose job it would be to ship the wounded from the front line dressing stations down to Al Jubayl and then back to the UK.

The RAF plan was that their Puma helicopters – capable of taking six stretcher cases and four seated wounded – would casevac the wounded from the battle-field to the front line field dressing stations, and the bigger Chinooks would transfer them to field hospitals or the RAF hospital. Wg Cdr Mike Trace was in charge of the Puma wing, drawn from 230 Sqn at RAF Gütersloh and 33 Sqn from RAF Odiham. One problem that he had to sort out in 'exercise after exercise after exercise' was having more aircraft than the field dressing stations could cope with: 'The army medics hadn't seen that weight of support before, because they were used to operating primarily by vehicle. We were also working over fairly short distances so the aircraft were rattling around. Nor did the medics immediately appreciate the effects of weather, particularly sandstorms which slowed us right down – and flying at night, which was very tiring.'

The desert sand took its toll of helicopter engines but spares arrived remarkably quickly. Not so parkas: 'It was bloody cold and I had frost in my tent on three consecutive mornings. So we demanded 250 Canadian parkas. Fifty arrived. Where the rest went, goodness only knows.'

Working as a medic with the Chinooks out in the desert was Sgt Ian Tervit from RAF Cottesmore: 'There were only six of us so we formed our own little group. We weren't allowed, under the terms of the Geneva Convention, to do guard duties but we set up our own area and dug our own trenches'. Their main role was dealing with 'the little infections and personal hygiene' – and giving all the extra jabs required to provide immunity against biological agents: 'There is a course of vaccines. The first gives a degree of protection, the second takes it up further and the third to 100%. If the equipment we had was worn correctly, we wouldn't be affected anyway so it was a belt and braces job. But it made us very popular.'

Also working on the Chinooks was aircraft electrician SAC Andy Garton. 'They said, "It hasn't rained here for two years". I thought, "Fair cop," but as soon as we got there it rained. It wasn't a shower. It rained and rained and rained. Everything was soaking wet and we lived in a quagmire. I'd had this feeling that deserts were cold at night, so I'd taken my European combats, just in case. But a lot of people hadn't and they were banging their heads it was so cold.'

There was, however, the pleasure of working side by side with 'that strange race', the Americans: 'They had their equivalent of a NAAFI shop wherever they were and one of the funniest things out there was this burger caravan about two miles down the road. They had free cheeseburgers for troops which were so bloody marvellous you couldn't resist trying them. Every time you went near it you had to have a burger.'

Even at Al Jubayl there were lighter moments. 'A lake developed between the tents of Blackadder Lines. There were naval elements on the other side so we decided to have a boat race', explains Gp Capt Charles Newrick, consultant pathologist at 32 Field Hospital. 'The Navy built a pretty impressive construction, vaguely like a ship, while the RAF and Army TA put together some plastic water bottles. But theirs sank immediately on launching while ours sailed across the lake . . .'

Christmas was celebrated at a score of RAF bases in the Gulf in as many different ways. Flt Lt Alexander Gordon, of 43 Sqn, had taken the precaution of cele-brating it a month early on 25 November with his wife and friends back in Leuchars. 'We really went for it,' he remembers. 'We had the full nine yards. Turkey, Christmas pud, lots of booze, everything. Then we sat down in front of the television and watched a 1940s vintage black and white weepie. We had tea, exchanged presents and that for us was Christmas.'

Christmas Day itself at Dhahran was less memorable: 'The aircrew made a point of going down to the squadron with a load of parcels from the British Legion and various companies. We distributed them, as well as biscuits, mince pies and non-alcoholic beer, to our ground crew who were still working on shift. I'm still not sure whether they appreciated that or not!' What certainly was appreciated was the support given to wives and families back home and in Germany: 'The local Woolworths, Marks and Spencer and other stores gave out boxes of biscuits, pairs of underpants, little things – but it was brilliant, because of the good feeling it engendered both at home and out in the Gulf. I shall shop in Marks and Spencer for evermore because of that!'

Probably the most miserable Christmas was that spent by those who were caught in transit, like Cpl Kevin Grisdale and SAC Thomas Stafford, both from RAF Lossiemouth. 'We spent Christmas Day in the Gateway Hotel at Brize, which was closed,' remembers Grisdale. 'I phoned my wife and she was not impressed.' On Boxing Day they were told they could go home for 36 hours. 'But from Brize Norton to Lossiemouth is a long way. We'd have had an hour there before turning back again so we were hacked off with it.' Eventually, they ended up in Al Jubayl on local resource supply 'buying up everything in Saudi Arabia', building up contacts with local Saudi businessmen – and finding to their surprise that 'the locals were brilliant. We made a lot of good friends.'

Christmas Day on the Puma squadron followed traditional lines as closely as possible, as Mike Trace explains: 'We set up a "cooked food" area at the car park. We invited the Americans over, asked their cooks to come and help out and we had this combined party in the evening, outside on a night that the wind made bitterly cold. We had our own cabaret, which was good fun because we had to explain the jokes to the Americans. But that was it. It was over in one night and New Year passed by without our even noticing.'

Out in Tabuk Chf Tech Mark Norton chose to work through Christmas Day: 'It was a bit of an anti-climax. We tried to put on a show but people were so tired after a 12-hour shift they just went to bed. I volunteered to work, mainly so that I could use the phone to get through to my family.' At Tabuk, only queues to use the lavatories were longer than queues for the phone: 'The worst thing was having to book a cubicle, because we had five proper toilets and three out of five usually weren't working. If you were desperate you went out and scooped a hole and squatted in the desert.'

Life and Christmas were more civilised back at Muharraq – from which the BBC's Christmas Eve Songs of Praise service and link-up with service families in Fallingbostel and Aldershot was broadcast. 'Everything was all ready and ticketyboo,' remembers Sqn Ldr Peter Mutch, acting as the RAF's press liaison officer. 'Then half an hour before the programme, all the lights went out in Bahrain. Our emergency diesel generator was filled with petrol, but we managed to siphon it out and got them back on with about ten minutes to spare.'

In fact, the link-up depressed rather than lifted spirits, according to Geoff Davies: 'A lot of the army guys were in a real mess because it emphasised that they were away from home. I found one officer crying. So Christmas Day was pretty miserable. At the army hospital the officers served the food at the Christmas dinner and the troops went bananas, throwing food, which disgusted my lot. But after that we actually felt better, because we realised we could do better than that.'

SAC Scott Randall, an ops assistant in XV Sqn, has different memories of Christmas Day in Muharraq. He worked for part of the day before a cocktail party and Christmas lunch, followed by a swim: 'It was a terrific day but the biggest event was the Scud warning.'

It was Scuds, too, that interrupted the day in Riyadh.

John Ayers and other Hercules aircrews had celebrated the night before and anticipated 'a late lie-in till about lunchtime. We got the alarm at about seven o'clock and all dashed down to the cellar with our survival equipment and respirators on – and there we stayed – for so long that I fell asleep in my NBC suit. Some time later one of our number who thought this was going on rather a long time wandered out in his NBC suit and mask, the lot, to be met by the rest of the detachment sitting round the pool. The alert had been cancelled after it had been sounded but nobody had got the message through to us. Saddam Hussein had been doing a test firing in the direction of Israel. After that, the engineer in our crew devised an alarm system for the whole of the compound by wiring up a series of car horns.'

With Christmas over, the 15 January deadline laid down by the UN for the Iraqi withdrawal from Kuwait assumed ever greater significance. On 28 December it was announced that British nationals in the Gulf would be issued with respirators, and joint Army-RAF teams flew out to instruct them in NBC drill. SAC Fred Reid was part of a team of three based at the British Consulate in Dhahran. 'We did 3,640 civvies in five days,' he remembers. 'Kids, women, oil-rig workers, and we were saying amongst ourselves that if half of them survived that was a job well done. We were fitting them with respirators, briefly running over what to do if chemicals were used and where to go in the house if there was an air raid. The quality of the British NBC respirators was definitely better than the American models – we had Americans trying to buy them off everyone.'

Following hard on their heels came a 45-strong mobile field laboratory unit, whose job it would be to track down and identify any chemicals or biological viruses released into the atmosphere by shells, bombs or missiles. 'We came from different forces,' explains Cpl Steve Curme, a specialist lab technician from RAF Halton. 'We had nine teams of five, each with a Land Rover, made up of two RAF lab technicians to test air and soil samples, two REME technicians – a driver and an electrical technician – and a Regiment sergeant who was the vehicle commander.' They decided to call themselves 1 FLU, the 1st Field Laboratory Unit, and gave themselves a coat of arms based on a flu virus.

On 6 January the Prime Minister, John Major, began a three-day tour of the Gulf visiting British forces. 'I introduced him to the guys,' recalls Wg Cdr Jerry Witts, OC 31 Sqn at Dhahran. 'He called everyone together and he told us, "Look here, chaps, we're here to support the UN via the coalition, alongside the Americans. UN Resolution 678 must be upheld. Even now I hope it won't come to a fight, but even if it does I know that you're ready – and good luck". Something in the way he said it made me think he knew something I didn't.' The same unspoken message was delivered by 'a stream of Air Marshals who came down to wish us luck and say they wished they were with us – the sort of things that Air Marshals say – to which you reply under your breath, "Jolly glad you aren't!"' He continues, 'Then it was a race against time.'

It was the same everywhere. Out with the Chinooks in the desert, Andy Garton watched the pace pick up 'as we got closer and closer to the deadline. At Christmas we'd started 12-hour shifts so we worked three days and three nights, then changing round every week from nights to days, which was an 18-hour shift. On our off-time we just slept.'

Fg Off Rachael Berry had only recently become the first woman MAMS team leader and had a point to prove: 'It was a lot to think about, as the first woman doing the job.' Berry's concerns were not unjustified. Going through Riyadh on her first day, her flight was delayed. Hearing that people were busy loading equipment at the airport, she suggested to a senior NCO that she give a hand: 'I remember him standing smartly to attention and saying, "Well, with all due respect, ma'am, I don't really feel that movements work is the sort of work that a WRAF officer should be doing." So I said,' "Oh, and why is that then?" He said, "Well, it's all heavy work, and lifting and things. It's just not really ladies' work." I said, "I hate to say anything, but it's exactly the job that I'm going to be doing".'

In Muharraq, Berry got to grips with her job and had to make some difficult decisions: 'Going through officer training I'd thought, "Why on earth am I doing all this lead-by-example malarkey?" But in Bahrain I thought, "Well, it really is important", because I vividly remember having to pick somebody to carry on working. He'd already worked for 15 hours and I had to ask him to work another eight! I got people's backs up, I know I did, but generally, I was very conscious of morale. The working hours were very long, you'd finish at, say, six o'clock in the evening and then be expecting an aircraft in at ten o'clock. So you'd have your four hours off – not long enough to get any sleep. Working 24 hours, the next morning you'd think, "Oh God, I'm still here!"' She fell asleep at her desk more than once, usually when she was due to go home.

It was no different back in Britain, where every modification that had any relevance to operations in the Gulf was now being furiously implemented. There seemed to be an infinite pot of gold to be drawn upon: 'If you had "Granby" attached to any modification on a Tornado it would happen. You're talking millions of pounds that just appeared. They leapt two and a half years in modifications in almost the same number of weeks.'

On the Jaguar lines at Coltishall the set routines went

out of the window as eight or nine aircraft were worked on, all in different stages of modification. 'It was just a mass of moving panel racks,' explains Flt Sgt Gil Harding. 'Because you move the aircraft round you have to move the paperwork, all the components, all the spares. We ended up with a system where each aircraft had a rack and everything was mobile, even the desks. All the paperwork was on clipboards, because if you opened the doors, it all blew out of the hangar. Every morning when I came in after the graveyard shift, I had to walk round and find out where all the aircraft were. I'd go round shouting "Why is that cockpit empty?" because if one guy stepped out, I wanted another guy in, doing the job. By mid-January people were beginning to droop – but I can say of Granby that the airfields worked as they should have. Everybody was pulling together.'

On every flying squadron new aircrew were continuing to arrive. All had to make hurried adjustments to the unfamiliar environment, as well as learning to operate new items of equipment and familiarising themselves with new operating procedures. 'I can still remember that first trip down to the southern desert, the Great Arabian FA,' declares F3 pilot Alexander Gordon. 'It was classical desert, entirely featureless. It's very difficult to pick out any features because the sun's so bright and the sand reflects the glare back at you. I remember watching the shadow beneath my wingman getting closer and closer as he descended, just edging down below 250ft for the first time. We did three or four PIs [practice intercepts] over the same bit of desert and the same camel was there each time. It was the only camel and it became almost like a navigation feature.'

The Tornado GR1s practised a number of new weapons delivery techniques, as Flt Lt Colin Adair of 31 Sqn explains: 'We do a "lay down", which is where we fly at low level and drop our bombs as we go over, and we do

67

a "lock", when we pull up and throw the bomb. But we also practised new techniques with high angle dives at medium level, where we turn on our backs, dive down, see our target, release our bombs and pull away.' There were also vital briefing sessions with American survival and rescue specialists. These left Adair 'gobsmacked' by what the US forces were prepared to do if their aircraft crashed in enemy territory or if they had to bale out: 'They would be coming in with everything – sand-buggies, special radios, special lights. It was, "Don't worry, boys. You go down and we'll come and get you".'

Given the intensity of training it was almost inevitable that there would be casualties – and there were. 'We lost Kieran and Norman on the Sunday before the war started, on the 13th,' remembers GR1 navigator Sqn Ldr Bertie Newton: 'Somebody heard that a VC10 navigator had put out a Mayday at this position, so I had a look at the map and it was where we would have been flying. I thought it was almost certainly not a VC10 but a Tornado. This was in Oman, about three hours' flying away, so there was a long wait before we knew which one of the three crews had been killed.'

For their squadron commander Vaughan Morris, the deaths of Flt Lts Kieran Duffy and Norman Dent just days before the war started seemed 'such a waste. That was what gave me more personal grief than anything else. They were two young lads with lots of spirit but they were gentlemen, great friends of everyone. They were leading lights in the squadron junta, as it's known, the young men in the squadron who are the personalities, but they were both dedicated to their jobs. Both had been disappointed when they couldn't go in August and they were both really thrilled when they were given the opportunity to go in January.'

For Colin Adair the crash meant the loss of a close

friend: 'Kieran and I had gone through training together. He lived next door to me in the mess and he would always pop round for a beer or something and chat about his latest love problems. My wall has views of Scotland and the odd girlie pin-up but Kieran had aircraft all over the wall. He loved the Air Force and loved flying. I don't know if he knew any fear. He was so confident in himself, that he could do just about anything. Every time you saw him he was grinning for some reason or other. You could see his smile from miles away. He was a great guy and I miss him terribly.'

The crash undoubtedly came as a major blow to morale at a difficult time: 'It was a tragedy for the squadron and of course it knocked other people who were just about to go to war themselves – particularly the ground crew who'll never forget that they started the aircraft up and waved goodbye as it went off. But there was a closing of ranks and we bounced back very quickly.'

On 9 January, with the deadline for Iraqi withdrawal less than a week away, US Secretary of State Baker and Iraq's Tariq Aziz held talks in Geneva – to no avail. 'We were doing a survival course that day,' remembers Mark Richardson. 'We listened at lunchtime and they were talking. We came back in the evening and they were still talking and we thought, "They can't sit and talk about nothing for six hours". Then Aziz came on TV and said, basically, nothing had happened. I remember the jaws round the room thumping on the ground.' Angus Elliott continues: 'It was like a cinema. He just said four words, "I regret to say" – nobody spoke. We just sat and I thought, "Shit, this is it".'

Then came the moment when all aircrews were summoned to station commanders' briefings. 'It was just like something out of the Second World War,' is how Mark Robinson of 29 Sqn remembers it at Dhahran. 'I could have been watching a film. They pulled in 31 Sqn – the

GR1s. All the aircrew piled into this room, all the screens were pulled back and there was this map of the Middle East, classic Biggles-style. The station commander stood there and said, "Gentlemen, what you are about to hear is top secret, very, very secret squirrel, and if this leaves the room it will cost lives". When we heard that, 300 chins hit the floor. He gave us a brief overview of how the war was going to start. He couldn't tell us when it was going to start, but this was how. And at the end of that – it was only about fifteen minutes long – he said, "Gentlemen, this is the last time we will all be together. May I wish you the best of luck". And that was it. I expected some film star to walk in and say, "OK chaps, here we go".'

Angus Hogg was also there: 'I remember thinking it was incredible, looking round, again wondering how many of us would be here in a few weeks' time and thinking, "This is it. These are the guys who are going to go out and do the business". I must say I felt quite privileged to be part of it.'

Chapter 5

THE STORM BREAKS

'The skies are illuminated now by large flashes . . .
the entire city is blacked out. A bomb came down
near the hotel . . . you can feel it shaking the
building. There's a very bright flash at a refinery
building. There's something on fire . . .'

John Holliman, CNN
Baghdad, 0240, 17 January 1991

'I hung around until about 5.30 in the afternoon but
nothing seemed to be happening. There was nothing
more I could do, so I went back to the house I shared
with Wing Commander Ivor Evans and helped myself
to one of those alcohol-free beers. We were watching
CNN and chatting. I remarked that it was the end of
the 16th and nothing had happened. I thought that now
he'd faced off past the deadline, he'd start to pull out.
Then my phone rang.'

It was Jerry Witts' Ops officer: '"Can you come to
work, boss?" he said, "Straight away." From his tone
of voice I knew exactly what it was. I just grabbed my
kit and drove in. I was absolutely terrified. I remember
my knees were trembling, my foot was shaking on the
accelerator, I was crunching the gears. I was thinking,
"I can't believe this! I can't believe this!" I remember
looking at other motorists and thinking, "I wonder if
they know where I'm going?"'

That same afternoon Victor tanker pilot Sqn Ldr Dick Druitt was also being called in, 'I actually had a phone call with a particular coded message. "The mail is out" meant that you weren't needed. "The mail is in" meant you were needed to bring your crew in. So we all came in and then it suddenly dawned on everyone that we were about to do something unstoppable. We were actually about to start something. It was then that people became more serious.'

Up until the last moments, most had to be kept in the dark about the impending air attack, Witts remembers: 'Slowly, as the time ticked by, we let the curtain lift a little and let more and more people know that something was happening.' Even as the first wave took off some hours later, those who would form part of the second wave did not know exactly what was going on. 'I wandered in at eleven o'clock', recalls Flt Lt Neil Cobb, 'and the station manager said, "Oh, are you on this one then?" I thought, "I don't know what he's talking about", and said, "I don't think so, sir". "Jolly good" he said.'

One reason for secrecy was the proximity of the journalists. 'I got quite neurotic about keeping quiet,' recalls Witts. 'The last thing I wanted was for the media to get hold of it, they were virtually living on top of us. Charles Drago of CNN was staying at the hotel 100 yards off the end of the runway, and you can imagine what would have happened if he'd found out we were about to go.'

The running order for the first night was contained in an air tasking message, out of which commanders would take the small frag (fragment) that detailed their own operation. Wg Cdr Bill Pixton explains how the frag tasked his Desert Cats against a typical target. On careful examination of the cross-referencing notes 'I would find that flying top cover somewhere there would be four or six F-15s, and another half dozen Wild Weasel F4Gs and 16s to suppress surface-to-air missile systems. There would be tanker support, AWACS support, airborne command control posts and all sorts of stuff.'

In amongst this incredible display of air power, the Tornado GR1s (four from Dhahran and eight from Muharraq) that would make the first strike had been given a vital role to play. They were to attack the sprawling Iraqi airbases, aiming to destroy the taxiways which led from the HASs (hardened aircraft shelters) to the runways, so stranding the enemy air force in its shelters. They were armed with the JP233, the runway denial weapon which, according to Sandy Wilson, is unique: 'Whilst the Americans had an enormous number of weapons in their inventory, they didn't have anything quite like this.'

The principle behind the weapon is to make the runway as hard to repair as possible. Jerry Witts describes how it works: 'It drops two cartons of weapons. It drops a series of cratering devices which are like big tubes or rockets and float down on parachutes. When they are just above the ground they fire off. There's a shaped charge inside that goes through the concrete, then blows up, thus heaving the concrete up. It should excavate the ground underneath, which makes it extremely difficult to repair. And then, to make sure no-one can get to the hole, it drops a load of small mines.'

In the final hours of briefing and preparation, one pre-flight task that took on a special significance was the routine removal of all personal possessions. Flt Lt Malcolm Hammans explains: 'When we fly a war sortie, we don't carry anything that is personalised apart from an identification card with our name, rank and number. We take off things like wedding rings and put them in little plastic bags. That was the worst part: we knew we were going to go and do it, and it almost seemed that we weren't going to come back. A lot of us felt sick and very nervous.'

Two extra items had been included in the 'Go' bag of those due to fly across the border. The first was £800 in gold to help negotiate a passage to safety with local tribes. The other was the 'goolie chit', which promised, in Arabic, that Her Majesty's Government would pay a bounty of £5,000 to anyone who returned an airman – complete – to the allies. Intelligence officer Fg Off David Owen states: 'In conflicts in that part of the world in the 1920s, captured RAF aircrew had their testicles cut off and put into their mouths – which is apparently the most offensive thing an Arab can do to someone.'

Not surprisingly the mood was a sombre one as the 'time to walk' approached. 'We eventually went out to the planes at about one o'clock in the morning,' recalls Witts. 'I remember thinking it was strangely normal, as though I expected something completely different.' In addition, he had specifically asked for there to be no emotion at the send-off: 'I didn't want a load of gung-ho blokes waving Union Jacks. It didn't seem appropriate, because the effect would have been worse if we hadn't come back. I wanted the whole thing to be level-headed and serious. War struck me as a serious business.'

Dick Druitt, as pilot of one of the two Victors taking the first eight Tornados from Muharraq to drop JP233s, also considered the gravity of his actions. He remembers 'sitting in the aeroplane, starting the engines. I just sat there and thought to myself, "What the hell am I about to do? What can of worms am I about to open? I felt I could be starting the Third World War".' But, whatever his misgivings, he knew that 'it was my job, I had to do it, I wasn't going to stop from doing it'.

He also knew that it was his job to lead the way: 'The boss of the squadron was in one plane and I was in the other. We felt we should go first, since we didn't know what would happen. Contrary to the way the Army works, we send our officers in first, and our engineers were very pleased to see that. They all said they saw why we were worth our flying pay! I think they were very proud of us actually.'

Also on the first night's sortie – and sharing the tense moments before take-off – were four of the Desert Cats, the Jaguars operating from Muharraq. Bill Pixton remembers: 'We did all the pre-flight checks and start checks. Then, because we gave ourselves plenty of time but did everything twice as fast as we normally would, we ended up sitting in the cockpit listening to the clock tick. And you can start to think *too* much. Once you're airborne and you remember that this is what you do for a living you calm down a bit.'

The first air strikes were to be carried out at night because of the superior night vision capabilities of the allied aircraft and because they were going in low. 'It was one of those dark nights that you can only get in the desert,' Witts recalls. 'Very thick blackness. People talk about dark velvet desert nights and that's how it felt.'

It hid air activity on an enormous scale. Back on the ground Mark Richardson contemplated 'the sheer financial clout of launching 1,000 planes, each worth £20–30 million'. The sky was so full of aircraft it was difficult to find a slot to check in with the AWACS. Amongst them was Tornado F3 pilot Sqn Ldr Paul Brown, who remembers: 'We cruised out from Dhahran through the safe lane transit route. We were wearing night vision goggles. We had dozens of contacts on the radar and hundreds of sightings – all the lights milling around. With the goggles you can see lights to a range of about 80 miles. So we knew where most of the tanker tow lines were, where the aircraft were refuelling and forming up before they went on their first strike mission across the border.'

Jerry Witts was leading a fourship headed towards a large airfield in southern Iraq: 'I began to get quite excited. I thought it was fantastic. There were hundreds and hundreds of planes up there – we were going to stuff this bloke and he deserved it. And it was going to be OK because we were all there.'

The first major task to focus the minds of the pilots was tanking at night, a skill that some had only recently acquired. The tankers played a vital role, ensuring that the heavily-laden Tornados and Jaguars had sufficient fuel to reach their targets. 'If the opposition had been anything like military people,' says Druitt, 'the first planes they'd have taken out would have been the tankers and the AWACS, because without them the others could never have reached their targets. I went off as number two and I had trouble finding the other tanker,' he continues. 'When I actually did, I was almost in his underwing tank just to keep him in sight, because it was essential to have two tankers for that operation. One tanker for eight Tornados wouldn't have been enough. So the whole push of that first day depended on my not losing him. It made the adrenalin flow.'

H hour was set for midnight GMT (0300 local time). In order to achieve their required ToT (time on target) the strike force had to take off before the war started. Witts explains: 'It had been calculated that the Iraqis had an early warning line which extended into Saudi Arabia by a certain number of miles. So the routing plan was that we would take off and stay south of that line until midnight.'

The armada moved north and east towards the early warning line. F3 navigator Flt Lt Angus Elliott was flying a CAP and can still visualise what he saw on his radar: 'As we turned south, the number of targets – or shall I say pilots – on the radar increased dramatically. I thought, "This is a problem". Then I realised it wasn't, that this was a mass raid from all sides, all levels, heights, every-thing, running up towards the border and aiming to cross it together in a blanket push. They reached a certain point, switched off their IFF [Interrogate Friend or Foe] and in they went.'

With the lights off and radio contact at a minimum, the Tornados dropped down to low level and pushed ahead towards their different targets – described by some as 'like being in a simulator: quiet and almost unreal'.

Malcolm Hammans (who was on a later raid) gives an evocative account of a war sortie across the desert: 'When we go to war we're in the middle of nowhere and it's absolutely pitch black, there are no lights of villages, of roads or anything. It was a dark night, hardly any moon, a few stars, and we were at 200ft without seeing anything until we came to the target area.

'As we came towards the target there was nothing. We were rushing into this black hole. Our first aircraft attacked the field and all of a sudden there was a wall of triple A [anti-aircraft artillery]. It seemed that everyone on that airfield was firing at us. It was going above us, below us, down both wings. The whole place was lit up. We were very close to the other aircraft and we could see their weapons going off – we had to grit our teeth and keep going.'

Paul Brown saw the triple A from the safe distance of his Tornado F3: 'Suddenly the whole sky literally lit up with triple A, SAMs and airborne explosions. With the night vision goggles I could see everything. I remember thinking that it was like walking through Trafalgar Square with all the pigeons – walk through them and they all get airborne. That was just how it looked. There were SAMs zig-zagging up into the air in salvos of three or six, triple A explosions going on all over the place. There was tracer everywhere. It was the biggest fireworks display I'd ever seen. All I could think was, "God, are those poor bastards going into that?"'

The Tornado pilots on that first attack had plenty to

think about apart from the triple A. There was no experience of using the JP233 in anger, as Jerry Witts says: 'It's one thing to talk about and read about a particular weapon, but another to fire it. There are physical sensations involved and it's nice to know what they are.' He remembers his final run: 'We ran in at it and I couldn't see a thing. My navigator had it on the radar and the auto-pilot was doing the work. I threw all the switches and we let the thing go.

'It takes a few seconds. It was like going over a cobbled road very quickly. It seemed very important to me to stay very low, because if anyone did start shooting that's where I wanted to be. All of a sudden we were up at about 800ft and I was fighting like a dingbat to keep the plane down and get away as fast as we possibly could.'

He avoided what flak there was and headed for home. As he did so, he was witness to an unforgettable scene: 'It was some miles away to our right. All of a sudden there were a couple of orange explosions. They were totally silent. And the desert seemed to light up in a big orange flash.

'Then, milliseconds later, there was a wall-to-wall incandescent white curtain of light, which was barrage triple A firing up into the air. I asked Adie [his navigator] what was over there and he said an airfield. It was horrendous, it was solid – I could draw it better than I could describe it. I felt sorry for the poor buggers who were going through that.'

Witts next remembers 'heading back across the border – doing elated barrel rolls and designing the perfect English breakfast – I've never felt so high in my life. That was followed by a big low – what the doctors would describe as a post-adrenal low. Then absolute fatigue. We didn't think about it at the time but we'd been up for 30 hours.'

One of the first to know that all had gone well was Flt

Lt Paul Smith, flying a VC10 tanker and holding a race track pattern near the border, waiting for his 'chicks' to return. He had set his receiver to the same wavelength as that of the Tornados: 'All of a sudden we saw this piece of equipment burst into life – and we knew they were on their way back.' Once they were back into Saudi airspace, the pilots broke radio silence: 'We're back. Hope you've got some fuel for us.'

They landed in the full glare of press and television attention, as Peter Mutch, press liaison officer at Muharraq, remembers: 'The aircraft returned at about six o'clock in the morning and we had a film crew and some newspaper reporters out there. The first aircraft touched down, taxied round and there was a pause of about five or six minutes. Normally they come back in quick succession. We were all very worried. Then all of a sudden the other seven arrived, one after the other, and the crews climbed out.'

The international media had already relayed news of the first night's raids – as they occurred – to the waiting world. For Mark Richardson, a frustrated F3 navigator who was not airborne for the first night, the reports acted as a channel for his emotions: 'I was sitting listening to it all on the radio. I remember hearing Peter Arnett saying there were bombs falling in Baghdad and, quite barbarically, thinking "They've hit Baghdad. Bloody brilliant! It serves you right, you bastard. You started it, now you finish it!"'

His frustration was shared by others who had not taken part. Flt Lt Mike Warren had been forced to turn back from his sortie when his GR1 developed radar problems. It was 'definitely the biggest feeling of disappointment I have ever had, for some strange psychological reason that I don't understand. I still can't come to terms with why I thought it, but it was all part of the atmosphere that had built up. Once you're there, there's nothing worse than coming back and saying, "Yes, I went on the first night but had to turn back because of problems with the aircraft."'

For Mark Robinson, part of the significant air defence presence, it was hardly less frustrating to miss out because the other navigator of his constituted pair had better things to do: 'He's a squadron leader as well as a flight commander, so he was on the desk making sure that people were doing what they should. He couldn't fly, so I couldn't fly. I was going to him every hour saying, "Get me off the bloody ground. I can't sit here. I can't bear this anymore!" We were sitting at QRA [quick reaction alert] on the ground and we could hear them on all the frequencies – all the bombers mounting up. I just wanted to be there, to be part of it. I was so close but I was just missing out. I don't think I slept for two days because I was too keyed up. I don't know what I expected – something more than actually happened.'

But as Wg Cdr Mick Richardson at Air Headquarters in Riyadh makes plain, the frustration of the F3 crews was all to the good: 'The long-term goal was to stop Iraqi aircraft attacking our forces on the ground. Now if that means his not flying at all and keeping his aircraft locked away, that's great by me. You're diluting Iraqi effort all the way through. If that means there's nothing to dilute by the time it comes to the F3s, I'm very sorry, guys, but you still did a good job. One must never lose sight of the fact that, although they *didn't* shoot anything down, they were there if they needed to. They worked long hours, and the amount of concentration required doesn't diminish because they're sitting with nothing to do.'

Mark Robinson gives a graphic account of just how much attention is needed on a war sortie: 'When you got off the ground you'd been taught to do your checks religiously, and you were hyped up. You would go round on CAP, eyes wide open, can't see anything, on the first sweep all the way down. Four hours later – phew! nothing happened again. By that time you've realised you weren't really missing anything, but for the first hour or so you're completely tensed up, knotted up, eyes out on stalks. You expect to be shot at all the time, hordes of enemy planes coming over the border. And it didn't happen. It was kind of frustrating, I suppose.'

By the time the first GR1 crews were returning to base, the second wave were in their outbrief. Flt Lt Mike Toft from XV Sqn found his time on target was 0930 local time – broad daylight. He was late taking off, had to change aeroplanes twice due to technical failure and, once airborne, had to tank twice to reach his distant objective. The sun was over the horizon three hours before he was due to reach his target.

Toft soon came to the conclusion that they hadn't trained low enough 'because the desert on the way to the target was as flat as a pancake: 130ft felt like 1,000ft does in Germany. We crossed the border at 50ft; speed not below 450 knots. It sounds crazy but I suppose we averaged 30–35ft. There's very little time to look at a map, we were looking ahead for undulations or enemy fighters. There was a bedouin with a herd of three or four hundred goats – we went straight over him.'

Malcolm Hammans was not flying until the second night, so he could benefit from the experience of the crews who had returned: 'We went down to breakfast and the guys who'd been on the first raid were just coming in. Obviously we were badgering them for as much information as possible. They told us what it was like, that they'd all come back, what the threats were and what their feelings were. Unfortunately we had to hang around until one o'clock in the afternoon before we could go to work – four or five hours with nothing to do and nowhere to go. It seemed interminable.'

'It was a very worrying time, very nerve-wracking. A

lot of us got together in our rooms to watch the TV, to have a chat about how we felt and what it was going to be like. It was very frightening. Anyone who says they weren't frightened is lying.'

In some ways the first night's attack was easier to approach than subsequent sorties. Fg Off Mal Craghill recalls that 'in one of our regular ground training sessions, the boss had said that if it came to a war, his personal opinion was that it wouldn't be difficult convincing guys to go on the first night. It would be the second trip and thereafter that would be difficult, because then they'd know what it was like to be fired at. He was right – the first night was just a big step into the unknown. It was just a shot in the dark.'

He and pilot Mike Warren were able to make up for missing the first night's action when they were tasked to H3, one of the bigger military airfields near Baghdad. After the previous disappointment, 'once I left the tanker I thought, "Great! At least there's nothing to stop us getting across the border".' He had no trouble seeing his target: it was lit up by triple A for about 15 minutes before he reached it: 'I found it incredible to watch, it was almost a fascination. Because it was our first night, as we turned towards the target we were all set to go, no matter what. But the boss turned us away because there was no way of getting through. He'd been there the night before and was able, with that very, very limited experience, to say that it was much worse. With hindsight it was the best decision he could have made. When we came back, we found that two American jets had been shot down going across the airfield. If we'd been on our own, or in front, we would probably have blasted through it and who knows what might have happened.'

The incident highlights what was known as the White Cliffs syndrome. Jerry Witts says: 'The brief that I'd been given was that we were there to use our assets as efficiently as possible, without losing aircraft or lives. I think our outlook was slightly different to how it would have been had we been defending British territory. We were there to do a job of work and we were quite happy to do it, but none of us intended to die in the process.'

Yet it was during the second night that, as Witts recalls, 'we started to hear about the losses. One had been lost from Bahrain. Then someone else was lost. After a couple of days we were certainly suffering a bit in the Tornado world and we'd lost at least three planes which, in percentage terms, didn't look very good.'

Flt Lt David Waddington and his navigator Flt Lt Robbie Stewart from 27 Sqn witnessed one of those losses. They were number two of a fourship, with Wg Cdr Nigel Elsdon and Flt Lt Max Collier behind them at number three, flying on the second night against an airfield called Shaibah, near Basra. Waddington recounts how 'we went in over the sea, in a gap of land called the swamp, between the top of Kuwait and the Iraq/Iran border. That was the shortest way in and, we also thought, the least well defended. However, as soon as we coasted in over Iraq, the triple A started up. It was incredible. There was so much triple A that we were picking a route through and basically slaloming the aircraft between them – a bit like a video game.

'I was amazed how calm I was. I was giving a running commentary to Robbie in the back: "Triple A over there, just coming right, coming left". All I could see was light, I didn't think about there being three inches of lead behind it. We got to the airfield and I remember we were flying manually over the target to keep it level for the weapons release. I put the bomb foreline through the target bars and concentrated only on that, not worrying about anything else.'

In the back seat, Stewart 'knew I was going to be on target. The thing went off, we turned a corner and, just as we turned, number four shouted "Aircraft crash!". I looked out and saw a huge explosion. I thought initially it was bombs but then I realised it wasn't. It was the boss going in – how we don't know.

'We climbed up – we weren't quite sure what had happened. We knew an aircraft had crashed and number three hadn't checked in. Eventually I spoke to the AWACS, "Look, can you see three or four aircraft?" We had our IFF on and the guy came back and said "There are only three". Then it began to sink in – my God, we've just lost one.

'It hit our number four very badly because he'd actually seen it. He was in tears at the debrief. He's a young lad – it was his first bombing mission – and he'd seen somebody crash and get killed right in front of him.'

When someone is killed in action, there are rituals to be observed by the survivors, as Waddington explains: 'We took all the beer and spirits out of Max's room and the boss's room and down to the bar. It's an Air Force tradition – you either go to the bar and fill up the guy's bar book or drink whatever he's got in his room. I found it very hard actually. We were drinking their beer and they weren't coming home.'

'Max I had known for a long time,' records Robbie Stewart. 'Quiet, sincere, a good operator and a very nice bloke.' Nigel Elsdon, however, had not been with 27 Sqn as OC for very long. 'Nigel had pitched up because the previous boss had been killed [in a training accident] and you're always apprehensive about somebody new, because the last guy was a great bloke. But Nigel was of the same mould fortunately.'

Everyone remembers where they were when they heard about the first combat losses and, so compact is the RAF as a 'family', that many knew those who were lost – either personally or through a friend. Mark

Norton, a chief technician based at Tabuk recalls: 'The moment we knew we'd lost a plane will stay with me all of my life. It was especially difficult for the two men who'd seen it off. They stood outside for ages waiting for it to come into view. I think we all knew that it never would.'

Throughout the Gulf, the effect of the early losses was dramatic. Bill Pixton remembers how 'the mood completely changed. All of a sudden the younger guys who'd been pestering me to get some targets said, "No rush. We'll go when they want us to go".'

Many, like F3 navigator Fg Off Tony Beresford, had to come to terms with the reality of conflict: 'If you go to war people are going to be killed. It's one of those facts that you have to accept. So I had to get on with the job and try not to let it affect me.'

But, Sandy Wilson points out, the losses had to be seen in perspective: 'We did lose some aircraft, but to lose so few, in view of the risks involved, I thought was quite outstanding. When we stopped flying low level and went to medium level, that wasn't because we felt we couldn't take any more losses or were hurt by public opinion or anything else. It was a straightforward operational decision that at that stage we didn't need to go down and drop weapons at low level. It made more sense to bring our aircraft up, so we changed tactics and got into the precision-guided business.'

In many ways the losses were lighter than might have been expected, because, as Vaughan Morris explains: 'Over the desert there's nothing to hide behind when you're operating at low level. There are no trees, very few hills, and people can normally see an aircraft coming from a long way off.' He confirms that, contrary to press speculation, the move to medium level was a pre-planned operational tactic: 'Within the first couple of days we'd identified that we would probably be going to war at medium altitude, but first we had to establish air supremacy. We kept an open mind, but trained for both the high and low option during the three months we were out there. I felt that we were well prepared – flexibility is the key to air power.'

The events of the first two nights allowed the allies to achieve command of the air. Mick Richardson, at Air Headquarters in Riyadh, recalls staying awake for 36 and 48 hours at a stretch at this stage 'because we all wanted to make sure that things got off on the right foot. We had to plan on entering a long campaign. We had to consider – what if we're not successful there, what if the weather changes, what if . . .' As things turned out the first air strikes 'went according to plan. It was then a question of not relaxing, of keeping it all going "on a roll" – as the Americans would say.'

Chapter 6

THE VANGUARDS OF VICTORY

'The army of Saddam Hussein is wiping out the renegade invaders and knocking out the forces of infidelism, corruption and treason. The vanguards of victory are levelling the positions of the forces of the tyrants of Khafji . . .'

Baghdad Radio

'We were on nights when it started,' remembers nurse Cpl Julie Pugh. 'We were sitting outside and heard all the planes taking off – the noise was spectacular. I went away from everybody else and just sat and listened. It was a horrible feeling, really eerie. I think we all knew then that something was going to happen.'

Geoff Davies, commander of the RAF hospital at Muharraq, was equally aware that the war was about to begin: 'It had been all quiet on the airfield, no flying that day. Everyone was apprehensive and you could feel it. But I still thought it wouldn't happen. I thought he [Saddam Hussein] would back down at the very last minute. I shall never forget that first night of the war. At 2.15am my number two went for a briefing with the detachment commander who said, "In five minutes' time the first aircraft will hit Baghdad. You can tell your troops". So I did – it was a very charged atmosphere. The biggest fear was "Would we be able to do the job if a lot of horrible casualties came in?" I spent half an hour in each

WRAF block, a lot of them were 18-year-old kids and one of the girls asked if the padre could say a prayer.'

'We were all very quiet,' comments Julie Pugh. 'Some people had a few tears then, but it would've been fine if they hadn't asked the padre to say anything!'

The effort involved and the accompanying sound of over 2,000 aircraft getting airborn and into position to launch the first waves of airstrikes alerted service personnel on every airbase. At the hospital, Flt Sgt Alan Bear was on night duty when he heard the sounds of 'aircraft obviously labouring to take off, lots of them. Sure enough, ten minutes later the detachment commander tannoyed and asked for heads of department to go to a briefing. Later that night we had several Red Alerts and we knew that the Iraqis had fired missiles. We moved into the sandbagged air-raid shelters and people were particularly frightened that night, a few of them in tears. We spent two hours lying face down in our colpro [collective protection] hospital, waiting for a bang and thinking a lot.'

Everyone had to wear their NBC suits: 'You had to have two layers of clothing on underneath – you had cotton gloves, rubber gloves, your respirator and your helmet on, so it was very hot and, because they're charcoal impregnated, you got absolutely filthy. You ended up looking like a coalminer.'

In Riyadh VC10 tanker pilot Paul Smith had been given advance warning, since his crew was one of the few in his squadron not flying that night: 'We were sitting in the planning room drawing maps and charts up for the second mission when the air-raid siren went. Everyone was totally surprised. We looked at each other and then everyone – at the same time, it seemed – reached for the gas masks and NBC kit. There were gloves and masks and protective suits flying in all directions. I was petrified and I don't mind admitting it. We all knew that something was going to be thrown at us and, in the event, there was a multiple Scud missile launch in which three or four missiles were targetted at Riyadh.

'About ten minutes later we heard a series of mighty bangs. The ground shook and my initial thought was that we'd been hit by a bomb or a missile, such was the force of the shockwave. We could feel it vibrating the walls and the floor. My heart was in my mouth when I heard this series of bangs but, in fact, the shockwaves were caused by outbound Patriot missiles. It was only after the eight or ninth went off that I realised it wasn't bombs falling on us.'

Most people, however, had no advance warning and received very rude awakenings as the sirens went off in the early hours of 17 January. In Riyadh Fred Reid was woken by his hotel's fire-alarm being sounded: 'I opened the door and there was a bloke standing there in full kit – respirator, gloves, boots, the works. He said, "Get your respirator on! Get your respirator on!" I said, "Is it a drill?" "No," he said. "It's an air-raid". The war had kicked off. So it was downstairs into the cellar, where it was a case of just sitting and wondering if an eight-ton rocket was going to land on us, because – let's face it – the guy's a nutter and no one knew what he was going to do. There were about 50 of us, and I could see the guys' faces through the respirator eye-pieces. What I wanted to do was just to get up and run away, and it took a lot to actually sit there on the floor. I was nearly physically sick – I felt as if I'd had a bad curry. My mate was also feeling sick and I thought, "Oh God, he's had a whiff of something", so I checked his respirator, but he said, "No, no. I feel sick because I'm scared."

They passed the time playing cards. 'Then it dawned on me, "Why sit here where four floors could come down on top of you when you could sit in your bedroom and just have two?" So we went upstairs and lay on the bed watching the telly – CNN, the "mouthpiece of Iraq" – because we could actually see what was happening in Baghdad.'

Flt Sgt David Field and Master Air Loadmaster Mike Mead from 216 Sqn, air-to-air refuellers, were newly-arrived in Riyadh – and both had problems with their NBC kits. One found himself with a broken zip on his smock and spent the night trying to hold the two sides together – while the other tried 'furiously to get into an NBC suit that was two sizes too small. It must have been hilarious to everybody else but I thought it was going to be the death of me.'

The threat of nerve gas was a very real one, especially to those like Reid, who had spent the previous weeks teaching others what to do in the event of a chemical attack. While on gateguard at his compound he had seen two fireballs in the sky which turned out to be Scud missiles: 'As we looked up two Patriots came across and took the Scuds out above the compound with the biggest bang you ever heard in your life. The last thing I wanted to do was to stand under a chemical shower so I ran into the block to be under cover and to get my kit on. It may sound stupid now but I decided that if I got a whiff of it I was going to shoot myself with the weapon I had. There was no way I was going to flip about on the floor like a kipper for 40 minutes.'

At Al Jubayl, which the Scuds overflew on their way to Dhahran, things were a little easier. But Cpl Ian Showler, sharing a room with five other medevac (medical evacuation) team members, experienced the same shock as he woke to the warbling of a siren and felt the 'fear and horror that war was upon us. That was the time I was thankful we'd done our ground defence training. However, what with the confusion of six bodies all jumping out of bed at once in their boxer shorts and scrabbling around, it must have taken me about 30 seconds to get my respirator on and another one to five minutes to get my undergarments and suit on.' Having no shelter to go to, they put their mattresses against the windows and 'sat around telling jokes' until the all-clear was sounded.

Medical administrator Ian Tervit was in charge of a block 'full of young lads aged 17 upwards. At 28 I was probably the oldest. They got up and got dressed and there was a deadly silence. There was no monkeying around. Everyone knew that the war had started.'

When daylight came the mood changed dramatically. At the hospital in Muharraq there were feelings of 'incredible elation' when it was learned that the first wave of Tornados had all come back. 'They opened the bar back at the compound for the night shift to go and have a beer because it had been such an emotion-packed night. We had a briefing and we were told that most of the Scud sites had been knocked out, so everything seemed to be going brilliantly. We all thought, "Two or three days of this and he's had it". That was a peak but we warned the troops that there would be peaks and troughs, good news and bad news.'

The bad news began to arrive on the second night of the war when it was learned that a Tornado GR1 had been lost – and as it became clear that the Scud threat had by no means been eliminated. This was brought home to Dick Druitt in no uncertain manner as he flew his Victor tanker out of Bahrain towards Dhahran: 'I'd just got clearance to climb from 6,000 to 8,000ft right over the middle of Dhahran when I saw this great big yellow flash just south of the city. I thought it was a flare and that's what I said to my crew. But a few seconds later it was fairly obvious that this yellow flare was coming up skywards and getting stronger. I said quite loudly that it looked like a missile and veered the plane away very, very quickly – though I'm not sure that it would have done any good. It went right in front of the plane, rose to just about 8,000ft – then it started to dip down and there was this massive ball of flame as it exploded.

'I radioed straight back to Dhahran that it looked as if we'd been shot at by a missile, assuming that it was a terrorist who'd listened to us taking off and tracked us. I left it at that and got on with my task and everybody calmed down. But when we landed there was still no report of any terrorism. Next morning I switched on CNN only to hear the reporter talking about a Patriot missile fired at Dhahran at 1.30 Zulu [Greenwich Mean Time], half-past four local time, that had hit the first Scud coming in. If it hadn't, it would probably have hit me, so I was quite pleased they were so accurate.'

It could have been the same Scud that caused problems for Tornado F3 navigator Mark Robinson and his pilot as they returned to Dhahran from a six-hour CAP along the Iraqi border: 'We'd just landed and my bum was a bit numb. I climbed out of the jet and was looking up at my pilot as he was getting out when there was this bang and a whoosh – and the sudden realisation that a Patriot had been fired. It went up, zoomed through the clouds and there was a huge flash of lightning as it hit the Scud right over our heads. My pilot let go of the steps he was climbing down and fell on top of me – we were rolling round on the floor desperately trying to get our respirators on. Then we ran like hell, pegged it to this pick-up vehicle which rushed us over to the air-raid shelters – where we dived in absolutely scared out of our heads.'

Like many aircrew not directly involved in bombing raids Paul Smith quickly came to regard the air 'as the safest place to be. If I saw myself dying at all it was dying on the ground being gassed. That was my chief nightmare'. The nightmare seemed to come true one midnight during a Scud raid when it was announced over the tannoy that the NBC state was 'Black', which meant the presence of chemical agents: 'The broadcast said, "NBC Black, NBC Black". That was one of the worst experiences of my life because it seemed that the chemical threat was real. We all climbed into our kit and my heart was beating at 120 to the minute. But five minutes later a rather sheepish voice on the tannoy said, "All clear, all clear". Thankfully, it was a false alarm.'

However, as the Scud attacks continued without any signs of NBC threat, attitudes changed. Aircrew, in particular, became 'very blase' about the whole business. 'We formed a Scud Watchers Society and had honorary members,' admits Robinson. 'When the Scud alerts came we'd run outside the shelter, not into it. We'd all sit outside with our respirators watching these things raining down. It was the first one that made you question life and after that you knew you were probably going to live.'

Others also created diversions to take their minds off the danger. 'As the air-raids came,' remembers Fred Reid, 'we'd sit on our beds playing computer games. We even had games where we tried to shoot aircraft down, which was pretty ironic really.'

At the hospital in Muharraq the musical director of the band devised a board game. 'It was called "Freedom Kuwait",' explains Sqn Ldr Francis Shannon. 'We had cards for Scud missiles, Patriot missiles, basic training and so on and we had soldiers that we moved around the board until we freed Kuwait. One of the cards to be picked up said, "Gas attack. Don respirator" and we actually had to put it on. On my left, John, one of the surgeons, got this card. He said, "Oh no. I don't have to do it, do I?" We said, "Of course you do. It's part of the game". So he put it on and the minute he did there was an air-raid. We didn't have our respirators on and we couldn't stop laughing.'

Out with the Chinooks at their forward base they

had their own, rather more basic, Scud attack game: 'If someone had his Walkman on and was just sitting around, everyone would pretend there was a Scud alert. We'd grab our chemical kits and tap the guy as we went past. We're supposed to be masked in nine seconds, he'd think he'd lost a few seconds already and his eyes would almost pop out as he tried to hold his breath and get to his kit.'

Aircraft electrician Andy Garton also remembers the character who 'wore a big orange cloak and a rubber thing over his head with "Captain Patriot" written on it. He ran around saying, "Captain Patriot's here". About three or four days later somebody came out with a big black mac and a big black hood saying, "Major Scud". We used to see them running round the site beating the shit out of each other. We went and dumped them in one of the American camps one night – the Americans found it totally amusing. One walks in saying, "Hullo, I'm Captain Patriot", and in comes Major Scud at the other end of the building and launches himself across the room, with tables and chairs going everywhere.'

Those flying CAPs sometimes had 'grand-stand views of the Scuds and Patriots battle', as F3 navigator Mark Richardson remembers: 'One night we watched four Scuds being launched from Kuwait. They showed up brilliantly through the night vision goggles as big balls of flame, just like shuttle launchers going up. You could see them going over the top, sort of fizzing in the atmosphere with little sparks like some sort of Buck Rogers space rocket. Right on cue, about six minutes later, you could watch them landing in Riyadh 250 miles away and the Patriots going up to intercept them. It was like an arcade game.'

On the ground familiarity bred contempt, even 'when the Scud landed on the American hangar half a mile down the road. The windows bulged, the house shook and the noise was deafening. I think at that point people thought, "Well, sod it! I think I'll just hide under the bed".'

Not everyone took Scud alerts so lightly. 'Stress changes people,' declares Cpl Eoin Selfridge, a squadron storeman in Muharraq. 'I had one instance when the air-raid siren went and I ran like mad. I cleared the 100 metres quicker than Ben Johnson. I got to the shelter and there was a bloke in front of me about six foot tall and built like a brick house. He was humming and hawing about whether to go in the shelter. I'm five foot nothing – I picked him up and threw him aside. "You can make your mind up after I get in", I told him.'

Although the direct hit on the accommodation hangar at Dhahran caused the most casualties it was Riyadh – 'Scud City' – that bore the brunt with 37 Scud attacks, almost all at night. Flt Lt Andy Bell was part of a team that went out to 'chase Scuds' in their specially equipped Land Rovers: 'As soon as we heard a Scud was inbound for Riyadh we'd get ready. In fact, we got very blasé about it, because the likelihood of one landing on top of us was about 4,000–1. To start with, a lot of them actually did land in Riyadh and we'd go out to see what they'd done and monitor the site for chemicals and radiation. We'd pull up at a good distance and if anything was clicking we wouldn't have gone near it. But in fact the best thing was the local chemical detector, the crowd of about 1,000 civilians, because if they weren't dropping we knew there was no problem.'

Another threat that failed to materialise was local terrorism from supporters of Saddam Hussein. But it had to be taken seriously. 'We didn't know where or how it was going to come, because the terrorist holds all the aces,' remembers Flt Lt Ken Beaton based at Muharraq. 'So we took all the normal precautions – checking vehicles, people, packages, but found nothing –

although one army chap got stabbed, we believe because he took a photograph in the street. The assailant was well known to the police and very quickly picked up. There were supporters of Saddam Hussein on the island but the locals were very friendly.'

Sgt Kevin Traynor of the Mobile Servicing Sqn also remembers a 'terrorist' incident up at Al Jubayl, when an American guard heard rustling on the perimeter fence: 'He shouted to us all to stand still and it carried on rustling. Then he shouted, "Stop or I'll fire" and it carried on rustling. So he shot his whole magazine off and a dead cat dropped out of the fence.'

Although the Scuds failed to wreak havoc they did affect morale in various ways. Some saw them as having a positive effect – 'because we banded together'. But they did wear people down. 'We were all getting very tired,' admits Julie Pugh. 'He would do it at half-past ten at night, then again at about two o'clock, then at about four o'clock. There were a few girls who were frightened and didn't go to sleep, and people who were frightened to go to the shower or the toilet in case they were in there when it happened. A girl in our room *was* in the shower when we had a Scud attack and we were all screaming our heads off for her to come out. But you had to carry on your normal activities, otherwise he would have won half the battle, wouldn't he – because the attacks were just to demoralise us.'

And, of course, there were minor Scud-induced casualties: a warrant officer who broke his little toe jumping out of bed and a number of cases of stress, as Sqn Ldr Les Hendry, SENGO on 31 Sqn, reports: 'We had a couple of lads who had to be casevaced because they didn't like Scuds going off near them and went to pieces. But the biggest problem was that you couldn't relax, couldn't have a beer and unwind after your shift. It was just 12 hours on, 12 hours off, so you were either at work or asleep in your hotel. On top of that, in the first four weeks of the war we weren't allowed out because of the terrorist threat, so it was a bit claustrophobic. And because we'd just pitched up two weeks before the war and had gone straight into it there wasn't time to explain all the job allocations. Some of the junior corporals felt they'd been messed around and reacted badly, so there were some morale problems.'

For the first few days of the war 'the boys were down on their knees', according to 31 Sqn's Chf Tech Frank Firth. 'Then we settled down and although the Scuds still came over, it eased off a lot. I should imagine it was like Bomber Command in 1942–3. The jets flew at night. In the morning we mended, in the afternoon the pilots would find out what they were going on, we would get our bomb load and load up. That went on for about a week and then they changed to daytime sorties where they were flying two or three waves a day. It almost got to the headless chicken stage because there were crews saying they had no bombs. My armourers were working down the line and I was working with two air-frame men, two engine men and a liney loading an aircraft with bombs because we'd run out of armourers. Then they wanted missiles fitted, which took more time.'

By this time the JP233 pods had been replaced by the 1,000lb 'iron bombs' with fuses that could be set to explode at different times: 'We might set five bombs to go off instantaneously and three delay bombs. I got the lads to think of three-figure numbers and we just plugged in some totally random delays.'

The armourers and ground crews also followed the World War Two practice of writing messages on the sides of the bombs. 'They quickly hit on the idea that they could make money out of this with messages like "To Saddam from Betty's Chip Shop",' recalls Sqn Ldr Greg Monaghan of 13 Sqn. 'What they were doing was thinking of every club, pub and shop in their home area. We had quite a number of bombs to be dropped so there were quite a lot of these messages. They took a picture of each message, with the idea that after the war they'd sell them to these places for a tenner a throw and make a mint.'

Such diversions served as light relief in a workplace where men were going out to be shot at and planes returning with battle damage. In Dhahran, Chf Tech Pete Waldron had only one seriously damaged aircraft for his repair team to work on: 'Having seen the extent of the damage I was surprised it came back at all. There were a lot of large holes in the tailerons – the small wings at the back – and a couple of holes on the damaged cables. To see them was quite frightening. We'd talked about it and practised on dummy aircraft but it was quite a novelty to have your own aircraft with battle damage and to get it back out to drop bombs again.' Four days and nights of repair work put the Tornado back into action.

The loss of five Tornado GR1s in the first week of the war – representing a quarter of the total allied air losses – also affected the morale of every squadron where aircrew went missing. Waldron was surprised by the way the ground crews coped: 'You'd see people going, "Blimey, we've lost another chap, I know him". Then for a matter of hours things went quiet and not a lot was said. But before you knew it things had picked up again, because the next wave of aircraft had come back and their successes were relayed down. You were back into the swing and away on to the next problem.'

The ground crews also had different perspectives on the conflict: 'The pace of the war was very static, two waves a day. The pilots flew once a day, worked four days and then had a day off. All right, those guys were putting their bums on the line and it was right and proper that they should have a day off, but the rest of us were working an 84-hour week, seven days a week, and as time went on that was starting to wear us down a little bit.'

Both night and day shifts had their stresses and strains, as SAC Jason Hedges and Eoin Selfridge remember when working at the supply desk. 'People very often lost their tempers over small things. There'd be 10 or 15 guys waiting for stuff and maybe just two or three of us to do it. There'd be a lot of shouting but it was just their way of releasing the pressure. Someone would get what we call a Wendy on. He'd start shouting and jumping about and we'd say, "He's throwing his teddies out of the cot again". Then ten minutes later you'd be sitting in the crew room with him, having a coffee and playing cards.'

The war helped to narrow the differences between those who stayed on the ground and those who flew – and who in peacetime drew 'a bit of stick as the master race'. It was 'always a bit of a joke with us that we're the only service that sends our officers to war,' explains Jaguar SENGO Phil Goodall. 'They put their little pink bums in the planes and go off to get shot at. But when push came to shove my guys didn't think like that anymore. There's certainly a division, and they knew that was the case, but they also knew the pilots were very brave to go out and do what they did every day. They were wishing them good luck when they came out and waving to them when they went off.'

Identification with the aircrew extended far beyond the flying squadrons. At Dhahran Rachael Berry, in her role as MAMS officer, never got to know any of the Tornado pilots but often watched them take off on their missions: 'They would take so long to get off the ground because they were so heavy with the JP233s and bombs that they were carrying. They'd usually go in groups of eight and I remember counting them out – seeing the afterburners burning off down the runway.

I remember actually phoning home once and saying, "Listen to this!" – I found that quite emotional; the noise and the vibrations. They'd travel down the taxiways and quite often you'd be going somewhere in a vehicle and have to wait for them to pass. I remember I used to sit at the steering wheel and fold my arms, saying, "Please all come back!"'

When the first losses were announced it was difficult to know how to respond, as Geoff Davies admits: 'The second day I asked some of the female nurses to go and see the aircrew but none of them wanted to, because they didn't know what to say to them. So we did a card for each squadron, everyone signed it and I took it over to them.'

Julie Pugh believes that she and the other airwomen stood up to the stresses of the war well: 'I found the women stronger than the men. They were more friendly, cheered people along and if anybody was upset we'd go and see them and talk, whereas it's very difficult for a man to communicate.'

In this respect, Berry found that 'sometimes people used to come and speak to me because I was a woman. It was female company. I remember an army staff sergeant who kept showing me photographs of his family and his wife. Just before the land battle started he showed me a poem he'd written for his wife. It was about how he felt about her, thanking her for always being there and, if he didn't come back, how he loved her. He said, "Do you think I should send her this?" I said, "Well, if you want her in tears, yes". Even now thinking about it still brings a tear to my eye.'

Being a woman in a war zone had its drawbacks. Both Pugh and Berry had to suffer the attentions and misrepresentations of the press. Berry, an air movements officer, found herself appearing in *The Gulf Times* as 'Rachael, the sweetheart of all RAF Hercules pilots' and 'misquoted as saying, "I can lift and haul as well as the rest of them", which I've never said, because I've never believed that. But it was faxed through to Riyadh and round the Gulf. I remembered I phoned somebody up and they said, "Well, ma'am, you haven't done very much for women coming to the trade, have you!" And that genuinely upset me.'

This was not the media's finest hour as far as most service personnel were concerned. Francis Shannon felt that the press 'hyped up' the situation and cites the instance of a radio reporter on Muharraq airbase: 'He was saying that Muharraq was under attack by 12 aircraft and this went out on the radio – and the families were listening to it. One man was on the phone to his wife and she said, "I've just heard you're under attack!" He said, "I'm having a pint of beer". It was our lads coming back from a sortie and circling the airfield before coming in to land!'

Many worried about the lack of definite information about the progress of the war. As Sgt Adrian Davies puts it: 'Morale went up when we knew what we were doing and down when we didn't'. Despite jokey newssheets like *Tabuk Today* ('for a brighter tomorrow'), and such local forces newspapers as *The Sandy Times*, there was an apparent lack of hard news. 'Compared to what people saw in Britain, the general flow of information to us out there was poor,' asserts Hercules OC Wg Cdr Peter Bedford. 'I think that's always the case in a war but very little of the basics of the war filtered down to us. We had a television in the hotel which showed little clips from CBS and the briefings in Riyadh but Saudi television tended to be rather insular.'

Ian Tervit found Saudi TV difficult to follow: 'Smack bang in the middle of *Neighbours* the screen would go blank and the announcer would say that it was now time for prayers. There would be prayers and then it would go back to *Neighbours* – but ten minutes further on than the point where it had left off.'

At some bases satellite links allowed the blanket coverage of the war given in the USA and the UK to be followed. Out in the field it was usually a case of tuning in to the news bulletins of the BBC World Service, the British Forces Broadcasting Service or the American Forces RTN radio, where 'at least you could hear what they thought was going on'.

However, when Tervit moved out into the desert with the Chinook squadron, he had access to briefings from the two Army intelligence officers on site: 'They gave all the site personnel two briefings daily but their theory was that until they'd heard it confirmed by their sources in Riyadh it wasn't true.' This cautious 'need to know' approach led to the worry in some quarters in the early stages that the war was not going as well for the allies as they were being led to believe.

The lack of news made contacts with home terribly important – and here most people had the advantage of access to phones. As far as Tony Beresford of 43 Sqn was concerned 'communications were very, very good. We could dial straight to the UK and we just got billed at the end of the month, so I could talk to my wife at least once a week and sometimes three times a week. The worst part about it was the horrendous bills when we got back, which we're still paying off now.' The morale-raising went both ways, as Beresford's fellow crewman Brian O'Connor recalls: 'My wife's support was tremendous. She always related the good things that were happening with the kids and spared me the bits I couldn't do anything about. So when I'd finished a call I had a clear mind about home and felt that she was doing all right. Even though all of them were sick as dogs and could barely get out of bed, you wouldn't have known it by talking to her! I tried to do the same with her, keeping it light and airy and not talking about the situation.'

But sometimes this policy backfired, as Eoin Selfridge remembers: 'My wife told me later that she had been frightened at times. The worst moment was when I was phoning her and we had a Scud attack. She heard the klaxons going and asked what it was. "It's an air attack", I said, "I have to go". Once it had finished there was a queue a mile long for the phone, waiting to tell people we were OK. I was away about 20 minutes and when I got back to her she said it had been the longest 20 minutes of her life. As soon as she'd heard the klaxons she'd probably had the mortgage out, looking for a new house!'

Not everyone was in a position to make regular telephone calls though at least there were the 'blueys' to fall back on and 'letters became a lifeline and if they were held up there was great anxiety.' Sgt Steve Wyatt, stuck down in Seeb with the Nimrod detachment, says: 'There was a huge outpouring of emotion from the UK. Thousands of people wrote, to "a pilot in the Royal Air Force" or to "somebody on 43 Squadron". A two-foot cubed box would arrive, full of letters. The guys just grabbed a handful and started opening them. For instance, all the kids in a class would write letters – a lot were almost the same word for word – but it was still immensely rewarding to read these letters. What was even nicer was that some were from eligible young ladies. One I got was from a woman who was in her early forties who gave me her life story. She said she was actually writing in the hope of striking up a correspondence with a single man of the same age. If I was not in this category, but knew somebody who was, could I please forward this letter to him. She had twin daughters aged 18, and if I did this, she would get one of them to write to me. I suggested to the boss that as he fitted the age group, perhaps he'd like to write to this woman but he declined.'

Inevitably, there was places where the mailing system worked less well. 'We only got mail every five or six days,' declares SAC Brian Aitken, whose job as an MT driver took him away from the big bases. 'And we only had two videos, so everybody knew the dialogue off by heart.'

But hearing from home was not always cheering, as Francis Shannon recalls: 'Ely Hospital sent a video out with the families on it. Some people were really cut up that night as it brought back to them how much they missed them. It wasn't a question of not coping with the war. It was more of a domestic thing. They really missed their families.'

However, the work of the Gulf Support Groups was enormously appreciated – even if some gifts went to the wrong places: 'The Red Cross sent 230 Sqn detachment four huge boxes of tampons when we were at King Khalid Military City. Three hundred and thirty seven blokes and four boxes of tampons. We had Tampax parties, Tampax fights and fed Tampax to the camels. We couldn't get rid of the things. But they made great firelighters.'

The Victor tanker detachment from RAF Marham based at Dhahran did rather better with Biggles the Bear: 'The local scouts sent out this little teddy bear which came with a leather helmet and goggles and a flying jacket. We produced a flying log book for him and rations, which consisted of small jars of honey and marmalade and this bear flew on an enormous number of missions, not just in our own Victors. He flew on quite a number of raids with the Jaguars and Buccaneers and the Tornado crews. Everybody dutifully filled his log book in.'

Chapter 7

WAR IS A PROFANITY

'War is a profanity because, let's face it, you've got two opposing sides trying to settle their differences by killing as many of each other as they can. You don't just go out there and say, "OK, let's have a nice war today" . . .'

General Norman Schwarzkopf

The aim of the second phase of the air war was to capitalise on the disarray caused to Iraqi defences by the initial massive attacks. It took Operation Desert Storm to a wider range of targets, with an ever-increasing range of weapons and tactics. Although the broadening of the war was in line with planning, no-one could have forseen its exact development in the early days. Indeed, everyone was hoping for a rapid conclusion, as Jerry Witts confirms: 'I thought we'd go in on the first night, hit him for six, and he'd realise he'd bitten off more than he could chew and stop the war. But he didn't seem to do anything – he just lay there and let us poke him in the eye.'

That 'poking' took the form of some 2,000–3,000 sorties each day – approximately one bombing raid every 30 seconds. Mark Richardson voices the feelings of many when he says that 'the vast majority of us thought nothing would ever equal the air power of day one. Well, it did – day two through to day 40. If anything, it got more and more. I've never seen so many aeroplanes – you couldn't fly for 20 seconds without seeing at least another dozen planes flying past you.' His pilot, Angus Elliott, echoes the sentiment: 'Through night vision goggles, you can see everyone around you for miles and miles and yet, if you just lift your goggles up, it's pitch black. Drop them back down and there they are: 80 or 90 pilots all over the place, stacked up wall-to-wall aeroplanes. I was certainly amazed there were no more blue-on-blue midairs.'

Part of the reason for that impressive safety record was the quality of control coming from Riyadh. Victor pilot Dick Druitt was concerned before the operation began about whether so many nationalities could 'actually go in one direction. There was only one way and it was extremely impressive. It could have been the English way, it could have been the Kuwaiti way, but it was the American way and it worked brilliantly.'

Malcolm Hammans puts the British contribution into perspective: 'Without doubt, the Americans carried out the bulk of the difficult tasks out there – they had the major role of attacking Iraqi installations. Having said that, as a proportion of our national capacity we gave more than anyone else and they were fairly impressed with the results we produced.'

The American way involved a very strict adherence to the 'need to know' principle. Sqn Ldr Bertie Newton, navigator with 31 Sqn, declares: 'I got the feeling that we weren't given quite enough of the big picture, that the balance wasn't quite right – I think because the Americans were running it and they're obsessed with secrecy. But, as one of the guys laying their lives on the line, I personally would like to have known a little bit more about what was going on.'

As an American pilot seconded to 43 Sqn, Capt Brian

O'Connor had a unique view of the conflict from both points of view: 'From my standpoint it was a tremendous opportunity to deploy to a combat theatre with the RAF as well as being able to watch the USAF operate – seeing it through another nation's eyes.' He readily admits that information was 'sanitised' – particularly following the unfortunate incident when classified plans were stolen from the back of a car in London. 'It was noticeable that there was a decrease in information flow to the allied forces after that, especially when it came to the overall game plans, because they didn't want to compromise them. Consequently, we came in to the war with about half a day's notice of what the game plan was going to be next day.'

But as the second phase began, the emphasis of the planning changed to ensure sustained pressure on Iraq. For Jerry Witts, it was a matter of common sense: 'After a few days everyone had been once, and it became blindingly obvious to me that we should have a plan to pace people so that the work was shared out equally. Also, to give people a chance to pace themselves, to know when they'd be required to go, when they could psyche themselves up and when they could relax as much as possible.'

In Muharraq Bill Pixton was coming to a similar conclusion about his Desert Cats: 'I couldn't ask my pilots to fly more than one sortie a day, and perhaps every fifth day they should have a day off. The engineers went on two equal shifts to fix the aircraft and to bomb them up.'

With the change in shift patterns came a significant and hotly debated change in tactics. By 21 January, low-level JP233 missions gave way to a medium altitude strategy and the daylight dropping of 1,000lb iron or 'dumb' bombs. Like any strategy, it had its pros and cons. The Tornados had suffered three losses in action in the first three days of low-level attacks – though none had actually been shot down by triple A. By flying at over 20,000ft the aircraft were above all but the 100mm guns; however, their bombing was inevitably less accurate as well as being more exposed to surface-to-air missiles – as events were to show.

For the Tornado in particular, the switch was not entirely appropriate, as Flt Lt Neil Cobb explains: 'It has a very small wing, which is ideal for low-level flying, because it cuts through the air like a dart and is very stable in relation to the ground – which makes it a very good weapons platform.' But the turbofan engine operates less efficiently at higher altitudes. 'So there we were operating this wonderful low-level aircraft up at twenty-odd thousand feet, where it's rather outside its element.'

From the point of view of Sqn Ldr John Page, commanding the Rapiers at Muharraq, the tactic had been thought out in advance: 'Before the war started, Bill Pixton came to me and said, "What do you think as an air defender? Should we continue to fly low?" We came to the conclusion that, for the sort of targets he was going after, they should still fly low because they could achieve surprise.' Two factors were to reverse that conclusion. Low flying became dangerous as the element of surprise was lost, because 'in Iraq, they weren't short of small arms, anti-aircraft artillery and people'. The second factor was that 'we weren't prepared for the accuracy and capability of the American anti-radiation missiles. Their efficiency meant that the Iraqis couldn't turn on their radars. So flying high was less dangerous than flying low.' Despite some initial concern from a few Tornado aircrew, the move was generally welcomed.

Bill Pixton was certainly very happy with the performance of the Jaguar at altitude: 'It went a little bit higher than I thought it would with that war load. It certainly managed to get me out of enemy territory faster than I thought it might have done. And it was remarkably serviceable – we flew 617 combat missions and we only had seven "duty not carried out" missions – due to engineering problems. I guess the Jaguar likes hot weather and it likes flying high.'

Another reason for the relative safety at altitude was the success of the strike aircraft in taking out Iraqi airfields in the initial raids, resulting in an almost complete lack of opposing fighters. Flt Lt John Ayers, by now based in Riyadh as a planner, explains the dilemma that faced the Iraqi air force: 'They realised fairly early on that if they were going to get airborne at all, they'd be shot down.' The response of many was to fly to Iran: 'I'd like to think it was Saddam's air force being sensible because they weren't safe in the shelters and they weren't safe in the air.'

The Iraqi air force was equipped with Floggers, Fishbeds, Foxbats, Mirage F-1s and Fulcrums. The last is a high-tech aeroplane by modern standards but Paul Brown believes 'they obviously didn't really know how to use it, their technology wasn't as good as we'd believed'. He was surprised when they did not react: 'I think if people are bombing your country and you're a fighter pilot, you have to get airborne to stop them, otherwise there's no point in being there.' His point is reiterated by Flt Lt Alexander Gordon from 43 Sqn: 'I'm still amazed at the way they fought the war, because if you're going to design a strategy to lose, it's got to be pretty close to what they did.'

Angus Elliott suggests that an early engagement between six Iraqi fighters and four F-15s had a decisive impact on enemy morale: 'I think all the Iraqi planes, bar one, had been killed before they even merged. If that happened on this squadron – if you picked the six best pilots and sent them in six of the best planes against four of their adversaries – and none came back, when the boss told you, "You're next", you'd tell him where to stick it.'

Nevertheless, no-one underestimated the dangers of flying over Iraq: the enemy was still in possession of a fearsome range of SAM missile systems, appeared to have unlimited triple A ammunition and, potentially, still had many capable planes on the ground.

Keeping them there was the job of the allied air defenders, among them the Tornado F3 crews of 29 and 43 Sqns based at Dhahran. According to Brown, most of the F3 crews flew 'getting on for 30 live war missions in the 42 days of the war – proportionately more hours than any other unit in the war'. Alexander Gordon explains that, 'For the first two months I was out there, I flew 60 hours a month, which is roughly three times what I'd expect to fly in a month back here.'

The F3 crews, despite the long hours they worked, did not face the concentrated attentions of the triple A and SAM systems that plagued their GR1 colleagues. Flt Lt Mark Robinson declares that he never really felt he was in that much danger – though he does remember one sortie when 'we got shelled on the CAP, then we got shot at by surface-to-air missiles. They then launched four Scuds nearby, which was quite interesting. Then we got home and got Scudded just as we landed as well.'

Mark Richardson remembers those missiles too but comments that 'without the NVGs we probably wouldn't have seen them for a lot longer. They looked huge and very close but in fact, thank God, they weren't. It gets the heart going a bit. I guess it's like when you were a kid driving along with your dad in a car, and you stick a pair of binoculars to your face: everything looks terribly close and fast. It's a bit like that with goggles: you see an awful lot more than you really want to at times.'

Because the Iraqi air force had chosen the path of

discretion, much of the air defence work in the Gulf was fairly routine, as Gordon recalls: 'We stayed airborne for about four and a half hours at a time, which is a long sortie. Aside from the embarrassing things like suddenly wanting to have a pee, there was hunger, there was boredom and there was cramp. The ejection seat is very hard and you have a very sore bum after that long.'

So, apart from the occasional moment of excitement – like being told to move out of the way of friendly missiles on their way to Iraq – how do aircrew pass their time on such long sorties? 'We took up a travelling game of Trivial Pursuit,' says Gordon, 'and, for the record, I won! The Tornado has a high-frequency radio so we'd listen to the World Service and to the Voice of America. We also had a data tape system to record details of sorties for the debrief. This was largely redundant because of the video system, so a lot of people took up audio tapes: rock and roll, classical music, revivalist hymns. Somebody actually had a 70-minute tape with sounds of the Amazonian rainforest – just rain and the occasional squawk of a tropical bird. You only listened to that one once.'

Gordon knows that such activities may sound flippant during a war and admits that they are frowned on in peacetime. However, they were tacitly approved of in theatre 'because it was so boring and people were getting fatigued. The cumulative effect was such that there was a risk of dropping off.' On days off this was indulged to the full: 'My navigator was famous because he used to go to bed and not get up for 16 hours.'

Over at Tabuk, Flt Lt John Hogg realised what could happen if one started to relax: 'My wingman heard the missile fly over his cockpit before he saw it. He was a gibbering wreck when he came down. We gave him a lot of banter; everyone was laughing at him because he couldn't stop talking. That sharpened everyone up not to get complacent.'

There was certainly no complacency among the GR1 and Jaguar aircrews who were adopting a variety of different tactics as the air war continued. Dive bombing was tried in order to improve accuracy. Bill Pixton describes what this felt like in a Jaguar: 'Time seems to stretch. I don't suppose I was in a dive for more than 10 seconds from top to bottom – and the bit in the middle where I was actually concentrating on the weapon aiming could only have been about two or three seconds, but it seemed forever. I seemed to have time to make a couple of switch selections, pull on the ECM pod [electronic counter measures], put out some chaff, change my weapon selection maybe, adjust my weapon aiming. As soon as we came off my major concern was, "Are we all still here?" and I checked people in almost immediately – although you shouldn't be gassing on the radio really. I did it once and my number four hadn't even dropped his bombs yet. He said he was still going down in a dive – sorry.'

Dick Druitt followed their war on the radio of his Victor tanker: 'The Jaguars were doing strikes on boats over in the Gulf. We'd just refuelled a Jaguar and he zoomed off. His missile blew this boat out of the sea – I was actually listening to all this going on, which was fascinating.'

While the Jaguars attacked sea and land targets, the prime task of the six Tornado GR1As in the Gulf was observation – reconnaissance. From their base in Dhahran they worked a three-shift standby system: one from 1500 to 0300, another from 2100 to 0900 and the third on a rest day. This allowed up to six sorties each night – and all the reconnaissance GR1As' work was flown at low level and at night.

The recce crews operated very much alone. Sqn Ldr Roger Bennett points out: 'We had our own tasking officer down in Riyadh, who was very much part of an

Jaguars lined up at RAF Coltishall ready to be painted 'desert pink' *(41 Sqn RAF Coltishall)*

Ready for the worst: NBC kit offered an uncomfortable but vital protective system *(Major N Evans)*

A familiar sight in the Gulf: the Hercules, affectionately known as 'Fat Albert'*(Flt Lt John Ayers)*

'We'd pick him up on radar, roll in behind him, take the fuel': the silent meeting of a VC10K tanker and her chick (*Wg Cdr Oli Delany*)

'Mighty Hunter': the elegant Nimrod MR2, originally based on the de Havilland Comet *(MOD)*

Monitoring shipping movements: a vital part of the UN imposition of sanctions on Iraq (*Wg Cdr Andy Wight-Boycott*)

'Like something out of a Lowry painting': a Nimrod flies over the smoke of the newly-liberated Kuwait City
(Wg Cdr Andy Wight-Boycott)

RAF musicians performed a dual role in alien surroundings
(Sqn Ldr Francis Shannon)

Night vision goggles in use(*Patrick Allen,Peter March)*

The control panel of a Nimrod
(Peter March)

Tornado F3 detachment on the flight line, Dhahran
(Sqn Ldr Chris Newsome)

Pumas in the desert (*Stu Black, Peter March*)

The ageing but much loved Victor tankers supported British, Canadian, French and US aircraft(*Peter March*)

Tornado aircrew Flt Lts Jerry Gegg(left) and Ian Long return from the first strike to face the media(*Sqn Ldr Chris Newsome*)

Tornado F3 *(Flt Lt Ian Black)*

Battle damage: repair teams pulled out all the stops to keep aircraft operational
(Sqn Ldr Chris Newsome)

Two 'great blokes': Max Collier(right) and Nigel Elsdon, killed in action in Iraq on the night of 18 January
(provided by the families of Flt Lt Max Collier and Wg Cdr Nigel Elsdon)

'One in the eye for you, Saddam ...': messages on bombs ranged from invective aimed at the enemy to slogans photographed for profit
(Sqn Ldr Chris Newsome)

What might have been: this was all that remained of one Scud downed by a Patriot
(Sqn Ldr Chris Newsome)

Armed up with overwing Sidewinders, 1,000lb bombs, cluster bombs and ECM pods, the Jaguar force harried the Iraqi navy *(Peter March)*

'Alone, unarmed, and unafraid': the Tornado GR1A carried sophisticated video equipment and extra fuel tanks in place of weapons
(Public Info, Brit Forces Germany)

The paper that backs our boys: *The Sun* provided welcome support and news that was 'free to all you heroes' *(The Sun)*

'The Hercules was doing exactly what it was designed to do ... landing on desert strips a quarter of the length of a standard airfield'
(SAC Dave Pearce)

'It's vast; there's no shelter': the Pumas of the Support Helicopter Force, Middle East operated alongside aircraft of the The Royal Navy and Army Air Corps
(Patrick Allen, Peter March)

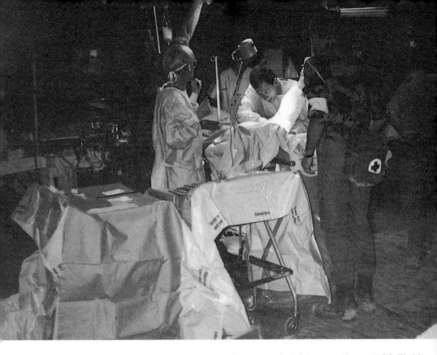

An unusual sight: operations at 32 Field
Hospital were rare *(Gp Capt Charles Newrick)*

'All the dirty water was used to water these plants': hobbies were
an important part of hospital life*(Gp Capt Charles Newrick)*

Kate Adie was one of the reporters respected for the rapport she built up with the forces *(Sqn Ldr Chris Newsome)*

Nose job: ground crew took pains to provide the Buccaneers with individual decoration *(Peter March)*

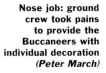

Ready for the off: Mal Miller(far right) and friends model what well-dressed Buccaneer aircrew are wearing this year *(Flt Lt Mal Miller)*

'An inaminate object that slowly comes
to life...'*(Peter March)*

**Norman Browne kitting up
for his first mission
*(Sqn Ldr Norman Browne)***

'In the air it looks the bizz': the
Buccaneer over the Saudi desert
(Peter March)

For many Iraqi PoWs, boiled sweets handed out on RAF helicopters were their first food for days
(Cpl Clive Darwood)

'They got rid of any bit of military kit they could': the debris of war surrounding this Iraqi bunker included one of the many discarded boots
(Major Mark Kitchen)

Examples of precision bombing of Iraqi HASs
(Peter March)

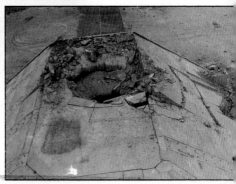

Seeing the results: evidence of a successful attack on the Al Nasiriyah road bridge across the Euphrates *(Sqn Ldr Norman Browne)*

Iraqi vehicles fleeing ʳom Kuwait were forced into ever-wider detours off 'Hell's Highway' *(Flt Lt John Ayers)*

ᵗhe entrance arch of the Ali-Al-Salem airfield ᵧmbolised the destruction of Kuwait's capital *ᴹajor Mark Kitchen)*

The final act: Iraqi generals meet General
Schwarzkopf and allied commanders to
accept the conditions of the ceasefire
(Sqn Ldr Chris Newsome)

Dave Waddington(second left) and Robbie Stewart(third left)
on their return to RAF Marham *(RAF Marham)*

American intelligence-gathering cell down there. Unlike the mud movers who went through their missions in large packages with American support, we were generally going in on our own. The only thing we had to do with the Americans directly was to use their AWACS.'

The aircraft themselves are standard GR1s but, as Flt Lt Angus Hogg points out, 'the guns have been taken out and the reconnaissance system has been put in'. This system consists of an infra-red line scanner under the aircraft and two sideways-looking infra-red sensors, giving a horizon-to-horizon view. The space normally occupied by the cannon holds video cameras. So were they unprotected? Fg Off Jerry Spencer from 11 Sqn suggests that the old recce maxim – 'Alone, unarmed and unafraid' – was at least two-thirds correct. His partner, Angus Hogg, confirms that he prayed, 'frequently, the whole time and at all stages'.

The recce crews worked largely as quick reaction units, responding to instructions received only two or three hours in advance from Riyadh: and could be checking out military activity on the ground, 'blind' reconnaissance for special forces or – particularly in western Iraq near the politicall sensitive border with Jordan and Syria – Scudbusting. Both Hogg and Spencer remember how satisfying it was 'to get a good picture of a Scud out in the open, because they were very good at hiding them'.

For both men, the Gulf experience confirmed the importance of reconnaissance work in a modern war. 'I think the guys were genuinely surprised at what we could do,' says Spencer. 'Outside the recce world our work tends not to get publicised very much, it's a bit of a sideline. But now it's been put on the map.'

Back in the midst of the action, the effects of stress were beginning to show. Mal Craghill remembers a particularly vivid instance: 'One of the guys in our

113

formation had a fit on the morning after we'd flown the first trip, which eventually the medics put down to a combination of lack of food, lack of sleep and the stress of being fired at for the first time. Fortunately we had a radio in the villa and called for medical support. They arrived in a couple of minutes, by which time he was coming round, but he had no idea what had happened.'

That such reactions were so rare is in part a tribute to the release valve that operates throughout the RAF: humour. Neil 'Crusty' Cobb speaks for many when he describes how he coped: 'You make fun out of it really. If you can make fun out of dying, that's the way through. My attitude was just try and enjoy it while you can. Go out and drop your bombs and, if you get killed, that's tough.'

Most aircrew jokes hone in on a weakness: when Mike Warren and Mal Craghill returned from a mission where they had missed a bridge (their bombs falling harmlessly into the river), they found two sardines awaiting them on the bar. The F3 crews, bereft of opportunities to engage the Iraqi air force, were mocked by the mud movers. Yet the flippant rivalry between squadrons masks mutual concern. An engineering officer tells of a message received in the early, difficult days of the war. It was from the Phantom crews, grinding their teeth away from the action. It read: 'God speed. Wish we were with you.'

Flt Lt Colin Adair's fourship called itself 'The Leper Colony', after the film in which 'the misfits and outcasts of the squadron are put together in one bomber under James Stewart. We were a mishmash of people from different squadrons, and we lived our lives like a Hollywood movie really. It wasn't that we didn't care; we just didn't want to get worried about it all. We took our actual business very seriously. We tried to relieve our stress on the ground by being stupid.' Alexander Gordon remembers that 'some of the humour was completely puerile. It wouldn't be considered funny at all in this country by the same people who found it hilarious out there. It was a method of releasing tension. The situation was exceedingly unfunny but as a defence mechanism, people had to find something to laugh about.'

Films of the 1940s and '50s have successfully perpetuated traditional Air Force values to a new generation. Warren is one of many who admit to being strongly influenced by Pinewood and Hollywood: 'You watch the World War II films and see the attitudes of the Spitfire pilots, with their banter, and you feel that the same sort of thing is happening but 50 years on.'

The GR1 crews could banter about death in the abstract, but their mood was sombre after the loss of friends and colleagues. David Waddington recalls the atmosphere after Nigel Elsdon and Max Collier had been shot down: 'The guys were obviously talking about it, but there was nobody in tears, nobody breaking down in the bar. It was a very quiet grieving. And you wonder if you're going to have to do it again the next night.'

They did have to – for Waddington himself.

Their next mission was against the huge Al-Tallil airbase near Basra, a target which presented obvious dangers, of which navigator Robbie Stewart was aware: 'We knew there'd be triple A, and we knew there was a Roland missile site on the airfield. We were very apprehensive: Dave and I used to look at one another, we didn't need to say much, we'd just look.'

However, the approach was quiet, as Waddington describes: 'We were only flying over Iraq for about 30 minutes until we hit the target. Absolutely pitch dark, nothing around us – just like doing a training sortie. There were eight aircraft in the formation. We were carrying 1,000lb bombs, trying to toss them into the airfield to suppress the triple A so that the last four aircraft, who were carrying JP233s, would have an easier time.

'We were just coming up to the pull-up point where we would release the bombs, three and a half miles from the target. I remember the missiles being fired at me, seeing it at 12 o'clock, which is the worst position. My exact words were "***! Missile!" I broke left and shouted, "Chaff!", at Robbie. All I could see was a flame like a very large firework coming towards me but once I banked the aircraft we lost sight of it. Then there was an enormous white flash. I remember an enormous wind – I think the canopy was shattered – and then I was unconscious very quickly. My last thoughts were that I was going to die.'

Stewart, further back from the blast, had a split-second to react instinctively: 'I ejected on the command eject system. The back seat goes first, half a second before the front seat.' Others on the raid were convinced that both had been killed.

Sadly, the losses continued. On 22 January, during an attack by eight Tornados on Ar Rutbah radar site, Sqn Ldrs Garry Lennox and Kevin Weeks of 16 Sqn, based in Tabuk, were lost. And the following day Flt Lt Simon Burgess and Sqn Ldr Bob Ankerson of 17 Sqn, operating from Dhahran, went missing, one of their bombs having exploded prematurely – bringing the total of GR1 losses in action to five in seven days.

In broadcasts which quickly became infamous, the Iraqis paraded a number of captured aircrew on television, amongst them Flt Lts John Peters and Adrian 'John' Nichol. Although in some ways this fulfilled everyone's worst fear it was, at the same time, strangely reassuring, as Bertie Newton remembers: 'I was certainly convinced that, if you were taken prisoner, you wouldn't get out alive from Iraq. I was very glad when I saw the two guys on television because I knew them both quite well. I thought, "Fine, excellent – because they've been on television they're the most likely not to get topped".'

Most of the crews had discussed what they would do if they came down in what they called, after the *Blackadder* television series, 'sausage side'. Newton reports that 'some people in the early days had decided that if they did land they'd top themselves. I'd never ever think of doing that because I'm an optimist. You'd feel a real plank if peace was declared about ten seconds later.'

That was, however, still a distant prospect. In early February the main thrust of the air strikes moved away from airfields and towards industrial centres, power stations and ammunition dumps. Many of these were less well defended and produced satisfyingly impressive explosions when attacked. Jerry Witts remembers that 'the landscape was punctuated by massive fires. On the way back I remember thinking that they were really taking a bashing. I wondered how this bloke could carry on. It was ridiculous. His country was being dismantled before his very eyes; fortunately – despite what anyone says – without huge loss of civilian life. The stupidity of the whole thing struck me.'

Despite the huge amount of damage being done to Iraqi targets, the conventional iron bombs being used had their limitations, as Neil Cobb points out: 'You ran in, dropped your bombs and – however many seconds later – there was a "Kerrrumph" from the ground and you thought, "Ah, the bombs hit the ground. I wonder whether they hit the target."'

There was a growing demand for some of the 'smart' technology which the Americans were using to such good effect – on the enemy and on public opinion. But, as General Schwarzkopf had warned, no technology could deliver 'a nice war'. On occasions the bombs missed their targets and hit civilian areas.

Alexander Gordon explains how smart weapons, like smart people, sometimes made mistakes: 'The Americans made a big thing of how their precision munitions could take out a cheese sandwich at 200 miles. Perhaps they kicked themselves for that, because in reality you *cannot* have a surgical war. There is no such thing. For a bomb to go down an elevator shaft is just luck. It probably has a CEP – a computer error probability – of maybe 30-40 ft. That can make the difference between hitting the place you're aiming for and the one next door which is full of civilians. We felt there was an awful lot of wingeing back here about civilian casualties and our attitude was, "We're at war with them. This is what happens in war. People die".'

Sqn Ldr Phil Goodall is emphatic: 'We carried out a gentlemanly war. Despite the propaganda about baby milk factories, the rules on our side were strict: we hit military targets. I'm not just giving you the party line. I was in the briefing room when targets were looked at and taken away from us on a day-to-day basis because of the civilian population. It was right and proper that we did carry it out that way but, of course, we were playing to one set of rules and Saddam has always played to another.'

One response to the demand for precision bombing was to use Buccaneer designators with Tornados carrying laser-guided weapons. Another was the TIALD [Thermal Imaging and Laser Designation] pod. Greg Monaghan from 13 Sqn based at RAF Honington was involved from the beginning: 'When this project came up in November, they looked around the Air Force for someone to do it. I was on a sort of standby standby team. So we had to learn how to use the kit and work out our own tactics and so on.'

The TIALD had been ordered in June 1988 and was going through the lengthy process of being developed, tested, and evaluated when Iraq invaded Kuwait. With the combination of goodwill and a more or less open cheque book – both of which solved so many Gulf War problems – the system was short-circuited: 'Everybody concerned with the project came together at Boscombe Down: the software writers, Ferranti, the pilots. We worked seven days a week until ten or eleven o'clock at night. The engineers were working almost 24 hours a day. The pace was quite startling – we did, effectively, two years' work in a month.'

Four aircraft and two pods were taken out to Tabuk on 6 February. Following the briefest of test runs – just one sortie – they were put to use under the names of two characters in *Viz* magazine: Sandra and Tracy. Monaghan explains the result: 'By day or night we were 1,000% more effective. The chaps were missing [at medium level], because the Tornado wasn't designed to do that – and what was worse, they couldn't see by how much they were missing in order to correct. So in one fell swoop we were hitting the targets a very high percentage of the time – and we took film to prove it. So morale went sky high.'

If morale in Tabuk was less than sky high before the arrival of TIALD, it was in part due to the crowded accommodation provided on this isolated desert posting. Aircrew were living in an apartment complex previously used by British Aerospace. Each room had four bunk beds, a shower and virtually no privacy. Neither was there much in the way of entertainment, as Gordon explains: 'On local television they would normally spend the first 15 minutes talking about what the local sheik did today. And when they ran out of things to say about it, rather than just stop the piece, they'd show him walking down a line of soldiers, or opening a baby milk factory or whatever, and they'd have martial music playing – for 15 minutes!'

Those in Dhahran and Muharraq were undoubtedly better off in many respects, although their situation seemed bizarre to many. Colin Adair, stationed in Dhahran, remembers 'the unreality of it all. You could be at the sports complex, sailing, water skiing, sunbathing. You'd come back at night, plan it, get dressed in your war suit; you'd have your gun, all your other secret bits and pieces on you – map, all the good stuff. You'd jump in your jet, go off, blow up a power station and come back home in time for tea and medals.' Roger Bennett was also based in Dhahran, living in an apartment complex, and admits: 'We were looked after by the apartment staff, who were generally Indian or Ceylonese. The food was very good quality and we also had a field kitchen from the base.'

Many felt their way of life was very insular, as Alexander Gordon explains: 'It was very difficult to concern yourself with anything external. We became very boring flyers. Our entire life was in the cockpit, sleeping, eating and at the squadron. There was very little outside this world event that we could be bothered with.'

Dick Druitt also admits to a certain amount of introspection: 'You get very lonely in a hotel room for three months. In that loneliness you have time to consider yourself and your priorities. What use are the material things of life if you're not alive to enjoy them? I try to enjoy life and my family a bit more now. My wife finds me a lot happier.'

Druitt was stationed at Bahrain with the Buccaneer, Jaguar and Tornado crews for whom he tanked. He felt being on site helped build up a good relationship: 'We'd go over and brief them with the maps in front of us, with the blokes who were actually going.' He is a strong believer in the importance of service camaraderie – this was one of the reasons for his joining the Air Force. He would often 'go over to their hotels, go out for a meal with them, get pissed and fall over each other.'

Another important morale booster that everyone remembers were the letters from home. Bennett remembers: 'Old ladies were spending their pensions on tins of chocolate to send out to anybody. That was a great lift to the guys. It was fantastic to see that support.' Even when it came from a schoolboy who wrote to 'an airman in the Gulf' and ended his short message of support with the memorable postscript: 'PS. Please write back if you aren't dead.'

The press too played its part in keeping spirits high. Bennett remembers that '*The Sun* was fantastic, not just for us but for all the troops out there. They supported our lads and it was a great lift. They sent out a special edition to us regularly.' In particular, the aircrew became friendly with the TV crews, as Neil Cobb explains: 'The thing they had in their favour was that they'd video you, so you could see it straight away, as opposed to a press interview which you might see ten days later. So the guys were popular. They also had a fairly good hospitality budget. I think the room bill of the TV-AM guy was about £45,000. His fridge door was never closed.'

As the air war continued, the focus of media attention switched to the impending ground offensive. The relentless build-up of forces was also clearly visible to those in the air: 'It was just an endless stream of tank tracks, personnel, camps, APVs [armoured personnel vehicles] and it went on as far as you could see,' remembers Paul Smith. 'A never-ending convoy – not only in length, but also in width,' adds Tony Beresford.

Angus Hogg and Jerry Spencer vividly recall seeing the advancing land assault: 'With NVGs, we'd been seeing this massive build-up of kit on the nights before, but it was all in the dark – we were flying over this black space. But that night all the lights were on. They were just driving through into Iraq, lights on, the lot. It was just like the M25 on a Friday.'

Bill Pixton believes that the correct balance between the air and ground wars was achieved: 'I think a lot of people estimated that the ground war would have started a couple of weeks before it did – but, in my view, the plan was wonderful. We hit the right things. We took it in slow time. We coordinated it all and we kept it up 24 hours a day until we were 200% happy that we'd inflicted about as much damage as we could and he was on his last legs. We might have been able to let the Army go in maybe a week earlier, or even two, and they probably would've got to Basra only a day later than they did. They might only have lost another 50-odd troops on the way: but you tell the 50-odd troops' families that.'

Chapter 8

WHAT NEEDS TO BE DONE

'Unless Saddam Hussein gets out of Kuwait we will invite you to remove him. Whatever needs to be done could not be in better hands . . .'

Prime Minister John Major

With their supremacy in the air secured, the allies were free to redeploy ground troops in huge numbers. The scene created by mobilisation on such an enormous scale was best appreciated from a tanker pilot's vantage-point: 'Looking down, it seemed like the whole of the desert was peppered with compounds of various different nationalities, and crossed with the tracks in the sand of tanks, armoured cars, carriers, artillery, troops. There was a main road that ran roughly east-west – and that was just a continuous stream of traffic in both directions, day and night.'

The air war had continued almost unabated for a full 38 days in preparation for the inevitable ground offensive. This was to be a ground war fought by tanks, artillery and infantry – but under the cover of an air umbrella, with US helicopter gunships riding shotgun, and with a full supporting cast of more helicopters to bring troops and supplies forward and to take back the wounded. Air power was to play a vital role in the push into Iraq and Kuwait and, as far as the RAF was concerned, that meant working on a 'hub and spokes principle' from Riyadh. As well as looking after the Tristars and VC10s freighting and transiting through Riyadh, Peter Bedford's Air Transport Detachment handled the in-theatre Hercs – which now came into their own: 'The Hercules is a most forgiving aeroplane and it was doing exactly what it was designed to do – operating very short sectors, landing on desert strips a quarter of the length of a standard airfield – and flying low-level as a matter of routine, because we had no self-protection.'

Perhaps even more vital was the role to be played both by 205 General Hospital, now set up in the terminal building, and the auxiliary aeromedics of 4626 Sqn, as Sqn Ldr Chris Hewat explains: 'We could have had in-theatre and out-of-theatre Hercules, a VC10 and a Tristar, all either bringing injured in from the front or taking those who'd been stabilised to Cyprus or the UK. In the case of the VC10 you're talking about a 51-stretcher fit – that was probably the most complex aircraft to load. I think in my heart of hearts that, had we been faced with thirteen to fourteen hundred casualties a day, there would have been pandemonium – but the system we set up would have coped.'

The system relied on field hospitals from which the assembled teams could use waiting aircraft to fly the wounded in and out. This meant moving the helicopter squadrons forward from their base at Al Jubayl, together with aeromedics, musicians turned medics and hospital staff from Riyadh and Bahrain. Most of the latter were sent forward to Al Qaysumah, a desert airfield about 230 miles north-west of Al Jubayl and only about 60 miles south of the Iraqi border. The mobilisation began two days after the start of the air war. The lucky ones flew up by Chinook or Puma but the great majority took to the road.

Some were lucky to get there at all, as pathologist Gp

Capt Charles Newrick recounts: 'My lasting impression of the Gulf is that whenever we set off to go somewhere we got lost. Driving up to Al Qaysumah took us 21 hours. A driver took a wrong turning and the convoy ended up in a rather impressive-looking place where there didn't seem to be anybody around. The officer in charge got out and started strolling through this arcade of Islamic design while we all sat in the coaches. Suddenly Saudis appeared from everywhere – they obviously didn't want us there. It turned out that we'd actually managed to get to the Kuwaiti border hundreds of miles from where we were supposed to be. Not only were we on the Kuwaiti border, but apparently there was an Iraqi gun emplacement about 200 yards away which had the border crossing in its sights. It was encouraging in a way – we had red crosses on the coaches and they didn't open fire on us.'

Flt Lt Rachel Johnson and SACW Connie Dale, with the aeromed evacuation detachment that was going to work alongside 32 and 22 Field Hospitals, had a more orthodox journey in 4-tonners to Al Qaysumah. However, this party also had its problems. 'When we arrived it was about two o'clock in the morning,' Johnson remembers. 'From being in a five-star hotel we found ourselves in freezing cold, pouring rain and thick mud. We couldn't find our advance party and we could hear gunfire. It was friendly fire but we didn't know that. The next day we found our lads and started building the evacuation centre.'

This was sited at the end of the runway where the helicopters could unload casualties for the Hercules to pick up. 'We started from scratch. We put our tents up and they got flooded so we had to dig trenches round them. We were expecting lots of casualties and needed somewhere to put them so we had to build massive air-raid shelters which the Royal Engineers helped us with. It was very hard work and I felt like a council worker digging the trenches.'

Digging in the sand proved tough, as medic SAC Gary Woods discovered: 'I dug about seven or eight trenches there and the sand was awful stuff. It was more of a dry, dusty type of soil. I remember reading about the old Desert Rats – they said how hard it was to dig out and it was true. You'd dig about two feet down and then it was hard and solid. It would take an hour to dig down two feet and a day or two to dig the rest of the trench.'

Conditions were basic for the 100-strong RAF party, as Dale describes: 'I was living in a tent with three men: an MT technician and two musicians. We put up a blanket on a piece of string so I had my little piece of privacy where I could change. The Air Force supplies everyone with a bum roll, about an inch thick, for sleeping on. But when we first got there, we were sleeping on stretchers because the bum roll was damp and our sleeping bags didn't dry because of the continuous rain. And we didn't have any showers. That was sad because next door to us were the Americans and they had everything – wooden floorboards, and hot stoves inside their tents that they could cook on. They had showers, mirrors, sinks – we couldn't believe it, because all we had was a bucket. However, we traded some of our kit with the Yanks and got their cots, which were canvas and metal, so at least we could sleep above the ground and not get damp. Later I moved in with the other four girls and we tried to make it as much our home as possible. I had a compo box next to my bed with a scarf over it and my candle on that. I even stuck pictures from home on the tent with elastoplast. You had to keep up your standards, because if you let them drop then your morale would have dropped as well.'

At night a blackout was enforced: 'We had to use torches and we mainly played cards, but that was fun and kept the conversation going. It was amazing how we became really good friends with everybody from cooks to MT drivers. And we got friendly with the American Apache crew that were next door to us. That was good because we were like a family.'

As was so often the case in the Gulf, the Americans at Al Qaysumah turned out to be friends and providers. 'There were about 2–3,000 of them,' remembers Johnson. 'They looked after us and swapped kits with us. I swapped my beret for a Parka jacket because I was so cold. I also got an American cot as well as an American poncho and within a week I was well-equipped. The Americans also built some shower units and once a week we used to go across and queue to use their showers.'

The Hercules aircrew also provided a valuable link with the outside world, particularly since Johnson's husband was in the Gulf as a Hercules pilot: 'I knew a lot of them and they provided us with lots of things that we wouldn't have got otherwise. I used to say, "I'd like some fresh fruit, Persil and cleanser for my skin" and the next day they'd come with a shopping bag. It made our life much more comfortable.'

Ironically, one of the biggest problems at Al Qaysumah turned out to be a shortage of water: 'The colonel in charge was a nice bloke but he was quite strict. There was a complete ban on washing combats and we were only allowed to wash our undergarments. Showering was once every three days. The colonel was into gardening and had plants and all the dirty water was used to water these plants. He built up sandbag squares and planted palm trees in them, so it looked nice when you drove into the hospital. There was a big sign there saying "The Desert Rose", which was a terrible name because a desert rose is what you pee into. You dig a big hole, put a tube in the ground, fill the dirt back around it and stick a funnel on the top.

Because these funnels were mainly red they were called desert roses.'

Charles Newrick found that trying to set up his pathology unit in these circumstances was not easy. It was 'a very unethical environment', as far as he was concerned: 'A lot of the stuff we were supposed to get had been diverted and never got to us. So we were very, very short. Much of what we had to do was scrounge – first come, first served – which was probably the worst thing about the war. We had 20 different units there so it was a little bit fraught for the first fortnight until we settled down.'

However, with the ground war expected to start within a fortnight everything was geared towards preparing for the arrival of casualties: 'Throughout the whole of the air battle canvas was going up, canvas was coming down, being relocated – and exercises were going on: exercises in the air, exercises with chemicals, exercises with everything. We were doing exercises for two massive dumps of 140 casualties twice a day. In fact, it was in many ways harder work than we had to do when the ground attack started.'

Also sent out into the field were the Chinook and Puma squadrons from Odiham and Gütersloh. Their main operating base was moved westwards to King Khalid Military City – known as KKMC – a vast open camp sited some distance away in the desert north of Riyadh. As Wg Cdr Mike Trace explains, this was all part of a move to bring the British ground forces across Saudi Arabia to the west without alerting the Iraqis to this fact: 'We left behind a radio unit on the coast north of Jubayl which transmitted the radio traffic from one of our false exercises to give the impression the Brits were still on the coast and still exercising.'

The move was carried out partly by air and partly in convoy along the notorious MSR, which Chinook electrician Andy Garton describes as a 'deathtrap. The MSR – the main supply route between the east coast and the west where the big party was going to begin – was the equivalent of the M25 but the width of a C class road, and going down it you had the largest tank transporter to the smallest Arab car. The average was seven deaths a day and it was like the Indie 500 really, because everything was nose to tail all the way but at 55mph with lorries, cars, buses, everything weaving in and out.'

Driving a 4-tonner on such a road was 'quite hairy. If you met a tank transporter coming in the other direction with a tank on the back you had no option but to get off the road, where there was a two-foot deep rut. You'd try to edge out as far as you could and cringe away from the window – and hope that nothing would hit you. You'd put a personal stereo on, turn the volume up and drive with your eyes shut, thinking, "If it's going to happen, it's going to happen".'

KKMC was an entirely military area made up of camps filled with allied forces – and without comforts: 'We were dumped in the bondu [wasteland] at the back of the city and we used the same set of 20 showers as about ten and a half thousand Americans, a few thousand Egyptians and Syrians and whoever else was down there – so we smelled like the back end of an elephant in the rutting season.'

The lack of toilet facilities at KKMC also provided a rich vein of military humour: 'Instead of toilets, we had sort of garden sheds with half of a 45-gallon drum at the bottom, the contents of which were burned the following morning. We didn't have much idea how to burn them – so we just went for it. We got some fuel and made a few Molotov cocktails but that was a bit dangerous, because we had one or two drums exploding. The door springs on these toilets had had it. You'd be sitting there and the door would flop open and there'd be shouts of "Morning,

Tom!" The only claim to fame that I have from being out there is that I used the same toilet as Kate Adie, because one day we ferried some newscasters in and Kate Adie went to this sacred area.'

Even more memorable than the lavatories was the harshness of the desert all around them, as MT driver SAC Dave Pearce recalls: 'It's flat as a pancake with little bushes here and there. There's different-coloured sand, swept in different ways by the wind. It's vast; there's no shelter. There were no wind breaks, especially when the helicopters came down. We would just get covered in sand. We had to turn our backs and hope that we didn't get mouthfuls of it. Sand got everywhere. We had to clear out our tents every day, and weapons three or four times a day. When it rained, everything was muddy and filthy.'

Some aspects of the desert surprised Gary Woods: 'I expected to see millions of camels, but I only saw a few small herds. Another thing that amazed me was the price of fuel. We were bombing along the MSR towards Kuwait and missed the TSW refuelling point. We decided that we would all have to chip in and buy some. We pulled into a garage and asked for diesel and an old Arab filled up the whole tank for something like £1.10. That was something to be experienced – filling up your tank for a pound.'

The helicopter squadrons had their own camp sites north of KKMC which they shared with medics brought in to assist them, and RAF Regiment gunners to guard the camps. Cpl Clive Darwood was one of the latter: 'We set up our site next door to some American Chinooks. The only thing that had been done for us was that a berm had been dug by the Americans. They were on one side and we were on the other. We had to dig air-raid shelters by hand and we installed the NIAD chemical sentry – a big square box that had to be replenished every 12 hours and have the batteries changed.'

However, their chief duty was guarding the camp: 'When 1 Sqn came out with a flight they set up about four OPs [observation posts] about a kilometre and a half in front and we patrolled inside their OP screen, mostly at night – when we patrolled every hour. One of the lads, Benny Evans, came back from patrol and said, "I'm not going out there again". Apparently, he'd heard something moving, had gone to ground and moved forward, got to where the noise was – and there was a big snake looking at him . . .'

By day the most serious hazard, as the rainy season ended, was the sandstorms: 'The worst sandstorm we had was in the middle of the afternoon when it went so dark it was like night. We had goggles but we couldn't see more than 20 metres in front of us and, of course, we had to stay in the position.' There were also the flies: 'There was nothing in the desert so we could never understand why there were loads and loads of flies. But they were very docile, unlike the British fly, so killing them became a pastime. They used to be everywhere, so we had a lot of fun killing them.'

It was decided that the usual three-man Puma crew of pilot, co-pilot and crewman should be supplemented by a medic, partly to assist in casevacs and partly because 'they could look out to the side and rear of us, because we were frightened of an enemy air threat'. This was how Ian Showler, Ian Tervit and a number of qualified aeromedics – 'you get little wings to wear on your sleeve' – came to fly as constituted crew-members on the Pumas. They both regarded themselves as very fortunate.

'I felt safe with those two guys in the front,' declares Showler, 'and the crewman was excellent as well, a good lad with a sense of humour. I said, "It's going to be a big learning curve for me, obviously – where you want me in the helicopter, what you want me to do". And he said to me, "It's going to be a big learning curve for me as well". So that established right from the start that I would help him out and he would help me out, which was great.'

In flight there was always plenty to do: 'You don't just sit in the back and pick your nose. You're an extra pair of eyes. You have your bonedome on and you're on intercom with the rest of the crew. I would take the port side and the crewman would take the starboard side and I'd be constantly scanning the air and calling up any air traffic that I could see. If I saw anything I'd click on the intercom and say something like, "Helicopter low, two miles, eight o'clock, same heading", or "Tornado, nine o'clock, very high, no confliction". And they'd say, "Copied", or "Good spot", things like that. So you were involved in the crew right from the start.'

The Pumas were dealing with casevacs right away, as Tervit describes: 'The next day a lot of injuries came in – people who'd been working long hours making mistakes with their tools, falling off the backs of lorries. Then there were cases of diarrhoea and vomiting as a result of the change of food and the conditions we were living in. But it was quite a while before we got the first serious casualties.'

Also on the move were small parties of RAF personnel attached to one group or another, or sometimes making up their own little band. Cpl Dave Pullen was one of 24 RAF caterers who ran the kitchen at a desert Forward Maintenance Area (FMA): 'We had everybody coming through us to go to the front lines, with four serveries going at the same time. The queues would go on for an hour or two hours. At one point there were just under 3,000 people and I've never catered for that many on that sort of equipment. The main hardship was the serving of the customer, not the cooking of the food. Being Air Force caterers we knew how to sort them out. If they had a go at us, we just told them to wind their necks in.'

They lived – and cooked – in tents: 'We were working in very cramped, very hot conditions with all the burners, gas and petrol inside the tents. That was the main drawback, because there are only so many sides to a tent that you can lift up. However, there were more people doing one job than would have been expected in the UK, which gave you more time to take a break. You just looked forward to the end of the day when you could say, "This is my time. I'm going back to my little tent".'

The field laboratory teams with their NBC testing equipment travelled from one unit to another. 'It was a bit like being at Scouts, because you had to be in the gang,' says Cpl Steve Curme. 'First we were part of the 7th Armoured Brigade, so we had to stitch a desert rat onto our uniforms. Then they moved forward and we became part of the FMA. They had their own Blackadder badge so off came the Desert Rats, out came the needle and thread and on went the Blackadder. Then shortly after that the 1st Field Laboratory Unit adopted its own insignia, which was two crossed palm trees with laboratory glassware at the bottom. That was just for our own 45-strong unit.'

Members of Tactical Supply Wing worked in pairs rather than teams, as suppliers or truck-drivers. As drivers, their job was largely to transport aviation fuel from refineries to fuel dumps or to tactical refuelling areas, driving by night and day along the MSR highways and often sleeping in the cabs of their vehicles. 'We were very mobile,' explains Sgt Mick Johnson. 'You'd go through periods of a week where you wouldn't do anything and then in a couple of days you'd be moving a million litres of fuel.'

Others, like SAC Brian Aitken, were on resupply

– bringing up stores when necessary, but also turning their hands to whatever was required, whether it was digging trenches, building defensive sangars or doing the cooking. 'My first time was a disaster,' admits Aitken. 'We were using small Saudi stoves which we filled with the jet fuel we were shipping around. Whoever had filled it up for me had left fuel all round it. The whole lot went up in flames. I'd already put the dinner on the stove and the whole lot caught fire. Somebody used a fire extinguisher on it so the dinner was ruined. After that they found another job for me to do.'

Their food was usually from compo rations or from the larger packs swapped with the Americans: 'You got a box which had nine meals, ranging from goulash to spaghetti. You had a package which you diluted into a litre of water and that was your drink and you had a package which was your main meal, which you cooked on the top of the radiator of your vehicle when there were no other cooking facilities.'

One of the camps that Aitken resupplied was just south of the coastal town of Khafji, overrun by the one Iraqi military advance of the war: 'We were told there were 70,000 Iraqi troops there who could advance on us at any time, which was quite frightening. If you were on guard you could see loads of planes flying over and hear the bangs and the sight was just like a firework display. Different aircraft made different noises according to the loads they were dropping: thuds, cracks and bangs. The loudest bang went off one afternoon when a Hercules flew over with a pallet bomb, which exploded over the Iraqi lines and sucked the oxygen from the atmosphere.' This was the 15,000 lb 'daisy cutter', capable of clearing an area several times the size of a football field of mines – killing everything within it.

As the weeks passed the days grew warmer. 'It was cloudy in the morning when we started digging a sangar,'

Aitken remembers. 'It brightened in the afternoon, you were sweating and the grit was on you, but you felt stupid going back to your tent to put sun cream on – everyone would think you were posing – so you just got on with the job. That night I felt my arms cooking and they were scarlet red because I'd rolled up my sleeves. I never made that mistake again.'

In fact, living in the desert had no serious effect on the health of most service personnel. At Al Qaysumah Charles Newrick noted that the main problems were 'respiratory things like runny noses and coughs, which we put down to the fact that we were taking NAPs – nerve agent protective tablets – terrible nasty things.'

There were, however, problems with the NIAD toxic substance alarms in camp, which were always going off: 'There was a big burn-out on the bunker about half a mile away, where they burnt a lot of things including plastic bags, which gave off cyanide gas. These nasty substances would drift across our camp and the NIAD would go off, so we were forever putting on our noddy [NBC] suits left, right and centre two or three times a day. In the end we decided to get some canaries to act as gas detectors, though whether canaries were the right bird species to react to a nerve agent we never really discovered.'

Wild dogs also caused problems, according to Gary Woods: 'We were dumping food and although we incinerated it, a lot wouldn't burn. Eventually we had a pack of four or five dogs coming round quite regularly. I would stand on the top of this bund and they were all quite playful. But they reckoned they carried rabies and hepatitis and they shot them. I thought it was cruel but I suppose it was the correct thing to do.'

Out in the field and back in the main bases the steep learning curves gave way to the refining of new skills and drills. The musicians attached to the RAF hospital at Muharraq were no exception. Their Director of Music,

Flt Lt Rob Wiffin, became a communications systems expert: 'I must admit I loved the challenge. I had phones, tannoy systems, intercoms coming out of my ears. We were telling the musicians in the band who were good at car mechanics, "You're in charge of the collective protection area. You must find out how it works – the air filtration, the air conditioning". A lot of the musicians got involved with hands-on medical work and did courses to improve their skills. We did have a great affinity with the medics, probably because we're musicians first just as they're doctors and professional people first. What was strange to us was that the rank structure out there meant nothing at all. It was complete familiarity – but it didn't breed contempt because we gave them respect for their skills.'

Soon 'boredom and stagnation' began to set in and a number of off-duty activities and sports were organised. Here the musicians were able to put their musical skills to good use: 'We managed to get our instruments out under the guise of medical instruments – if we'd just asked for the instruments they wouldn't have got there. Some of the boys preferred to forget their proper role and just concentrated on getting through the war but others were happy to pick up their instruments and they called themselves the Red Cross Arm Band. There was a new bar in the complex for the junior ranks which they called the Red Red Red Lion – after the Red Red Alerts – and they played there. We even had a barbershop quartet singing messages over the tannoys. We had one area of the hospital which was very bumpy and dusty, which was called Lord's, and the chap who organised the cricket came in and said he wanted to announce the Test Match for that morning over the tannoy. So someone got a keyboard and we did the music from Test Match Special with four of us singing crowded round the microphone.'

Another memorable announcement was the morning reveille: 'We'd been on the night shift and at five to six the officer in charge came to me and said, "Right, wake the hospital up". So we put "Nessun Dorma" – which is "None Shall Sleep" – sung by Pavarotti, over the tannoy. We put it at really high volume and apparently you could hear it on the other side of the airfield two miles away. What the locals thought of it I don't know.'

As the air war entered its fifth week, anticipation after the huge build-up had given way to a sense of anticlimax, with 'a lot of people just sitting round doing nothing'. For the aeromedics it was a case of 'just waiting, twiddling your thumbs, checking kit every day – but you can only count tablets so many times'.

Back in the UK many families shared the sense of frustration – which, perhaps strangely, was relieved by intensifications in the conflict, as Sqn Ldr Bernice Emmett, commanding the Personnel Management Sqn at RAF Brize Norton, found: 'When the air war started, there was almost euphoria. The release in tension was quite dramatic. Although the families were worried, it gave them some light at the end of the tunnel. It was going to be all over and done with.' Many of those from Brize Norton were out in the desert, which meant difficulties for those back home in keeping track of them: 'We had people in about nine or ten different locations, and we didn't know where others – special forces – were.'

As Dick Druitt states, being at home was harder in some ways than being in the Gulf: 'They had to sort out not only their own emotions but also their emotions about us, knowing that we could easily have been shot at. And they had to live their own lives and get on with their own problems. I do respect the people back here a lot.' He adds that the backing of his station, RAF Marham, was crucial: 'The support was tremendous. They held what they called "Granby Meet" every day; even if only one person turned up, they would be met and could find out what had been going on in the Gulf that day.'

Setting up mailing lists to distribute information posed unexpected problems, as Sqn Ldr David Battley at RAF Coltishall recalls: 'When we asked some of the single airmen if they wanted us to send information to a girlfriend, some of them – possibly because they felt they ought to have one – gave us a name of someone who didn't realise she was a girlfriend. We had a couple of puzzled responses from a woman wondering why she was getting all this stuff about the Gulf.

'We had another problem from one lad who had rather more than one girlfriend. We finally convinced him that we would only accept one contact. We didn't want to ask any more questions than that, but we certainly weren't going to flood the local town with information.'

Many bases set up special all-night phone lines which gave out news and responded to offers of help. Reassurance was what most people wanted, as Battley remembers: 'We expected everyone would be delighted to have the phone picked up by a man or woman. In fact, many of them wanted to hear a pre-recorded answerphone message. We learnt that there were a number of women who would phone just before they went to bed to see that everything was all right, and that would give them a good night's sleep.'

Those at home were sometimes more reliably informed than those on the spot. In the Gulf rumours were rife: 'The Hercules crews told us things, the Americans told us things and visitors told us things. You never knew where they came from and you never knew what to believe.' But it was obvious that the great assault was poised to begin: 'It was awesome to see all the armament. They were always on manoeuvres, always practising. You'd fly over and wave and even if they couldn't see you they'd wave back anyway. It was good to know you were part of that force, that vast amount of armour and trucks going north. There was nothing going southbound. You felt really good and thought, "These guys are really going to do it".'

Chapter 9

NOTHING EXCEPT
A BATTLE LOST

'Nothing except a battle lost can be half so melancholy as a battle won . . .'

Duke of Wellington,
Waterloo Despatch, 1815

'The next thing I remember is waking up on the desert floor.' When David Waddington recovered consciousness, having been ejected just south of Al-Tallil airfield, it was still night. 'It was very quiet and I thought, "Am I dead? Is this death?" Then I remember looking behind me and seeing a parachute. There was a slight breeze and the parachute was semi-inflated I thought, "Oh God, maybe Robbie ejected us!" And that was the first inkling that I was still alive.'

Waddington found that his left elbow and right shoulder were dislocated, and was also aware of injuries to his face which had suffered cuts and swollen up. He attempted to put out a radio distress call and began shouting for Robbie Stewart, his navigator. Getting no answer, he decided to start walking south, first releasing his parachute harness – and losing the attached survival pack in the process: 'Because my arms were very weak I couldn't overcome the force of the canopy being inflated, so I had to let it go. Then I tried to pick a star and walk towards it. But I was still very much in a state of shock. I'd try to make a radio call then I'd forget which star I was looking at, so I'd have to pick another star and walk towards that. Also, there were a lot of fences, which I couldn't get over because I couldn't lift myself up on my arms. So I had to walk along them.'

After four or five hours 'I saw some triple A coming from an airfield in front of me and I thought, "Ah, there must be another airfield around here". In fact, I'd done a sort of U-turn. I guess it was about three or four o'clock. I was tired so I just sat down and had a drink of water because I had one packet of water in my leg pocket – the only pocket to survive the ejection. I tried to dig a hole to hide in but I couldn't use my arms. I had to dig with the heels of my feet and couldn't get very far.'

Eventually, concealing himself between two pipe-lines, Waddington activated his emergency locator beacon – 'hoping that any guys flying over would hear it' – and attempted more distress calls on his radio. However, his injuries prevented him making use of the radio aerial tucked into his Mae West (life jacket) and again his calls went unanswered. He reflected on what this might mean for his family and his fiancée and 'the thought of the knock on the door was absolutely horrendous; very, very hard for me mentally. I was alive, but they wouldn't know that.'

When daylight came Waddington began to doze off. 'There was some stagnant water there and a flock of birds, seagull-sized, around it. I heard some rifle fire and I thought that somebody was trying to scare the birds away – but it was two guys actually firing at me as I was lying down. Once they got to within 100 yards of me they gestured to me to stand up. I wondered if they were going to kill me, but in a way it really didn't matter because I thought I should have been dead anyway. They were very wary of coming close and wanted me to put my hands above my head – but I couldn't, so I started shouting, "*Salaam alalekum* – peace be on your family", which is a strange thing to say when you've just been bombing someone. There was an old guy and a young guy and the older one came up covered by the other with a rifle. I showed him where my pistol was and I pointed at the pocket where I had an extra clip of ammunition. That told him that I wasn't going to try to kill him or anything, and he was reasonably friendly – and I thought, "Well, that's it. You're not going home tonight". I'd seen footprints on the other side of the pipe which I'd assumed to be Robbie's, so I thought he'd done a runner. I had no doubt that he was alive.'

Robbie Stewart was indeed alive – but had suffered far worse injuries ejecting at a height of less than 200ft travelling at 600 miles an hour: 'There was a huge explosion as I was shoved out by the ejector seat, but I can't remember lying on the ground. I woke up 12 hours later. It was broad daylight, about eight or ten in the morning. I was suddenly aware that in my left hand I was holding a radio, in my right hand I was holding my mini-flares and I had some water lying on my stomach. I thought, "Good old Dave, great lad. He's been round, seen that I was unconscious, put these things out for me and he's gone to try and get away".'

In fact, during the night Stewart had managed to climb out of his G-suit, extract and assemble his radio, battery and aerial himself – suffering from a broken shoulder, crushed vertebrae in his spine and a leg that was broken in three places: 'I must have kept passing out with the pain. I still can't believe I did it. I really feel like there was someone sitting on my shoulder doing it for me – but I must have done it myself, even down to the water.'

Stewart's leg injury was causing him so much pain he was hardly able to move. 'My first thought was "Thank God I'm alive", because it was a real miracle to get out at that speed and that height. My next thought was "I'm the only guy that knows I'm alive. My poor wife and kids. They've got no idea". Then I did actually cry for my family and the old tears were flooding down. I knew I couldn't escape but it was like God had said, "Well, you're going to need these," because there in my hand were these mini-flares.'

He was lying not far from a road and by firing his flares was able to stop a passing lorry carrying civilian workmen. Putting him in the back of their truck they drove him into a nearby town where he was handed over to men who 'might have been Ba'ath Party, though they wore green uniform'. They transferred him to a car, and 'stood looking at me, staring at their prize exhibit. One of them opened the door and prodded my foot, just to see what reaction he'd get. I started to vomit because of the pain.'

Following some perfunctory first aid, he was blind-folded and taken to 'what I realised was an interrogation bunker because I could hear an American being inter-rogated in front of me. The treatment was beginning to get a little worse now. They started asking me questions and the guy obviously wasn't happy with the way I was answering them. He said, "Mr Stewart, you're not answering our questions. Somebody else will come", and he went out. I was lying on a stretcher and I could see underneath my blindfold when he came back in that it was the same bloke. He started speaking in a deeper voice, which was quite funny. Unfortunately, he brought his mates, one of whom was carrying a big stick with some sort of ball at the end. He started hitting me with this thing and said he'd break my other leg. I was vomiting and in such a lot of pain from my leg anyhow that what they were doing to me was just on the same level and didn't feel any worse.'

The interrogation was far from subtle: 'One thing that

had annoyed me earlier was all these articles in the papers telling the world precisely what we were doing out there, who we were, how many aircraft there were, what aircraft we were flying and where we were based, and I thought, "That's what I'm going to give them". So I actually gave them the full story out of *The Sunday Times*. I told them I was from Bahrain but that we were carrying JP233, because they were anti-runway devices and not anti-personnel. I also told them we were flying at 500ft – when we were flying at 200ft – and I said we tanked at 20,000ft – which we didn't. There wasn't one technical question asked so I was quite happy – and they did say they'd got my pilot, which was a great relief because it meant he was alive.'

Initially, David Waddington was taken to buildings close to the airfield he had so recently been attacking: 'They made me go into this pit. It was about seven feet deep, with sides that sloped in, and they pushed me down into it. They were all looking at me – there were about ten or fifteen of them. They all had rifles, and I thought "God, what's going to happen here?"'

But he was simply searched – 'they took everything of value, like the radio, and just left me with my flying suit and boots' – and handed over to the Iraqi air force. Like Stewart, he was taken to what was probably the town of Nasiriyah, but given basic medical treatment: 'They cleaned up my face, put stitches over my eye and cheek, put my dislocated arm roughly back into position and plastered it all up. At one stage they were going to give me an anaesthetic, because my face was absolute agony, but the military guy stopped them. They wouldn't allow me to have painkillers or anything like that.'

Unlike Stewart, his initial questioning was relatively benign, and took place once he had been taken back to Al-Tallil airfield: 'I'd have liked to have stayed there,' Waddington admits. 'Six aircrew guys tried to ask me questions and they were quite civilised towards me. They said, "You're another pilot. We know what it's like. We've flown in the Iran-Iraq war". They brought me food, which was very well-presented, a plate with bread on it, tea, a side salad, and a plate with all this meat cut into triangles like the spokes of a wheel. They asked me questions and I was just saying, "I'm sorry, I can't answer that question". Eventually, this guy said, "We'll have to take you to Baghdad".'

It was in Baghdad that Waddington – still believing his navigator had escaped – was subjected to the brutal inter-rogation machinery that John Peters and Adrian Nichol had been through 48 hours earlier: 'I was blindfolded all the time. This guy started to ask questions – name, rank, number. And then, "What do you fly?" "Sorry, can't answer that question". Immediately I was hit on the head, hit on my back and some sort of truncheon-like thing cracked across my legs. They did this twice, then they said, "What do you fly?" "Sorry, can't answer that question" – and it happened again. There was a sort of acceptance on my part. I knew it was going to happen and then it goes past the stage where it hurts. It's just happening. Eventually I thought, "Well, 'I'm going to tell them I fly Tornados", so I'd tell them something. Then they'd go onto a different tack and I'd say, "I can't answer that question", and they'd beat me up again".'

This interrogation continued throughout the night. 'Sometimes they'd beat me to the stage where I'd go unconscious. Then I'd come round and they'd ask me another question and beat me up again – blows to the head, the back and the legs. A couple of times they tried to hit my dislocated arm but of course it was in plaster so it didn't really affect me that much.

'Eventually, at the end of it, I'd answered everything they wanted to know. I remember there were two points where I really tried to hold out. One of them was when they were asking about Robbie. I really didn't want to give that information away, but eventually they beat it out of me. I was worried about things like addresses in the UK because of the terrorist threat but they never did ask anything like that. All the information that I gave them was the stuff that had been in the papers; they'd have found out more from reading *The Daily Telegraph*. It had gone past the stage of hurting. But there was real fear that they were going to pull fingernails or burn my legs – which happened with the military guys because they were much tougher than we were and they did hold out for a period of time.'

Between bouts of interrogation Waddington was taken out into the corridor of the building and became aware that other allied prisoners-of-war were being held in the same building: 'There were eight or nine bodies there with blankets over them. I could hear the Americans and I thought I heard one of the English guys at one stage during an interrogation, but I was drifting in and out of sleep at this stage.' The next night he was taken to a hospital on the outskirts of Baghdad where, unknown to him, Robbie Stewart was also being treated for his injuries. Although guarded in isolation from each other and handcuffed to their beds at night, both men were treated with considerable kindness by the medical staff. Stewart recalls one instance: 'A lot of guys took their rings off [before combat missions] but I felt mine was part of me so I had to wear it. In the hospital they pulled it off, by winding cord round the inside, but they were very gentle about it. The bloke looked at me as he did it and said, "You'll be getting this back". And I have still got it.'

Stewart spent two weeks in hospital, and Waddington a week, before being returned to prison. Waddington briefly joined some other allied prisoners-of-war in a military prison, where at least he was able to communicate with the American PoW in the next cell: 'We chatted away one night for about five or six minutes. It was absolutely fantastic to be able to talk to somebody.' He also found something in common with his captors during the 15 minutes exercise he was allowed: 'They were mad on football, and although one of my arms was in plaster they kicked this football over to me, and I juggled it about a bit on my feet and knees and kicked it back to them. I told them I came from Manchester, and they said "Ah, Manchester United, Bryan Robson", and from then on they called me Bryan Robson.'

His treatment deteriorated again after being driven back to Baghdad on the night of 30 January: 'They moved us to what was a Ba'ath Party Intelligence HQ in the middle of Baghdad – a very high security place on the top floor of a building'. All the allied prisoners were brought together in this central interrogation centre which Stewart describes as a 'classic prison with a long corridor and cells going off it, each with a big steel door and a flap in it. The walls were very thick so you couldn't communicate. It was all the noise of keys locking and doors slamming and steel tips on the guards' boots as they walked up and down on the stone floor. We had two bowls, one for water, one for food and we got fed once a day.'

The food usually consisted of 'half a mugful of greasy soup and a piece of pitta bread' – and here Waddington fared worst of all, being at the far end of the corridor: 'They used to start at one end and work their way up and quite often by the time they got to me they'd have none left. After about two and a half weeks we had fried rice one day instead of soup – the first solid food we'd had. But by the time they got to me they'd run out of it. They just gave me this piece of pitta bread and I almost burst into tears. My weight was reduced from 11 stone to eight and a half, and I was trying to work out how long before I starved to death, hoping the war would be over by that time.'

Waddington had been singled out for ill-treatment because he was suspected of being an Israeli masquerading as an English pilot: 'I got the punishment cell. This was ten feet by six or seven feet with a hole-in-the-ground toilet at one end. When I first got there, they used to keep the light on for about three or four hours a day but then they just turned the light off. There was a tap and where it came out of the wall there was a millimetre crack – I used to get diffused light from that. As this light came and went I scratched a mark on the wall to mark off the days. It was incredibly hard coping with being in the dark. After six or seven hours, I'd get a sort of strobing behind my eye, which was there whether I closed my eyes or opened them. It was there all the time – in the pitch black.

'And this would drive me crazy, so sometimes I'd knock on the door just for the guards to open the face plate. Even though they'd go mad at this and punch me, it was worth it just to open the door and see something. The only way I coped was by thinking of blind people – people who are like this all their lives. I also thought about all the starving people and how I was getting food once a day. Even if it wasn't enough to keep my body weight up, there were other people worse off than me. And the other way to cope was that I thought, "I'm not going to be the first to give in to this. Nobody else has yet and I'm not going to be the first to give them that pleasure".'

Robbie Stewart also had his low moments – suffering a lot of pain from his leg. 'Eventually when I got a doctor I said I needed a plastercast on it and he agreed, because I could hear the bones clicking every time I moved. He took me out one day, put me in a chair and this guard came up, gave me a vicious look and pulled out a knife which he whipped round my face. Then he brought out a revolver, showed me the bullets, put them in and put this pistol to my head. The doctor, meanwhile, was plastering my leg. The guard started hitting me on the head with the butt of his pistol and this went on for a few minutes. All the time the doctor was doing my leg. Then an Iraqi prisoner came in and the guard ran across and started beating two-thirds of whatsit out of him. Then he threw him in a cell and started on me again, with another bloke joining in. By this stage my head was down by my knees. I was actually helping the doctor by holding the plaster, while one guy was hitting me on the back of my neck and the other was hitting me on the head. Eventually, I couldn't take it anymore and I ran back to my room with the doctor running after me saying, "You shouldn't be running on your leg". It was farcical.'

Both men steeled themselves for a long imprisonment. 'I started doing geometry,' explains Stewart. 'I went through all the theorems I'd learnt at school. I sat there for hours on difficult ones and eventually I'd find the answer. I made myself a chess set from orange peel. I cut the shapes with a piece of wood, with the end of my crutch I could do circles for pawns, and I played chess with myself. I found a small screw and with that I sewed together some socks for my feet and a sleeping bag out of my blanket. And I actually discovered a tube of Crest toothpaste hidden behind a window. It was empty, but I found a little bit of toothpaste inside which I could put in my mouth and taste. That was nice.'

His sleep was disturbed: 'We all had the same dream. We'd be at home and we'd be with our wives and families or our mates and we'd have to say, "Look, I've got to go. I'm a PoW in Baghdad". My vision was of my wife Tange making tea. I'm dressed in my prison pyjamas and she's saying, "Where are you going?" And I'd say, "I've got to be back in Baghdad". And then I'd wake up – and I would be.'

Both Stewart and Waddington drew comfort from their religious faith. 'Certainly I prayed a lot,' declares Stewart. 'I prayed that the bombing would stop because that meant peace was on its way. But every night the bombing would continue and that was quite frightening.' Waddington – 'I'm not a particularly religious guy' – also prayed 'an awful lot. Most guys did. We made rosary beads out of blankets and things like that and whenever I was really down, when I really thought I couldn't stand it any more, something would happen like the light coming on or a guy coming round with an extra piece of bread. Something would happen to keep me going until the next time I felt really down. I remember praying "Wouldn't it be good if this building took some damage from bombing and they had to move us?" and three days after I prayed for that to happen, it did.'

The outside world's only clue to their condition was from the parade of captured aircrew, among them John Peters and Adrian Nichol, on Iraqi television during the first days of the air war. In fact, the Iraqis made videos of most of the PoWs, although not all were shown. Waddington was interviewed on film in hospital and in prison almost made another appearance: 'They took me downstairs to make this video, they shaved me, the interviewer looked at me and said "Do you feel up to making this video?" I said "No, I feel very ill" – my shoulder was incredibly painful, and hadn't really been treated. He sat me there for 20 minutes, and asked me again. I said no, so he said, "OK, we'll get you a doctor, and we'll come back in a few days". They wouldn't make it, because I looked so sick and my face was still battered.'

The broadcasts produced violently conflicting emotions among families and fellow aircrew. 'I found it very disturbing,' admits Jerry Witts, 'disturbing to the extent that if I knew it was being repeated on television I wouldn't watch it.'

Just as bad perhaps was the fear of 'the knock on the door' – something that probably caused as much worry among those in the Gulf as among their wives and families. Marrying into the RAF means joining a self-contained community that 'looks after its own'. The death of a husband can therefore mean suffering a double loss, as Rev Wg Cdr Ian Lambert – better known at RAF Marham as 'Padre Lambert' – explains: 'One of the factors that makes death even more difficult is that the Air Force widow not only loses the man she loves, but also her identity as an Air Force wife. Even though service families know this may happen, it's still devastating when a widow has to leave a community that's been her home. Her secure place is gone and she loses her set of friends because eventually she'll have to go from the squadron and the married quarters patch. She has to start all over again and that makes the death of her husband particularly hard to bear. And her husband carries that knowledge with him when he goes off to the war. It makes it even harder for him.'

Marham had to face the loss on the second night of the war of 27 Sqn's 'boss', Nigel Elsdon, and his navigator Max Collier, followed 24 hours later by the shooting down of Dave Waddington and Robbie Stewart. All four were listed as missing: 'A wife is in a dreadfully difficult position when her husband is missing. Until she knows he's dead she cannot begin to grieve, she's in complete spiritual limbo. There was an excellent wives' support group. It was fantastic – but in the end they were alone.'

It seemed that there was worse to come: 'When those casualties came through, people felt that it was the beginning of a lot more, and that caused a great deal of anxiety among the other wives. There was a sense of "Will it be my husband next?" because at the beginning we'd expected it to be a much more serious conflict in terms of deaths and casualties. But I can say quite honestly that everyone, even the bereaved families or the families of the listed people, still supported the cause. They were going to get on with this task and acquit themselves well because the cause was just. That was true of all ranks and families.'

Sadly, some of the British media felt obliged to 'doorstep' the families of aircrew posted as missing: 'The press think they've got a God-given right to get it all out of you,' declares Robbie Stewart. 'My wife found it very hard. She didn't want to believe. She didn't want to disbelieve. She had to walk a middle line. The press had pitched up when I went missing. Some of them were very intrusive as well, coming round pestering, pestering. There was one particularly bad time near the end when *The Lincolnshire Echo*, of all papers, suddenly produced this piece saying that two airmen had been tortured and executed – and that they'd been bombing close to Basra. Then they put at the bottom that Flt Lts Stewart and Waddington had been bombing close to Basra.

'That sort of thing appearing in the press was awful. Tange didn't want to talk to them because they might have used it against me in Baghdad – but the *Daily Mail* kept hounding and hounding. They wanted details. They'd got pictures of the house – even our nicknames. If they'd wanted to, Baghdad could have used this – "We've got your son, we've got Tange" – that sort of thing. That would have hit me badly in prison – but they didn't think about it.'

Even out in the Gulf, being part of 'the best show in town' was not easy. But it was as much a reality of modern conflict as 'smart bombs' or NBC threats. In Bahrain it fell to Sqn Ldr Peter Mutch as press liaison officer to keep the media happy with interviews and photo opportunities – while allowing the aircrews to get on with fighting the war: 'What the press and TV wanted was to interview crews as soon as they'd touched down. But obviously the crews were fairly stressed when they came back from a war sortie and didn't always want microphones shoved under their noses or cameras pushed in their faces. We came to a compromise whereby they'd interview crews after the debrief when they'd had time to unwind.'

It didn't take long for this difficult balance to be put to the test: 'On the second mission we lost the aircraft with Flt Lts Peters and Nichol – and the following day a report came out in the *Independent* about the loss of the aircraft and how it had affected people – including a few remarks that had been picked up by talking to people in the bar. That upset some of the aircrew so the following day Gp Capt David Henderson [detachment commander at Muharraq] had all the media in at his daily briefing. He said that if that was the way they were going to conduct their operations and report comments made in confidence then they would be given access to nothing. They wouldn't be allowed on the base and they could just sit and twiddle their thumbs. Because we were all living in the same hotel and drinking in the same bar, they had to realise that things were being said to them predominantly in confidence – and, to give the press their due, thereafter there wasn't anything adverse that they wrote about. The relationship worked very well.'

At Bahrain, in particular, a close relationship between aircrews and the British media developed: 'Close friend-ships were struck up, a lot of mutual trust developed – that meant they got a much better service and were able to report a lot more than they would had we not been living in such circumstances. At Bahrain we lost four aircraft – two on the second and third sorties, then a couple of days went by and we lost a third and then fourth aircraft – fairly well into the war. That was the one with Rupert Clark and Steve Hicks. Rupert Clark and Tony Birtley, the TV-AM reporter, used to play a fair amount of squash together. When that aircraft went down and Tony Birtley found out, he was particularly upset. That indicates the closeness that had developed between some people on the press side and our own.'

This growing trust was something that Flt Lt Mike Toft also witnessed: 'Initially we were very stand-offish. We didn't know how to treat them and I don't know whether they knew how to treat us. After Gp Capt Henderson had laid down the policy the press were fine – although someone from the gutter press ended up in the swimming pool. He deserved it.'

This trust was not extended to the American TV network CNN, whose reporting 'got up people's noses'. What Dick Druitt of 55 Sqn found appalling was the fact that CNN gave too much information: 'There was one occasion when a reporter was stood there and Tornados were taking off behind him [to fly on a combat mission]. Anybody can calculate how long it's going to take to fly from Bahrain to Baghdad and work out exactly when those planes were going to overfly. That was putting people's lives in danger.'

It was the 'gutter press guys' of the British press 'sniffing around for scandal' that particularly upset Wg Cdr David Hamilton: 'They weren't interested in the fact that the Tornado F3 was working well. I had my ground crews and aircrews complaining that their wives were reading "F3s are going to get shot down". How do you think a wife is going to feel when her young husband is flying a Tornado F3? It was complete rubbish and nothing short of scandalous. And for the troops it was the same. Their wives were thinking, "What the heck is my husband doing out there?" We wrote back to say that everything was fine and they thought, "He's only saying that to keep me quiet", because they were being bombarded every minute of the day by people pontificating about what might or might not happen. So when the RAF who were looking after the families on station tried to say, "Don't worry, everything's OK", they thought they were just saying that.'

It wasn't only the crews of the flying squadrons who had doubts about the way the war was being reported. Musician Flt Sgt John Williams became concerned about the effect that 'sensational' press reporting was having on his wife and children: 'Apparently the coverage they were getting was quite horrific. A bloke that was working with us had to go back to Britain for tests, and he wrote us a letter saying he'd just watched a television programme on gas and NBC and all of that. He said that watching these things was really frightening. They should have just given the proper facts and left it at that.'

The need to find new stories sometimes led to conjecture, according to F3 pilot Sqn Ldr Paul Brown: 'Once we had air superiority, the bombers could cruise over Iraq, drop bombs and come home. That was happening day after day after day. But just saying the same thing every day upsets the media. They do want blood and guts, they do want heroic tales and they do want different stories to tell. But the people at home just want to know the facts. They don't really want speculation – that if he starts launching chemical weapons 30,000 people will die.'

For Peter Mutch 'trying to find new angles' for the media as the war went on proved something of a headache. In particular, the television crews clamoured for pictures to illustrate reports on the air campaign, and here the technology that made precision bombing possible came to his aid: 'The Jaguars had a head-up display so we could use some of that, but the Tornados had nothing to show until the Buccaneers arrived on theatre with their laser-guided bombing. They had a video unit to do with the laser-tracking, so then what you were seeing was the Buccaneers doing the tracking and Tornados doing the bombing.'

Different commanders had different ideas about how best to handle the media. At Dhahran, Jerry Witts found the local permanent press team 'very co-operative' and 'very supportive. They became part of the big team. I was happy for them to go just about anywhere and talk to anyone at any time. I used to look for opportunities to get the guys on television. We even used to have chats to see if anyone had ideas. That was how the teddy bear came about. I was more than happy because, if the wives and girls could see the guys, then they knew they were all right.'

However, out in Tabuk, where there were no hotels and very limited press facilities, 16 Sqn took a different view. 'We hardly saw any of the media,' recalls Mal Craghill. 'At one stage we had some reporters who wanted to interview guys as they were going out. The boss asked around to see what the general opinion was, and the guys didn't want it. There could have been nothing worse for a family at home than to see their son on television and think he was fine, and then maybe get a telephone call later to say that he hadn't come back.'

For Bill Pixton, too, commanding the Jaguar detachment at Muharraq, there was a feeling that the media saw the war as 'a bit like an American football match. You want to see the line moving further forwards. I can understand that. But this was a bit too serious.' His aircrews, who were in different hotels to the Tornado aircrews, did not have their press breathing down their necks. 'If the media felt that the Jaguar guys were a bit stand-offish it was because they were concentrating on what they were doing. It was life and death, and I wasn't all that interested necessarily in talking to somebody from the BBC. I was more concerned about making sure that what we were doing was going to achieve its aim.'

Chapter 10

GOING BANANAS

Navigator	This has got to be the biggest target in Iraq!
Pilot	Just bear with me, Harry. I'm getting you the best angle. Speed's good, height's good. I'm shortly going to roll in. About 10 seconds to roll in. I'm 10 knots slow. Rolling in. Sight on. Stand by. Sight on.
Navigator	Sight on. Nothing seen. Just keep going.
Pilot	Sight on. Releasing. Bombs away. Pulling.
Navigator	Happy. Yes, that's got a hole in it now.
Radio	Yes, a splash for us.
Pilot	Well done Harry, fantastic.
Navigator	Good.
Pilot	That got the ******!
Radio	Flak!
Pilot	Coming up over the middle, about 10,000ft in the middle. OK, let's get out of here.

In 1990 the Buccaneer – known throughout the Air Force as the 'banana jet' on account of its vaguely banana-shaped appearance – celebrated its 21st year of service with the RAF. As the heaviest, least manoeuvrable and oldest strike attack aircraft in service it has its critics, but those who actually fly it speak of the Buccaneer with fierce loyalty. 'It's a wonderful aeroplane,' insists navigator Sqn Ldr Norman Browne. 'I'm on it by choice, I love it and I don't want ever to fly anything else.'

His colleague in 12 Sqn, pilot Sqn Ldr Rick Phillips, agrees: 'I've flown well over 100 different types of aeroplane and to me the Buccaneer is the finest plane I've ever flown. I think I've flown it more than anybody else who's currently still flying and I'll see it through to the end. Of course, the Tornado which is replacing it has a much better avionics suite, much better inertial system, much better radar, but as a pure aeroplane the Buccaneer can totally outfly it. There is nothing the Buccaneer cannot do.'

His loyalty, after 20 years of flying Buccaneers, is shared by 12 Sqn's Senior Engineering Officer (SENGO), Sqn Ldr George Baber. He also freely admits to loving his banana jets: 'The Buccaneer is an inanimate object which slowly comes to life. When the aircrew get in and turn the power on it's like the nerve endings coming alive. And when they start the engines and the hydraulics start going it's a bit like blood running around the veins. On the ground it's a bit of an ugly duckling but in the air it looks the bizz.'

However, the Buccaneer's designated role was as a low-level anti-shipping strike aircraft using the Sea Eagle missile and the American Paveway Pave Spike laser-guided bombing system. It appeared to have no useful role to play in Operation Granby. 'We were continually assured that the Buccaneer wouldn't be required' – but Baber did some pre-planning just in case. RAF Lossiemouth also has an Operational Conversion Unit (237 OCU) for training Buccaneer pilots and navigators and in late November 1990 it put together some experienced crews and started low-level overland Pave Spike training: 'We did a dozen or so work-up sorties, had leave over Christmas and then were told that there was absolutely no way the MoD would consider sending the Buccaneer to the Gulf. So we all relaxed, calmed down and all training ceased.'

When the air war started 208 Sqn was down at St Mawgan in Cornwall on a NATO joint maritime exercise and 12 Sqn was on detachment in Gibraltar with the Royal Navy. 'I was sitting in a restaurant drinking whisky with the owner, who was ex-Air Force, my boss and some senior aircrew colleagues,' recalls Baber. 'At 4am the owner's wife telephoned to say she'd just heard on CNN that war had broken out.' For the next week the personnel of both squadrons stayed 'glued to the television, increasingly distressed at the losses we were suffering'. Phillips and Baber shared the same mixed feelings of guilt and relief: 'Part of me wanted to be there, the other part thought, "It's nice and safe here".'

Then came the urgent recalls. 'On 23 January I received a telephone call at midday, from Lossiemouth, informing me I had to return the quickest possible way,' explains Baber. 'I wasn't told but I instinctively knew why. I was surprised by how shocked I felt. The steward standing opposite me sat me down and gave me a cup of coffee.' Phillips, too, felt shock and apprehension: 'Yes, I was frightened and anybody who says he wasn't frightened needs his head examining. The fact was we knew we were going out there to be shot at. Fear is ever-present and it affects people in different ways. The families were also frightened but, to be quite honest, the quicker we got away the better it was.'

The Buccaneers had now been given a job to do: 'When the Secretary of State for Defence was asked why he was sending this antique plane to war he said, "Because we need to improve the standard of precision bombing", and that was a tremendous quote for the Buccaneer. There had been no precision bombing by the RAF until we went out there.' Their specific role was to provide secondary laser designation for the Tornado GR1s: 'The GR1s had achieved the initial aims of the first low-level phase and were now flying sorties in a more benign environment at medium level. To regain accuracy the decision was taken to use smart weapons which we could provide with the Pave Spike pod fitted to our aircraft. Our secondary laser designator could provide the Tornado with the pin-point accuracy it had lost in the move from low to medium level.'

Baber was deputed to go ahead to Muharraq to carry out an on-site survey and prepare for the arrival of aircraft and equipment. He'd been met at Aberdeen airport on the evening of the 23rd and 'from then on it was mayhem. I spent a frantic morning at Lossiemouth rushing round collecting ID cards, dog tags and injections – which will go down in my memory for ever – typhoid, tetanus, yellow fever, whooping cough and cholera. One in my right arm, two in my left, one in each buttock and one in my thigh, all in one go. As well as a variety of pills; NAPs – pills which we had to take every eight hours, Paludrin for malaria and polio. I had half an hour at home packing, was thrown into one of my own squadron Hunters and flown down to Brize Norton. Then I was whipped over to RAF Innsworth for the rest of my kitting, to pick up a pistol and receive my morphine injections. Then back to Brize Norton to meet up with a Kuwaiti Airways 747 which was to deploy the Coldstream Guards out to the Gulf.

'I got onto the 747 at eleven o'clock that night and that was the first time I'd stood still for more than five seconds. On board I met a young army officer who spent the entire journey reading an old leather-bound Bible. He asked me whether it was all right to be scared. He'd thought about jumping in front of cars on his way to the airport so that he could break a leg and not have to go.

Towards the end of the journey a pretty Kuwaiti hostess pinned a "Free Kuwait" metal badge onto my uniform and wished me luck – which was a moving moment.'

At Muharraq George Baber found an airbase already at war and a war routine in full swing: 'They spoke their own built-in Muharraq-speak, the slang of the Gulf, talking about the "banana", and the "shade" – which turned out to be where we parked aircraft, and the "circus tent" – which was where we ate. I was pulled up a couple of times for not wearing the dress in the right way and for not having my NBC in the right position. We didn't feel overly welcome, we were just another headache for the station. I'm not sure people were convinced that we had a significant role to play. I knew the first Hercs were arriving with my troops and equipment at midday the following day and I thought to myself, "How the hell am I going to be able to manage?"'

Meanwhile at Lossiemouth, 12 and 208 Sqns together with the Buccaneer OCU were pooling resources to get the initial deployment of six Buccaneers out to Muharraq as soon as possible. It was left to Baber's counterpart on 208 Sqn, Sqn Ldr David Tasker, to supervise the preparation of the chosen aircraft and to make up the first 10 Hercules loads into 'chalks – a movement term where an area of floor is chalked with Chalk 1 for Herc 1 and Chalk 2 for Herc 2, so we'd know what should be coming out on which Herc.'

Other units were also involved in the ensuing 'organised panic'. Sgt Keiron Muzylowski was to lead a team of four 'squippers', the station's safety equipment fitters who looked after all the aircrew's survival and safety equipment – 'everything from oxygen masks to parachutes. The big rush for us was to convert all the personal survival equipment from temperate conditions into desert packs. That meant putting more water into the survival packs – very tough silver bags placed one on top of another as part of the ejector seat, together with a desert survival booklet. Then we had to disconnect the auto-activation of the personal locator beacon. When you bale out it automatically switches on, so we disconnected that for security reasons.'

The first 12 aircrew were chosen on the basis of 'most time and leadership status'. Norman Browne was to go as the first 'spike leader', having drawn up the laser designator tactics in training: 'It had been my baby, I'd worked with it and done the bombing trial at Aberporth over the sea with a Tornado and a Jaguar – but coordination with large numbers we'd never tried.'

Among the younger aircrew included in this first batch was navigator Flt Lt Keith Nugent. 'The Saturday night before I left was the worst night of my life. I hated it. It was lovely to be with my girlfriend Barbara but I didn't feel too well with all the injections and things. I hadn't eaten for 48 hours either because I was scared. We were taking off at about five or six o'clock and I left the house at about three o'clock. It was completely dark and Barbara just came down to the door to wave goodbye. I'll always remember looking back over my shoulder as I drove off and thinking, "Am I going to see her again?"'

The Buccaneers left in pairs: two daily on the Saturday, Sunday and Monday. Although still unplanned at this stage, a second deployment of another six Buccaneers was to follow them a fortnight later. Rick Phillips and Flt Lt Mal Miller flew the last pair of Buccaneers in the initial detachment: 'When we hit the Egyptian coast we saw desert for the first time. There was the big green Nile valley but everything else was just red – the whole of Saudi Arabia. It was a nine-hour flight but being in two-seaters we had somebody to talk to, as well as the tankers. But it was a long trip. We're given little "piss packs" – a kind of dehydrated sponge in a plastic bag.

We put our pins in our ejector seats, unstrap, use it, and the sponge just soaks everything up.'

For Phillips the 4,000 mile journey was far from boring 'because my mind was racing away to what I'd failed to get finished at home'. But he found the desert 'awesome, a totally inhospitable and ghastly place'.

They landed at Muharraq just after sunset: 'The first thing that hit me even in the dark under the floodlights was the intense activity. I've never seen such a concentrated mass of military hardware apparently scattered just willy-nilly about a very small corner of an airfield. I've never taxied a jet plane through a building site before but that's what it was like. To see all these planes, fully armed and bombs everywhere, and being refuelled at the same time, was amazing. The rule book had been completely thrown out of the window, because otherwise we'd never have got the job done. On the other hand, it wasn't a shambles. People were very careful. Everybody knew what they were doing and everyone was working.'

David Tasker had already arrived with a team of 30 on the first Hercules. His first problem was finding space for the six Buccaneers because there was nowhere to park them: 'Then it was a question of how fast I could turn them round and how fast I could prepare them to fly.'

Baber was now the local expert: 'I had the Gulf-speak and my headaches were alleviated as the men started turning up and I could delegate jobs. The Royal Engineers were contracted out to lay new tarmac and within a week and a half we had brand-new tarmacked areas with steel matting on top for the Buccaneers to park on, with huge 20ft concrete splinter protection units round them.' By that time the Buccaneers were up and flying.

Soon after arrival the aircrews were given an intelligence briefing – 'quite a morale booster', as Keith Nugent remembers: 'Basically, they told us that a lot

164

of people were looking after our interests. We would have the F-111s providing electronic counter-measures, the Wild Weasels with their anti-radar missiles, the AWACS giving cover and lots and lots of fighters just in case anybody did get airborne. So, yes, we were going in there well-protected.' But Mal Miller, looking round the briefing room, was thinking: 'Well, who's not going to come back out of this lot?'

They had a week of in-theatre training over the Saudi desert, flying with Tornados and Jaguars. There was new equipment to get used to – 'we had megaproblems with the Have Quick radio which we'd never seen before and for which we had no manuals' – and problems with the comparatively ancient Pave Spike laser designator spike pods. However, 'once the cobwebs had been blown away things started to tick'.

On 4 February, just 11 days after deployment, the Buccaneer detachment flew its first combat sortie. 'It was a very tense moment for all of us,' recalls George Baber. 'The crews that came out were very scared. No-one had been in combat before or knew what to expect. Some had a false bonhomie and others snapped at the ground crew. The ground crew understood the tension the aircrew felt and handled them like eggs. We all knew that the success or failure of the Buccaneer would depend on how well the aircrew did.'

Three Buccaneers flew on this first mission: two aircraft to laser designate for four Tornado bombers, led by the detachment commander, Wg Cdr Bill Cope – and a third to act as a back-up in case one of the first pair had to turn back. Norman Browne was given the prime role of 'spike leader' navigator, with Keith Nugent flying as back-up navigator in the third aircraft.

Nugent's fear was not of being killed, but of being shot down and captured: 'I think that was the thing in the back of everybody's mind. Death, although it leaves a lot of pain for people at home – your family and friends – is fairly instant and that's the end of it. But being captured and probably injured having jumped out of a plane – that was the biggest fear.' Browne, however, was afraid for a different reason: 'I was very nervous because the whole operation hinged on it being a success. It was a sort of Royal Tournament showpiece and we wanted to get it absolutely right.'

Built into the Pave Spike system was a video camera that would record what appeared on the navigator's screen as he guided the laser designator onto the target. These video recordings would be used to demonstrate to the world that this was indeed pin-point bombing designed to minimise loss of life. Accuracy was a political necessity.

Despite the 'need to know' rule being strictly applied, the entire 220-strong detachment seemed to know that the first operational sortie was being flown. 'It was quite emotional,' remembers squipper Muzylowski. 'We had two on a shift but all four of us went in for the first sortie. You do get very attached to the aircrew because you work with them day in and day out. You get to know their little habits and what they like and don't like. They got dressed and prepped themselves. Then they went into the brief, came back, picked their helmets up and walked out to the aircraft. We were so nervous, the four of us, we just sat there and didn't know whether to speak to them, didn't know what to do. On every sortie they went on, always in the back of your head was, "Please let them come back". And once I saw them all come back from that first sortie I was over the moon.'

The cockpits of the three Buccaneers taking part were stuffed with good luck charms from the ground crews – but only later did Nugent become aware of just how much support they had: 'You're fairly blinkered when you first start. You've got to go out there and somebody is going to start shooting at you. I realised later on that the guys were treating us almost with kid gloves. Everything they did was geared to taking the pressure off us so that the only thing we had to worry about was coming in, planning what we had to do, flying the mission, debriefing it and going home. The nicest thing was the ground crew waving us off when we went out and waving to us when we came back – saying, "It doesn't matter what you have or haven't done, so long as you're back safely". It helped.'

Browne's fear left him as soon as they crossed the border: 'The closer we got all that was removed. All I wanted to do was to hit the target. We went in trail – two Tornados with a Buccaneer, two Tornados with a Buccaneer – separated by two minutes. Pablo Mason was leading the first Tornado and we picked the target up in good time at about 10 miles.'

As soon as the target – a bridge over the Euphrates – had been located he locked his spike pod onto his pilot's bomb-aiming sights and went 'head-down'. 'Once you say, "Right, I'm going head-down to do the target", you realise in a couple of seconds that you're very vulnerable,' continues Browne. Their intelligence briefing proved to be 'brilliant. They'd told us exactly what was there and they were correct. The fact that there was heavy traffic on this bridge made us think this was a surprise for the Iraqis because later on the bridges had less and less traffic on them. The attack went incredibly smoothly. As we designated we did a sort of tear-drop round the bridge, away from it and back to contain the tracking. The pilot saw all six bombs dropping off the Tornados and then we had a nerve-racking wait. I saw exactly what happened. The first bomb went straight through a lorry on the bridge.'

The success of this first mission gave a great boost

to both the Buccaneer wing and the Tornado squadrons: 'From the station commander down everyone was amazed at the video and the results. But the biggest reaction of all was when we showed it to the Tornado guys at the debrief. They had no idea until then what they'd done, how effective it had been. It was fantastic to actually see the results. It was a big lift for them.'

Later there was a chance for the ground crews to watch the video too, with mixed reactions. 'That really brought it home – good Lord, we were actually killing people – and a lot of the guys grew up,' comments David Tasker. For better or worse, the videos gave those on the ground a sense of involvement. 'Seeing it on the television screen made me painfully aware that people were going to die because of what we were doing,' Baber confirms. 'As engineers we were as responsible as the aircrew who pushed the buttons. I found that difficult but I eventually accepted the fact. We knew the bridges were crucial and we saw the effect that knocking those bridges down was having on the Iraqi soldiers in Kuwait. Supplies weren't reaching them. I brought my ground crew up every night to show them what they were achieving. It made them feel part of what was going on.'

The second Buccaneer sortie was equally successful. 'My video was the first to be shown on TV,' declares Keith Nugent. 'It was shown nationwide on American TV and all over the world. But I didn't have copyright and I didn't get named.' Later some members of the detachment were 'a little peeved' at what seemed to them to be the minimal press coverage given to the Buccaneer.

On 5 February it was the turn of pilots Rick Phillips and Mal Miller to fly their first missions. 'Our pair was the last to go off,' remembers Miller. 'By that time I was keen to get one under my belt but when it came round I had all the emotions.' Everyone now knew that there was still plenty of missile activity and anti-aircraft fire waiting for them.

Phillips felt 'very frightened' as he sat in his hotel room in the early hours picking at his breakfast: 'We went to the briefing and I had this ghastly sick feeling. The attack was to be against a bridge at a place called Al Kut. We did the planning and I hoped all would be well but I'll never forget walking out to the plane. I felt terrible and wondered whether I'd have to stop and be physically sick but, strangely enough, as soon as we did all the usual things, got strapped in, then I became completely normal. I just moved into a kind of mechanical mode of operating and that proved the value of the training we'd done. I can't remember how many times I checked everything but there was never anything left out – and throughout the entire war we didn't miss one thing once.'

The two aircraft took off and checked that the AWACS patrolling above them were receiving their IFF signals: 'They told us that they'd got our contact and they had this wonderful phrase. They just said "Picture clean" – that meant there was no airborne threat.' They then flew west out of Muharraq to rendezvous with four Tornados coming from Dhahran: 'We were relying on accurate navigation to get to a point in the sky. We weren't using any radar, no ground control, nothing. We gave ourselves height separation so we didn't collide. Each mission had a tactical call sign and the call signs we used were town names. On that mission it was "Newport". The Tornados were Newport one and two, I was Newport three, the next two Tornados were Newport four and five and Mal Miller was Newport six. When they came across the frequency and said, "Newport check", we just said, "Two", "Three", "Four", "Five", "Six". My navigator, Harry Heslop, has excellent eyesight. He spotted them instantly and we just joined them in formation.

'We met the tanker about 45 minutes after take-off – it was daylight by this time – and the Tornados started tanking straight away. They tanked full and came out, we went in and tanked full, then the Tornados went in again. We took about 6,000lbs per Buccaneer where the Tornados would take on about 12,000. Those tankers were brilliant. There was never any occasion when a tanker either wasn't there or didn't have the fuel. Then we said goodbye to the tanker and we were on our own. It was very hazy. The sun came up and it was quite fierce and bright at our height. As we crossed the border nothing changed – except that our heads were on screws all the way round.

'Then for the first time in my life I had real radar threats coming up on the radar warning receiver [RWR]. Some of the noises that I'd listened to on training in the early '70s and on Red Flag in America when we first got the radar warning receiver came back to me; and I instantly knew it was a SAM 2 system or a SAM 3 or a triple A. We knew they were looking at us and we varied our height every time we were locked on. But the thing that worried me most at this stage was the height-finding system that they had – the Thin Skin. If we got a Thin Skin indication then we had to do something fairly quickly. If they worked out at what height the formation was coming in they were then in a position to relay that information on to all triple A batteries, who could dial their fuses to have a barrage of flak coming up to that particular height.'

Both Buccaneer crews were very aware of the 'package' surrounding them. 'Not only did I see these aircraft,' continues Phillips, 'but on one particular sortie a Harm missile from one of the Wild Weasels was fired literally 15 yards past my port wing and frightened the living daylights out of me. I thought it was something that had been fired at me but the thing went rushing down and took out a SAM 3 missile site further down.'

However, on this initial sortie the approach to the target passed without incident. 'We had about 40 minutes over the border and it was very quiet on the way in,' remembers Miller. 'From about 30–40 miles away we were looking for our target. The bridge that I was going for was on a U-bend on the River Tigris, so I picked that up quite early on – about 25–30 miles away. Then over the target we saw some triple A. All that appeared were little puffy cumulus clouds, well below us and I wasn't sure at first that it was triple A. It was just like watching it on television and it was all very quiet.'

Then came disappointment as Phillips in the lead Buccaneer put his sights on: 'What amazed me was that I couldn't see the bridge, although I could see the roads on either side. I told Harry and there was this expletive from the back cockpit that "some bugger" had bombed our bridge! The Americans had bombed it in the night. So we just made a bigger hole than was already there. It would have been a complete waste of time to drop more bombs there so I made a hurried radio call to the second team down the back. About a mile away, on the other side of the town, there was another bridge that was completely intact. I told them to go for this bridge and asked them if they could hack that.'

Miller, flying with Mike Scarffe as his navigator, made a hurried switch and dived towards this 'target of opportunity'. 'I put my cross-hairs, so to speak – my aiming group – on the target. The navigator then unstowed his Pave Spike pod, which was looking at the same point that I'd put my aiming group on. He said, "Right OK, I'm happy. I've got the bridge". He was now tracking it on his TV with a little thumb wheel to move the cross-hairs about. At that point I came out of my shallow dive and moved up into an arc, always keeping the target visual and constantly referring to my line-of-sight meter in the cockpit which told me whether the Pave Spike could also see it or not. When the navigator was happy he fired his laser. Then the Tornados ran towards the target and at the drop-point released their bombs. They have a laser seeker in the nose that looks for the reflected energy from the laser and they just followed it down to where it was reflected from. The navigator called "Splash" as the bombs hit and then switched his laser off, although he kept tracking with his Pave Spike pod, still filming for battle damage assessment.'

There was considerable elation as the flight made its way home but also some concern: 'We'd survived and we'd blooded ourselves, but there was the intense disappointment that having done all the planning and work we'd found our target already bombed – and I wondered how we were going to explain this change of target to Riyadh, because it was contrary to rules. In fact, they were delighted – but they said not to do it again.'

Over the next four weeks the Buccaneers continued to mount combined raids with the Tornado squadrons based at Muharraq and Dhahran. Keith Nugent flew on another 14 operational sorties and admits that 'it never got easier. It depended on where I was going. If I was going into southern Iraq or to the east where people hadn't been shot at too much then I knew it wasn't going to be too bad. But if they said, "Right, you're off to somewhere near Baghdad", that was a bit more scary. I was the most scared before my third mission, which was the first time I went up near Baghdad, because the day before when the boys had been up there, there had been a lot of missiles coming up.'

Norman Browne remembers that raid as a 'hornet's nest. It wasn't a nice area and it was very heavily defended. The RWR was very busy. We had missiles fired at us on the way and then at the target there were missiles all over the place. Everybody heard them and everybody saw them, is the best way to describe it. They appeared not to be coming for you and then suddenly they picked on you.'

Despite the allied successes, missions continued to be hazardous. After a first phase of bombing bridges the laser designator missions were directed at airfields and other more specifically military targets. 'Every mission got worse,' declares Browne. 'Every minute you spent over Iraq seemed to get longer. It appeared to us that every time we hit a target with little resistance they managed to find us ones that had lots of resistance. That obviously wasn't the case, but that was the way it appeared.'

To unwind between sorties Browne played squash in the hotel's squash court. One of his partners was Flt Lt Stephen Hicks of XV Squadron, the RAF's last casualty of the war, who was killed when his Tornado was hit by two missiles on a raid on an Iraqi airfield on 14 February: 'Two of our planes watched them going in, so we were convinced they were both gone and that was that. I knew the guy pretty well, obviously, but we didn't really have time to think about it.' In fact, the Tornado's pilot, Flt Lt Rupert Clark, was able to eject and survived.

For Rick Phillips, too, things seemed to get harder rather than easier: 'As we got more experienced with the flak and the missiles it became quite terrifying, no two ways about it. As more Buccaneers came out we took more inexperienced people out. We split up from our pairs, picked up a youngster on our wing and took him along, which was the only way we could do it. We always flew in formation, giving each other cover and when one of us was going in and bombing the target the other chap was watching out for anything that was coming up and calling it. As time went on my look-out ability improved enormously because if the thing is being fired at you optically, you have to spot it, otherwise you won't survive. Your eyes must be out of the cockpit.'

There was always the temptation to relax one's guard after completing the raid: 'We would exit as high as we could and on this occasion my number two had called back to tell me that I was trailing – putting out a condensation trail in the sky. I conned Harry onto some explosions on the ground and told him they were worth looking at. I then realised I was looking at something that was actually drilling a hole straight at me in the canopy. I instantly went down the hill and we went into some rapid manoeuvring, dispensing chaff and flares. I barrelled around this thing and it disappeared off behind me. We'd had no electronic warning of it and the reason we survived was that they were still aiming the thing optically at the end of the trail. The adrenalin was moving there for some time.'

Shortly before the start of the ground war the Buccaneers were finally authorised to load up with their own 1,000lb bombs and – much to the satisfaction of the aircrews – do their own laser designator bombing of Iraqi airfields. 'I dropped the first ever bombs in anger from an RAF Buccaneer,' claims Nugent. 'It's a two-man thing. I made the switches in the back to release them from the wings and Tony pressed the trigger in the front to release them. We were concentrating on HASs, runways, taxiways, intersections.'

The Buccaneers continued to fly operational sorties right up to the day of the ceasefire. According to David Tasker, 'the big high was amazing. For the first time we had the personnel to do the job we were tasked with. Back in the UK with fixed manning reduction levels we were down to about 80%. In Bahrain we had 100% and with that we proved we could do the job. The night shift produced the goods and we had just short of a 90% serviceability rate, which is outstanding for a Buccaneer.'

What it meant was that the Buccaneers never missed a sortie. 'It stood up brilliantly,' concludes George Baber. 'We were tasked about 115 missions and every mission was completed. We flew 250 sorties and not a single sortie was lost. That really surprised the people at Muharraq, Riyadh and GHQ. We had 18 crews and 12 aircraft out there and I'm eternally grateful that we didn't lose an aircraft and that all the crews came home.'

Chapter 11

KNOCK 'EM HARD

'Knock 'em hard, knock 'em fast, knock 'em out!'
General Norman Schwarzkopf

'In terms of taking back territory, there are probably no cases in history where there hasn't been a ground war,' says Wg Cdr Mick Richardson, one of those who had been planning the air assault from Riyadh. 'It was just a question of what we could do as an air arm to ease their path, to minimise their casualties; and then of what we could do in support of the ground troops as they moved forward day by day.'

There were a number of factors to be considered in planning the ground assault – Operation Desert Sabre. One was the weather: in March and April the Gulf enters a season of heat and sand-storms which would have made life insufferable for those on the ground. As it was, the weather in January and February was the worst ever recorded for that region.

Rob Wiffin explains that another factor to be borne in mind was that the Islamic holy month of Ramadan began on 17 March and, 'we had to get it finished before Ramadan, because that would have made things very difficult for our allies'.

Also to be taken into account was the extent to which the air campaign had worn down Iraqi defences. 'We

176

saw the bombers unloading their ordnance on a daily basis. 'By day five of the war we were thinking, "My God, they're dropping a lot of bombs",' remembers Flt Lt Angus Elliott. 'By day 35 of the war we were thinking, "My God, 30 days ago they'd done a lot; but now they've done that every single day". We'd been Scudded on maybe ten occasions and each time we got slightly more on edge – and Scuds were inaccurate. Psychologically, it must have been shattering to get bombed 40 days and nights by accurate munitions in their hundreds and thousands.'

On the ground they were ready and waiting. Sgt Mick Johnson remembers the amount of hanging around in the lead up to war: 'It was very, very boring. Imagine doing a 12-hour shift and not doing anything. We were operating in a hardened 4-tonner. With four people in it things were pretty cramped – we just sat there for 12 hours and twiddled our thumbs.'

The enforced inactivity left time to brood on what was to come. SAC Andy Garton remembers a major preoccupation: 'We rather expected a lot of chemical weapons to be thrown against us. Apparently one field commander said that Hussein wouldn't use them against us because he knew that we'd retaliate with something very nasty. I don't know what they were planning but they had a heck of a lot of firepower sitting doing nothing.'

Flt Lt Rachel Johnson was 'very NBC conscious. I was pretty hot on my NBC drills by the time the ground war started. Back here you do it with a pinch of salt. There I made sure I could get water out of my drinking straw. I made sure I could eat something. I made sure I could get it on quickly.'

'There were quite a lot of things where we were not totally sure what would happen if it really came to the crunch, one of which was biological warfare,' admits Gp

Capt Charles Newrick. 'We were in no position to say "This chap has got anthrax, or plague, or whatever", we just didn't have the equipment to do it. Fortunately it wasn't required.'

Musician John Williams had other concerns. In his war role as a medic he had been trained to 'tend to people, stop bleeding, resuscitate, put drips in', but drew the line at emptying bedpans: 'I just said I wasn't going to do it. I don't care what they do to me. I wasn't going to empty bedpans and that was the end of it. They said, 'You might have to', and I said, 'I won't.''

As Wg Cdr Mike Trace explains, the Pumas of 33 and 230 Sqns, together with the Chinooks, had practised for every eventuality: 'Some of our casualty exercises involved 400 people. We shipped whole battalions right through the hospital system so that they knew where they'd end up if they were wounded.'

'We could have evacuated about sixteen hundred casualties per day if necessary,' states Hercules commander Wg Cdr Peter Bedford. 'If there had been serious opposition, our aeromed evacuation plan would have gone into action on a 24-hour basis: we would have had a flight every hour and a half, outloading casualties. In fact we were put on standby for that for the first day of the war.'

As that day approached, the intensity of the artillery barrage on Iraqi positions increased. SAC Dave Pearce remembers being woken at three o'clock in the morning and seeing 'the whole horizon light up and hearing the artillery fire non-stop for hours on end', while SAC Shaun Hayward remembers 'feeling' the artillery rumbling in the distance for weeks beforehand.

Sgt Ian Tervit, as part of the administrative backup to the medical effort, recalls: 'A week before the ground phase started we moved up to the north-west of Hafir al Batan. As we moved nearer to the front, the sound of artillery in the distance got louder. Then it went quiet for a couple of days. Someone said, "Just listen for the night before and you'll hear the artillery".'

The noise of the barrage was a more reliable guide to impending events than press speculation. Andy Garton recalls: 'There were lots of cons. When we wanted to spread an idea we brought the press in and it went round the world immediately. Thanks to the press the Iraqis didn't know exactly which way we were going.'

Like any of the great deceptions in military history, Schwarzkopf's 'left hook' could easily have been revealed. Capt Brian O'Connor, pilot of an F3, appreciated the danger: 'We could see where everyone was flying, we could see the massive airlift that was going out to the west day in, day out. We had to be careful about what we were saying on the radios. I heard a couple of crews just chit-chatting about what the general state of affairs was. Finally I came up on the radio and said, "Put a lid on it".'

'As far as the eye could see,' recalls Angus Elliott, 'there was nothing but tanks, more tanks, more guns and more people. There was nothing but hardware. Then, the day before the ground attack, it had all disappeared – not one single item left. It was all in huge convoys next to the border.'

The air offensive continued up to and during the ground attack. Jerry Witts confirms that 'our role was to keep his air power off our troops. So we kept revisiting his air fields, going round HAS by HAS and destroying them.' The GR1s also carried out reconnaissance: 'We actually took binoculars so that we could look down and report what we saw on the ground. I don't claim to be a great strategist but it gradually dawned on me that there were more and more friendlies massing along the tapline road – the big road running south of the border with Iraq. There was also increasing interest in anything that we might see that side of the border.'

Mike Trace, based at King Khalid Military City, explains what happened just before dawn on 24 February: 'On G-Day itself, 18 Corps went in across the border to the left of us, and the Arabs went into the bottom corner [to Kuwait]. In fact they were slower starting and it was G + 1 before they got in.' To the west the allies – wearing full chemical protective gear – broke through a weak section of the Iraqi defence and proceeded across the country with incredible haste.

Cpl Gary Morris was 'due to move out about 1900 on the 25th. I remember I got up at about five o'clock that morning and we got everything packed up. I went off to HQ to give them a final brief and said, "Right, I'm off now. I don't know when I'll next talk to you" because communications just didn't exist at the time – there were too many people trying to use the radios. When I got back all my kit had just been chucked in the back of the wagon. I thought, "What's going on here?" It had all been brought forward 12 hours.' His team was swept up in the surge forward and was the first RAF ground team into Iraq: 'We drove 112kms in 30 hours. We just kept going and going.'

Rick Phillips of 12 Sqn, one of the pilots flying on the continuing war sorties, was impressed by the swiftness of the assault: 'It was just wall-to-wall clouds as this armada marched north through the desert. There were thousands of vehicles, all moving at amazing speed. It was a most incredible spectacle.' Fellow Buccaneer airman Norman Browne observed the allied artillery in action: 'I saw an MLRS [mobile launch rocket system] going off – it was so impressive. A puff of smoke and all of a sudden there was a perfect circle, like a little doughnut of explosions, like little cluster bombs going off.'

The much-vaunted Iraqi defences turned out to be

less formidable than anticipated. Alexander Gordon flew over the defences once they had been penetrated and reveals that 'they weren't that impressive. They'd been exaggerated, particularly by the media. But the High Command had gained intelligence and they knew pretty much how to get around and through these defences.' Inaccuracies in media reports were, however, not corrected – intentionally: 'It's not the military's job to correct the mistaken impression that the media are giving. If the media had been saying these trenches are 40–50ft deep, filled with highly flammable oil, there are huge minefields on either side and extensive military emplacements and the military had turned round and said, "Well, actually it's only a ten foot deep trench, it doesn't go the entire way and the minefield is almost non-existent" – then obviously you're implying that you know because that's where you're going.'

The absence of visible Iraqi casualties was also striking. An estimate at the time was that perhaps some 95,000 had been killed in the conflict, with many more injured. Peter Bedford is at a loss to explain why so few were treated by the allied medical services, but suggests: 'I think what happened was that the war progressed so quickly that whatever Iraqi casualties there were must have died in the desert, either of the heat of the day or the cold of the night. Throughout the whole war, the huge 600-bed hospital in our airport only handled 200 casualties, and most of those weren't battle casualties.'

The extreme weather conditions were an influence throughout the war. Flying over the advancing troops in an air defence role, the clouds took on a symbolic significance for Brian O'Connor: 'I was praying hard that we had the weather to support the ground troops. As we got near the ground war it got blacker and blacker and blacker. It was almost like, "I'm God. I am here. This is my war. I'm allowing you to participate in it". The radar was extremely degraded because of the amount of electrical activity in the clouds – we were almost a token presence, if you will.'

In addition to the murky blackness, the weather seemed to defy normal meteorological patterns for the area: 'This weather system was centred right over the battle area. It started to taper off up to the west, and down to the south and out to the east. But right over that battle area it seemed to be self-generating – it didn't blow with the wind, it just stayed right there – which was as odd as can be.'

The electrical activity was such that O'Connor's F3 was struck by lightning, twice: 'We were struck on the side and on the nose: one time so hard that it actually welded the torpedo probe in place – they had to hacksaw it off later. After being struck, all our systems shut down from the electrical surge. Then, when they came back up we tried to find some clear airspace to refuel. We got struck again going in to the tanker and that got struck as well. They've had tankers blow up doing that type of thing before.'

Despite the hostility of the elements, when O'Connor returned to base he remembers: 'They were getting intelligence reports from the ground troops saying, "The weather could not be better. We're hitting them and they can't see us".'

The pace of the allied advance surprised everyone and created its own problems, particularly in stretching the lines of communication and supply. Mike Trace recalls: 'The army covered 135 miles in 100 hours. Suddenly our chain of support facilities stretched to almost beyond breaking point. Communications certainly broke down because the network was no longer a network but a line. And when the line broke, the whole system went down.' The same problem affected supplies and the casevac operation: 'Aircraft were flying around looking for trade. They were plotting where the field dressing station was, then tracking where it might have gone and going to find it, then asking if they had any casualties to take out.'

Some of those casualties were caused – unnecessarily – by mines. Gary Morris remembers one particularly tragic incident: 'We'd just crossed the border and were in the middle of a minefield. All around us were little bomblets that had been dropped – about the size of a snooker ball with a little bit of ribbon on them. Nobody knew what they were. Everyone was under strict instructions, "Don't pick anything up. No matter what it looks like, leave it!" Then we heard this big explosion. One of these had exploded and killed a bloke.'

Morris admits that curiosity got the better of many, from the OC downwards, when it came to abandoned Iraqi bunkers: 'They said a lot of the stuff had been booby-trapped. I went into the bunkers – we all did, even the bosses. It was just human instinct.' In one case, there were signs of a hasty exit by the previous occupants – 'they got out of it that quickly they didn't even turn the tea lamp off.'

Apart from varied collections of ammunition, weapons, maps, food, water and bedding, one bunker contained a clue to one of the mysteries of the war: 'The people we kept seeing never had any boots on and we couldn't work this out. They were all in the bunkers. They got rid of any bit of military kit they could – just threw it away.'

SAC Brian Aitken came briefly into contact with some of the casualties as he refuelled the helicopters which were bringing them into the field dressing stations: 'They'd bring their casualties in, patch them up, pump them full of morphine or whatever because a lot of people were screaming in pain.' It was not an experience for which he felt prepared: 'My whole view of the war changed from there on. I started hating the Iraqis. When it's actually happening to your own people, then the adrenalin starts flowing.'

Professional nurse SACW Connie Dale found the sight of serious injuries less traumatic: 'Some of our chaps had nasty injuries, mainly shrapnel to their bottoms or chests. The PoWs had mainly head injuries and chest wounds. There were a few amputees who'd had legs blown off. There were some nasty ones but overall our lads' morale was quite high.'

Further back down the line, Flt Sgt Alan Bear and his colleagues in Muharraq and Riyadh were feeling frustrated by their lack of involvement: 'The casualties were so few and far between that they were dealt with by the field hospitals in the desert. We were visited by the medical commander for the Gulf. He said fairly bluntly, "Thanks for coming but you won't be used". We were totally deflated at this news, having worked so hard to receive casualties. Our OC spoke to us afterwards and said he didn't feel the commander med had put things very well. He felt that we might still be used, and he was genuine about that. He wasn't saying that just to stop us feeling pissed off because we really were at quite a low ebb then, after the amount of work that we had put into it.'

Plans for the treatment of injuries had been modified to include Iraqi casualties, as Peter Bedford explains: 'Initially, when we were working out the aeromed procedures, we were thinking totally along the lines of the Brits and possibly members of the other coalition forces. Suddenly it dawned on us: "What about all the Iraqi casualties? What's going to happen to them?" So they got fed into the plot.'

Though the number of Iraqi casualties dealt with

was small, the number of prisoners-of-war continually increased. Andy Garton describes circumstances in which Iraqi troops surrendered which were fairly typical: 'When the allies went in, they went in right at the far side of this Iraqi battalion which was lined across the border. They went round the back of it and this poor battalion sat there for days without anything. Everybody had forgotten about them. Eventually they decided it was no good, and they got out and tramped across – we had about 50 of them trying to surrender to a Drone that was flying across. These guys didn't really want to fight. We talked to some of them and they said they'd been told they were only 40 miles from Riyadh when, in fact, they were about three to four hundred miles away.'

An allied tank stuck in a ditch received help from an unlikely quarter, as Connie Dale recounts: 'This Iraqi came over and helped push the tank out of the ditch with his tank. Once he'd got them out of the ditch he surrendered. The lads couldn't believe it!'

On many occasions, Iraqis 'flagged down' helicopters to give themselves up. Mike Trace recalls what happened in one such instance: 'One of our crewmen is a very keen gun expert. One lone Iraqi was passed during the day and, as the aircraft came overhead, he threw his weapon away and put his hands up. He turned to face the aircraft as it was coming in and was most surprised when the crewman, instead of coming to fetch him, went straight past to get the gun!'

However, Trace's unit found that not all those assumed to be prisoners-of-war were what they seemed: 'One of our aircraft was recovering from Kuwait back through Iraq to King Khalid Military City. They spotted two prisoners-of-war, picked them up and took them to the compound at Al Qaysumah on the way home. He got back to KKMC and was just having a shower when he was summoned to retrieve these two PoWs. They'd turned out to be Syrians and therefore on our side! He had a lot of sweet-talking to do. He actually had the presence of mind to take a cake sent by his mother with him, and he managed to pacify the Syrians with that . . .'

Part of the reason for the Iraqis' surrender in such large numbers was their physical and mental state, as Trace explains: 'They were generally in a dreadful condition. They were poorly clothed, very cold, very wet, incredibly thirsty, and even more hungry. They hadn't been fed in many days. They thought they were 50 miles north of Riyadh when they were still in Iraq.' Cpl Clive Darwood was involved in ferrying PoWs in Chinooks to holding camps. 'They turned up at the aircraft and a lot of them had no shoes on – just plastic wrapped round their feet. They were limping, unshaven – and the stench was indescribable.' The officers were in a slightly better condition: 'They had boots on and some of them were better dressed. They used to thank us when they got off the aircraft.'

As Trace points out, the logistical problem of shipping large numbers of PoWs to safe areas was immense: 'The Americans planned for it. They had wagons and soldiers earmarked. But I think we all got more involved in PoWs than we actually thought possible. It was forecast there'd be half a million men on that border. It was always going to be a problem looking back on it – if you don't kill them, they're going to be PoWs.'

Gary Morris was struck by the contrast between his inactivity and what was happening only a short distance away: 'I was sitting in my wagon at three in the morning reading a book and there's all this artillery barrage going on. The battle was going on about 3 kms in front of me. And I was sitting there, having a smoke. I said to the lad I was with, "Hey Paul, what do you think is going on up there? It's funny. We've just made a cup of tea, we're having a fag and 3 kms up there people are getting blown apart". He said, "That's war, Gary, isn't it" and just carried on reading.'

The hasty advance continued across Iraq, troops encircling Kuwait – and, rather than slow down, some prisoners-of-war were taken forward to be flown back at a later stage. Flt Lt Andy Bell, following 4 Brigade and tasked with finding chemical munitions, was also caught up in the rush onwards: 'My sergeant said to me, "Do you know who were the first people into Berlin in the Second World War? It was the RAF Regiment. Come on. Let's be the first allies into Kuwait".'

Bell, reasoning that the best place to find Iraqi chemical equipment would be in the country they were now rapidly abandoning, agreed, and they set off in their Land Rover, armed only with a rifle each: 'I was scared, because we didn't know what the situation was. I knew that we were still surrounding Kuwait City but I didn't know how much fighting was still going on. We got on the main Kuwait road; it was very eerie because there were all these Iraqi tanks and APCs [armoured personnel carriers] – still with their engines running. All the Iraqis had run away. There was no-one around except for a few dead bodies. I was all for turning round and going back, when a searchlight came on us.'

It was an American border checkpoint, where they were told: '"Sorry, you can't go into Kuwait. Arab coalition forces only. The British army is 20 miles down the road". I said, "I'm not British army. I'm RAF Regiment".'

Andy Bell and his sergeant were allowed through. They were, they believe, the first western allied uniformed troops in Kuwait. They were shocked by what they found: 'I was expecting something like the Falls Road, but with modern buildings. What I saw in Kuwait was horrendous – the city had been completely raped,' recalls Bell. 'Every shop had been ripped out. Light switches had been taken out. Windows had been taken out. Everything that could be damaged or destroyed was.'

In the first hours after its liberation, Kuwait City was a dangerous place to be. They decided to find somewhere to 'hole up'. 'Our idea was to try to get to the British Embassy, and wait outside, because we knew the Ambassador would arrive at some time. But we didn't have a map of the city, and couldn't find it. There were no lights. Tanks strewn everywhere. Rubble in the streets. Dead bodies. We were pulled up by the militia in a back street, and I knew one of them – he was an interpreter who'd worked with British Forces Middle East. They took us out to the airport, where the Hercules had just started to fly in to set up an airhead.'

As the allied troops closed in around Kuwait City on 26 February, still holding total aerial domination, there was only one escape route for those who had been occupying the capital for the previous 206 days – the road to Basra. The Iraqis commandeered all available transport – much of it new Japanese cars straight from the showroom – and the massive convoy headed north.

The bottleneck that ensued on what became known as 'the killing road' provided the easiest of targets for allied air power. F3 navigator Mark Robinson saw the results from the air: 'The road out of Kuwait to Basra was an awful sight. There was no way they could get off the road to do anything, they were just slaughtered. It was better they died on that road than our boys died – we were all acutely aware of that. But it didn't reduce the horror of what we saw there.'

Gary Morris saw and smelt the convoy from the ground. In amongst the burnt-out wrecks, he found Kuwaitis repossessing the goods so recently plundered from them: 'There was this bloke with his wife – they'd got a suitcase and were going from vehicle to vehicle pulling out telephone answering machines and stuff like that. I just looked and thought, "What the hell's going on here?"'

Eventually the Kuwaiti militia arrived to collect munitions: 'There were guns littered everywhere. People were just picking guns up and firing them off. I thought, "We've not come all the way through only to get shot here".'

Above the scene of devastation was a cloud of incredible proportions, as Flt Lt Dick McCormac, a Jaguar pilot, recalls: 'There was a thick pall of black smoke a couple of miles thick which drifted around the high pressure system in the Gulf. Sometimes it would be there and sometimes it wouldn't but, as time went on, it got thicker and thicker over Kuwait.' On occasions the visibility was so poor that aircrew could not carry out or complete their missions, and as Bill Pixton found, there were not always enough missions to go round: 'Our target area was shrinking by the hour. There were simply too many planes and not enough targets.'

Even as Iraqi troops retreated or surrendered there were still many dangers. Britain's most severe loss of the Gulf War occurred at this time, when two troop carriers from 4th Armoured Brigade were accidentally attacked by two American A-10 aircraft, killing nine men. Cpl Ian Showler was on the Puma helicopters that took some of the wounded from the field dressing station to 32 Field Hospital. He recalls: 'We got the guys on, made sure they were still breathing and that their drips were running nice and clearly, made sure that they had adequate morphine. It was a very long flight, mentally as well as physically. I was lifting casualties around; perhaps turning them onto their side if they were having difficulty breathing. And while I was working on them, I had to keep my eye on the others, because they were all in the same situation.

'I'll never forget one guy from the Warrior incident. He was very badly burned and had a large tattoo on his chest. I find myself going back to that. I was talking to him, although he couldn't hear me because of the roar of the aircraft. I'd talk to myself and tell myself what I was doing – reassuring myself, hoping that the casualties might be able to hear me as well and know I was trying to do my best for them. There was obviously a lot of pain in things you had to do – you know damned well that it'll hurt them if you move a certain part of their body – but you know that, if you didn't, there was a possibility they could drift away and you'd lose them. I never lost anybody. Everyone that came onto my aircraft left alive.'

Afterwards, Showler admits: 'I cried. I didn't have time to think about it when I was in the aircraft. But afterwards I sat down and thought, "Jesus! Why? Why?" And it really got to me.'

It got to others too. SAC Gary Woods talked to the Staff Sergeant in charge of the section that had been attacked: 'He said that he got out of the vehicle because he heard something go off and started treating the casualties. Then the planes came round a second time. They were on the floor and nobody knew what was going on – obviously there were dead and injured. Even on the coach [from the hospital] nobody really explained to them that it was an A–10 that actually took them out.

'It hit me a little bit then', continues Woods, 'because when the Staff Sergeant was telling me, he was in tears and I never really saw a Staff Sergeant cry. He was in tears at the back of the wagon because he felt sorry for his blokes and he felt angry.'

The unilateral allied ceasefire was announced at 0330 local time on Thursday 28 February, only 100 hours after the land war had begun. It was greeted with immense relief on all sides. But since the Iraqis had earlier appeared to offer a ceasefire which had raised hopes only to dash them, there was scepticism too, as SAC Andy Garton recalls: 'I was stood in the desert having a pee. The Group Captain was as well. He wandered over and I said, "I don't believe this ceasefire will work". "Neither do I" he said.' As Garton says: 'There was still an element of, "I don't trust these buggers. I'll believe it when I'm on the plane home".'

Everyone had their own reason for remembering the ceasefire. For Chf Tech John Goodwin, the announcement came during a party to celebrate his 40th birthday. Dick Druitt takes a special pride in having been part of the first formation as well as the last sortie: 'I was actually airborne at two o'clock in the morning and landed about four, five o'clock in the morning. I was the last jet to land in Bahrain.'

Flt Lt Mike Warren also landed in the early hours of the morning the ceasefire was announced. He too was among the 'first and last.' In fact, he claims: 'We finished the war, if the truth be known, it was our final blow that did it!'

This 'final blow' was a successful mission against Habbanniyah airfield, as navigator Mal Craghill remembers: 'That day the number two pilot had a letter from his father, saying that he'd done his National Service in Iraq, at an airfield called Habbanniyah. He wrote back to say, "If you did any work building hangars, Dad, I'm very sorry – we just bombed them . . ."'

Jerry Witts was in bed: 'You probably won't believe me – but I woke up at about 4.45am and turned on my little radio just in time to catch Bahrain Radio saying that President Bush had just announced there would be a cessation of hostilities, effective eight o'clock this morning – provided the Iraqis stopped shooting at us. I thought, "Whoopee!"'

Gary Woods reflects on the success of the ground offensive: 'A lot of pride went into the 100-hour war. Everybody was proud at the end of it because we did the job and we did it properly – we didn't cut any corners, we didn't take any risks. We went there and we used everything at our disposal from the smallest medic to the biggest aircraft. Everyone thought it was a great job – we were so proud.'

In most places that pride could not be celebrated with a toast. For Cpl Nigel Phipps, a steward at Riyadh, the celebratory drink was an alcohol-free beer with lime in it. 'It was horrible stuff,' he remembers. 'Everyone was happy but we weren't that desperate!'

Nevertheless, the festivities still went with a swing, as Charles Newrick recalls: 'We had a cocktail party, which was very relaxed and laid-back. I don't know how everybody got so relaxed – as you know, there was no alcohol.'

The Buccaneer crews, in the more liberal climate of Bahrain, were able to celebrate in the traditional manner. 'We went down for breakfast about eight o'clock,' remembers Keith Nugent, 'and Carl Wilson, one of the other navs, came in with the glazed look he has in his eyes when he's pissed. It's a look I know very well. He said "It's all over – we're in the conference room". It was Guinness and Macallan at nine o'clock in the morning. By eleven, I was out of my tree.'

Chapter 12

DARKNESS AT NOON

'O dark, dark, dark, amid the blaze of noon . . .'
Milton,
Samson Agonistes

For the prisoners-of-war in Baghdad, the ceasefire announced by the allies on 28 February was signalled by the sound of small arms fire in the streets, though they were in no position to share in the celebrations. Only five days earlier, they had been lucky to escape relatively unscathed when the building next door was flattened by four accurately-placed bombs.

'I was absolutely scared stiff,' admits David Waddington. 'It was much worse than being shot down, because I could hear the aircraft and I heard the bomb two or three seconds before it hit. I didn't know whether I was going to be alive in the next few seconds. I just lay there thinking, "Please let me survive".'

The bombs also caused severe damage to their prison cells. It seemed to Robbie Stewart that 'the whole building moved about four foot. The blasts were sufficiently close to us to demolish some of the walls and blow the hatches of our doors inwards – even though they opened outwards. A fire started outside, which I could see through my little grille, and there was a terrible smell of cordite. But the guards had gone and we could speak to each other. I heard John Peters and Rupert Clark and the American next to me. Then I heard a little voice saying, "Has anyone heard Robbie Stewart?" And I said, "Yes, Dave, I'm here. I've got a broken leg" – which was the first time he knew that we were actually there together. There was no panic – just the opposite. John Peters was talking as if he were leaning over a fence on a Sunday afternoon. He was yakking away so much the Americans said, "Hey, you Brits, be quiet" – because they wanted to speak.'

When the guards returned they broke down the doors to the cells and took the prisoners out of the building one by one. Stewart believed he was about to be shot. 'I was carried down on a bloke's shoulder,' he continues. 'He handed me over to these two guys at the bottom who grabbed hold of my arms and dragged me hopping on one leg. They said, "Come on, we'll show you what your American friends have done", and took me across to a bunker which was completely destroyed. They were both carrying AK47s – they pushed me against a wall and stepped back and I thought, "Well, they're going to shoot me now". I wasn't frightened or anything like that. All the way through I'd felt fairly strong because I had a family that could look after themselves and two good kids. I was contented with what I was leaving behind.'

Waddington, too, was half expecting to be shot: 'The guy who got me out of the cell used a crowbar to open the door. He took me by the scruff of the neck and was running down the corridor in pitch blackness when he ran into one of the face plates on the cell doors and knocked himself out. I was actually laughing when another Iraqi came up the stairs and looked at me as if I'd done it – I thought, "Oh no, what's going to happen now?" But fortunately this guy came round fairly quickly and carried on as if nothing had happened.'

All the prisoners were blindfolded, herded into a coach

and made to crouch on the floor. Again Stewart feared the worst: 'I sat next to an American. He had his arms folded across his chest and so did I – and he grabbed my fingers. That was a lovely feeling – knowing there was someone else in the same boat.'

In fact, they were driven to a large civilian prison – 'we called it the Country Club' – where Waddington and Stewart shared a cell with four other allied PoWs. 'Dave was very thin and drawn in the face,' recalls Stewart. 'He looked very white, his shoulders were bad but he seemed all right. Of course, we all had moustaches and beards.' Conditions remained primitive – 'the water they gave us for drinking had already been used by the Iraqi prisoners to wash in, so a lot of us picked up infections' – but they were given three meals a day, which was for Waddington, in particular, 'an incredible luxury'.

A day later, however, it was back to solitary confinement, more interrogation, more ill-treatment – and more death threats. 'But they were asking stupid questions,' Stewart remembers. 'They wanted to know if President Bush would go nuclear if they used chemical weapons. They asked what I knew about Turkey and Syria and the ground forces. Well, by 24 February that was irrelevant. We'd heard that the ground war had started but this bloke was saying, "When do you think the ground war will start?" What could you say?'

The prisoners learned of the ceasefire on the day it was declared. Four days later they were moved to a military prison and their treatment began to improve. 'The next morning they were very nice to us,' states Waddington. 'We were told, "Anything you want, just ask the guys outside. They'll get it for you". They gave me some sandals, which was the first time I'd had anything on my feet except some plastic bags which I'd found in my cell.'

Other luxuries followed. 'We were allowed to wash

for the first time in six weeks,' recalls Stewart. 'We had meat, they shaved us and gave us five or six blankets so I was actually warm. Then the guy came in and gave me new shoes and a nice yellow suit. And then one day he said, "You're going to be free in five minutes", just like that. They sprayed eau de cologne over us and took us out blindfolded to a bus.'

Waddington, however, did not feel reassured: 'I thought, "If they're going to release us why are they putting blindfolds on us?" so I was a bit worried. They sat me next to Robbie and I said, "What do you think then?" He said, "I don't know". He reached across and grabbed my hand. What he meant was, "It's over. We're going home". But what I thought it meant was, "If I don't see you again, good luck . . .", that sort of thing. So I was very nervous for about ten minutes. Then they said we could take the blindfolds off and we got to the hotel and the Red Cross were there.'

The PoWs' return to Riyadh in an International Red Cross plane was a cause of great jubilation, particularly among their fellow-fliers. A flight of Tornado F3s from 43 Sqn was flying CAPs on the border when they came in and 'the emotion just flowed'. F3 navigator Fg Off Tony Beresford remembers listening in on the air-to-air radio: 'The Swiss aircraft had two of our other F3 crews on the wing – on escort – and two American F-15s. One GR1 guy said, "I've never been so happy to see an F3 sitting on my wing". There's a traditional rivalry between the GR1s and F3s and always will be, but there's a lot more respect for them after the fantastic job they did.'

At King Khalid International, the returned captives were transferred to a VC10 to be flown to Akrotiri for their debriefing. 'That's something I'll not forget,' declares Sqn Ldr Chris Hewat, 'seeing them get off the aircraft in their bright yellow coveralls, like contestants on the Krypton Factor. They certainly looked a bit shell-shocked and one of the guys, Robert Stewart, looked in need of a stretcher – but there was no way he was getting onto one. He was determined to hobble along on crutches – he was going to get off that aircraft and onto the next one by himself. They were obviously delighted to be amongst familiar uniforms and we were just over the moon for them.'

However, there were sadder transfers to be made, as Sgt Kevin Traynor and his mobile servicing team witnessed at Al Jubayl: 'A [Hercules] C1 arrived and the first 17 coffins came on. I was running the fuel truck and the sergeant-major gave me a bollocking because he wanted to hold a practice parade and the people marching couldn't hear the band playing. So I switched it off for ten minutes, and when he'd got the practice over and done with I finished refuelling the aircraft. When the actual parade took place we had to march onto the Hercules, lay the coffin down and go out the front door. The aircraft was all dressed in black with Union Jacks. It was heart-rending, with grown-up soldiers crying their eyeballs out. They were holding onto the coffins of their friends and they didn't want to let go. The same aircraft came back the next day and the smell of formaldehyde was still there.'

Although the ceasefire was announced on 28 February, it was not until 3 March that the Iraqi generals met with General Schwarzkopf to formally accept all the allies' conditions. 'There was a great sense of relief that it was over,' declares Sqn Ldr Roger Bennett of 13 Sqn.

There was also the widespread feeling that 'with Saddam you couldn't take any chances'. CAPs continued to be flown, sentries were still posted and respirators carried. For chef Cpl Dave Pullen, as for many others, it was business as usual: 'When it came over the radio that all hostilities had ceased we just looked at each other. Then it was, "Right lads, back to work". It made no difference to us if the war was over or not. People were still going to be coming in an hour and a half for their tea. There was uncertainty, because we didn't trust him.'

For those who were flying it was a case of 'everybody being on their best behaviour', as F3 pilot Alexander Gordon puts it. 'We had to be very careful because people were fatigued, and the last thing we wanted at that stage was to lose an aircraft through aircrew error – or something stupid like beating up an army encampment at low level and getting shot down by one of our own missiles. So everybody was told to take no risks, just to finish the job that we'd started and to go home.'

However, when it came to flying through the smoke of the burning oil-wells to reach forward landing strips, risks had to be taken. 'We didn't have a lot to go by,' remembers Hercules navigator Flt Lt John Ayers of one such trip. 'The way we did it was to use the navigational aids to position us roughly at the TAP [target approach point]. Then we flew on a heading towards the strip with no forward visibility. To see through the smoke, I had to lie on the floor of the Hercules looking out of the side windows, trying to pick out things I hoped to recognise on the ground. One was a bend in the road just north of Kuwait. I got a visual reference on a point at the bend, so I knew where we were. Then we ran in on a stop-watch, seeing nothing forward but having the confidence to fly lower and lower. There was a line of power cables on the chart and once we'd passed that we could descend to a low level. It was satisfying to come out of the cloud about a mile short of the strip, and there it was.'

Within days of the liberation of Kuwait, official and unofficial battlefield tours became a feature. Leading the first was Mike Trace, who took the opportunity to end what he saw as his 'Duke of Plaza Toro act' and get airborne when the allied Deputy Commander, General Sir Peter de la Billière, entered Kuwait City the day after the ceasefire: 'We were the first RAF aircraft into Kuwait and we landed on a football pitch outside the British Embassy. We were instantly mobbed, surrounded by thousands and thousands of Kuwaitis. They were all trying to say, "Thank you for releasing us!" and we were saying, "Well, it's not only us". Lots of the local militia on road-blocks were firing off AK47s into the air – just shooting in delight. I was worried that when we got airborne they'd be shooting at the aircraft.'

As part of their tour of the British divisional area they took the general over 'Hell's Highway' – the Basra road: 'The tanks had got further off the motorway than the other vehicles. Some were a mile and a half off the road, where the tank commander or driver had been killed and the thing had just kept going. It was a numbing sight and the General, too, was absolutely heart-struck by it.' That night, Trace and his crew slept at the British Embassy, flushing the toilets with water drawn from the embassy swimming pool.

That same day the first fixed-wing aircraft was able to break through the pall of smoke to land at Kuwait International airport, as Peter Bedford remembers: 'We were actually taking a few people to help open the British Embassy. Obviously we'd heard about the oil fires but we hadn't any idea what they were like. We went down from 10,000 to 5,000ft, flying above white cloud with a lovely clear blue sky, and suddenly went into pitch black. The day turned to night and we had to turn all the lights on in the cockpit. As we came down to about 3,000ft, we came below the base of this thick black smoke and there lay all the oil fires. The ferocity with which those oil wells was burning, the amount of smoke that was being pushed out and the number of fires, right across the whole horizon, was almost incomprehensible. It was the most awful experience I think I've ever had, because I immediately felt that one person had been responsible for all this. He'd said, "Yes, do it" – an act of mass terrorism on an international scale.'

Only two other RAF Hercs had already landed, their aircraft was the third onto the airfield. 'I felt very angry,' continues Bedford. 'Everything in the terminal that couldn't be taken away had been broken and vandalised – from the phones being ripped out to the potted plants being kicked over. It summed up the way I felt the Iraqis had behaved in Kuwait. They'd broken everything they possibly could before they left and the oil fires were the same thing.'

Another early eyewitness was MT driver Cpl Nigel Cassata, who had arrived on the same flight. He describes breaking through the smoke cover as 'like entering Dante's Inferno. We'd all been on radios and earphones and we just stopped dead. Nobody spoke. It was eerie. We virtually circled Kuwait City and there was one solitary electric light bulb in the entire city. When we landed there were no runway lights.'

As well as vandalising the terminal, the Iraqis had left behind some other unpleasant surprises: 'When we got there they said, "Don't touch anything because there are booby-traps all over the place". There were a lot on the airfield. There was a booby-trapped vehicle with a grenade tied to the door with a wire, and helmets booby-trapped with grenades under them.'

Brian Aitken came into Kuwait City by road from Iraq and for a while worked from a helicopter refuelling base near Hell's Highway. 'The road was treacherous,' he states. 'We had to have someone walking in front, because of all the armoured personnel trucks carrying explosives that had been blown to pieces. The stench of blood and bodies in the heat was disgusting, so I drove about in my respirator. When we got up there [to the Basra road] there was still the odd person alive and moaning. There were bodies of people who'd stepped on mines or been shot. There were people who had their hands over their ears – the blast had done something to the insides of their heads but their bodies were intact. The only thing that scared me was the quantity of flies there and the disease they might be carrying.'

That concern, however, was offset by the welcome they received when they arrived in Kuwait City: 'People had tears of joy in their eyes, women actually pulled back their veils and kissed you – that made you feel you'd done a worthwhile job. But the parentless kids pointing to their mouths really got to me – they hadn't eaten for days. We shared chocolates, sweets, anything we had left in the vehicle.'

Aircrew usually had the comfort of being remote from the destruction caused by their bombs or rockets: 'You never actually see what's happened. It's back in time for tea and medals' – but this was not always the case. Flying over the road to Basra, Angus Elliott was struck by the number of vultures: 'I started thinking, "Hang on a minute, if the vultures are up here, what the hell is down there?" If you see the pictures taken of bombed buildings and you assume that maybe a couple of people were in each building, then I suppose we did see a great deal of death – but we never saw any death close up.'

However, some fixed-wing aircrew did manage to go 'sightseeing' in Kuwait. Flt Lt Tony Binnington's Chinook landed at one of the Iraqi barracks that 'our own Tornado boys had shot up. Two or three of the guys who'd actually flown the raid were fairly interested in seeing their handiwork. We were in a hover and one of the engines developed a small problem, so we landed on what remained of their parade ground and had a walk round. We saw by the state of the place that the casualties must have been enormous – with three storey buildings where the bomb had gone straight through and exploded at the bottom, so all that was left was a shell. They'd cleared the bodies but there was still small arms ammunition and equipment around. It seems a funny thing to say but there was a certain element of satisfaction – not at the deaths but the fact that the target had been so clinically taken out – because the accuracy of the bombing was incredible.'

They were similarly impressed by what they saw when they went on to overfly a number of Iraqi airfields which had also been bombed by their Tornados: 'You were in the hover so you could virtually reach out and touch the shelters and see just one hole in the roof and the doors blown out and a wrecked plane inside – and think what an amazing phenomenon it was.'

This precision was in stark contrast to the random violence that had wrecked Kuwait City: 'The thing that amazed me was that all the cars had been burnt out – and what happened to all the wheels? Somewhere or other there's a damn great stock of millions of car wheels. There was also a little marina with pleasure craft in it – little dinghies, canoes and sailing boats – and every one had been quite deliberately destroyed and sunk.'

For Fg Off Rachael Berry, who was also on the aerial tour, the scale of the devastation was 'just unbelievable. Imagine seeing a house that's been burnt out, with a car turned over in the drive and a swimming pool that's black and has pieces of furniture floating in it. Then try to imagine a whole city like that. The desert was so covered with oil, it was like seeing an estuary when the tide's gone out and you just have the mud flats. Where there should have been sand, there was just sludge. The Chinook has a dome-shaped window and I remember kneeling on this thing, looking out and just shaking my head. There was a squadron leader beside me who was saying, "I can't believe this".'

Throughout the first days of peace, the business of bringing in Iraqi casualties continued. 'The army guys were going out finding vehicles, people in the middle of minefields and so on,' explains aeromedic Ian Showler. 'I remember carrying a casualty who'd been lying in a minefield for four days.'

Their treatment seemed to take many Iraqis by surprise: 'You could see the look of horror on their faces as they came onto the aircraft. They didn't have a clue what was going on, couldn't speak a word of the language and were very frightened. We'd had lots of sweets sent to us, so we used to have a jar of boiled sweets on the aircraft. Injuries allowing, I'd give them a sweet, saying "How d'you do?" shaking their hand, patting them on the shoulder – and a smile would come to their faces. I could do anything then. I could cut down, have a look at their wounds, make sure they weren't bleeding, alter drips, all without their having to worry about it. Some of them wouldn't want you to touch them because you were obviously the opposition, so I'd say, "Fine", let them calm down and I'd come back again later.'

There were still more prisoners-of-war to be transported, as Regiment gunner Shaun Hayward describes: 'We were picking them up from holding points at the front and taking them to PoW camps. We'd get as many onto the aircraft as we could but they'd be holding on to each other and not wanting to be parted, because they'd obviously made friends with whoever they'd been holed up with for seven months. They'd just sit there crying. But they didn't give us any hassle. We'd give out chocolate or rations and fresh water, but you had to be careful you didn't cause a big fight on the aircraft over the water. You had to watch the officers, because they'd try to use their rank – and the Republican Guard. They were well-fed and healthy and we didn't feel too sorry for them. They were winding us up all the time when we were moving around in the aircraft, pretending to get things out of their pockets.'

203

There was also the stress of carrying both those who were dying and the dead: 'It seems a bit weird,' confesses Gary Morris. 'The thing I found about the bodies was that you don't look at them. A lot of the lads, especially the younger ones, they'd just take the mick. They'd say, "Look at him. He don't look too happy!" But it wasn't being disrespectful. It was our way of coping – otherwise you could easily start cracking up.'

One of the last battlefield casualties Charles Newrick remembers being brought into the field hospital at Al Qaysumah was a Bedouin who had been forced into the Iraqi front line: 'As soon as the ground offensive had started, he'd got out of his trench and started walking back to his sheep. He'd wandered over the sand dunes for five or six days, stood on a mine and lost his leg. He came in and had to have an above-the-knee amputation.'

Together with some of the less serious casualties, the Bedouin was a witness to the hospital staff's many off-duty activities, which included a revue 'with a distinctly lavatorial flavour, because most people were worried about their bowels out there', a couple of fun runs, a sports day with an 'NBC relay' and a display by the guard dogs of the RAF Police: 'We took the Bedouin along to watch the German Shepherds doing their tricks and he was fascinated. Through an interpreter, he told us "I wish I had a dog like that to keep my sheep in order".'

The first fortnight after the ceasefire was, in Flt Lt Ken Beaton's opinion, a 'very difficult period. We found ourselves without a war. All of a sudden there wasn't the need to arm up all these bombs, to turn round all these aircraft, to provide the back-up and the equipment. We had all these bodies with nothing to do.'

If the 'troops' now had time on their hands it was very different for their commanders. In Dhahran, Jerry Witts found that 'all the problems we'd put up with surfaced, the niggly things that we hadn't had time to deal with – like the fact that the guys' quarters were very spartan. So personally I was very busy. There was a huge amount of written work to do. I don't think I'd written on a piece of paper during the whole war – or received many. Suddenly they wanted reports on this and that and they wanted it all yesterday. The poor old laptop was getting red-hot.'

For the 'rest of the team', however, it was more a question of 'mooching around getting very bored.' The peace had given 'the adrenalin a chance to settle down' but in Dhahran this was too much of a good thing. 'It's not a place you'd go for your summer holiday. Our families weren't there and there was no female company – not that we're all rabid womanisers but you begin to notice all those differences. You couldn't get a beer or a newspaper and there was no chance to get away.'

Escaping from the claustrophobic atmosphere of their living quarters was not easy, as Sqn Ldr Greg Monaghan reports: 'You're not supposed to travel in Saudi without special written permission. If you want to go to the Red Sea you have to apply for a pass to travel, a pass for the Red Sea and a special swimming pass. We had a few test runs and found that if we showed our base passes – which were covered in Arabic writing – at the checkpoints, they were quite happy. We were encouraged by this and went down to the Red Sea three times, swam, saw lovely fish, got some lovely coral – and had no trouble until the third trip. We were on the beach when the coastguards came along. We went straight up to them and introduced ourselves because we discovered quite early on that if you go up to them, shake their hands, say who you are and are friendly, they're quite happy. The coastguards invited us to their hut and gave us tea and dates and coffee. Then their officers turned up and invited us to their mess, where they gave us lunch. Then the local security chief showed up and he was a bit twitchy because we were so close to Israel and Jordan. But in the end everyone was happy, there was a lot of shaking of hands and we drove home. We were escorted by a truckload of heavies all the way back to Tabuk – so they were quite keen to look after us.'

Back in December all RAF personnel had been warned to expect to do six month tours in the Gulf to match Army practice. However, the Prime Minister, on a second visit to the region, gave public assurances to the troops that they would be withdrawn with all speed. To Geoff Davies, officer commanding the hospital in Muharraq, it appeared that 'they had no winding-down plan. The plan for the war and dealing with casualties was brilliant and everybody knew what was going on. But when it all finished, there were a lot of rumours about who was going back and when. I fully expected us to be the last to go and told all the troops so. But then they started chopping and changing – a different plan every day. The medical people couldn't make any decisions until they knew how many troops were going to stay and the army couldn't stay until the Government told them what the policy was. It was a difficult time and I got pretty angry.'

In keeping with time-honoured service traditions, there was a lot of 'whingeing, moaning and bitching until the day we were allowed to go home'. Nigel Phipps, catering in Riyadh, represents the view from the ranks that 'you'd worked your butt off for so many days, building up to a climax – the anti-climax was that nobody could be bothered with a sense of urgency any more. The biggest problem for us was that they started sending everybody from the front home and there must have been 15,000 of us still out there, with the papers saying, "All our boys are home". So morale went down and we were all pig sick. Because we were all together doing nothing, tempers built up. You'd worked with people for so many weeks, all of a sudden you had time to sit and talk to each other and you realised that you didn't get on.'

Letters that had given so much pleasure and comfort in earlier days now became something of a chore – 'because you had to answer every one. Although we were very grateful, a lot didn't get answered.' The days, for Andy Garton, were passed with 'a bit of sunbathing, lazing around, wrapping up the helicopters, drinking lots of coffee, lots of tins of Pepsi, more sunbathing, watching a few videos'. For SAC Thomas Stafford a highlight was a football match with the Kuwaitis: 'I'd been speaking to a local we knew – saying we'd like a game of football. He got the local semi-pro team and I got 16 guys from the supply helicopter force. We went to a nearby stadium and they beat us 2–0.'

Aircraft nose painting took on new dimensions as ground crews used their artistic talents to portray lurid mascots, and sortie tallies, on the planes in their care: 'The Tornado ground crews started to paint them after they'd lost the first couple of Tornados and morale went down,' explains Buccaneer SENGO David Tasker. 'When we got there the Tornados, Jaguars and Victors had already got girls painted on the side. So they looked around and said, "Boss, can we do it?" The boss said yes, so we all had girls on the side – black bombs, red bombs, all sorts of things for different missions. Cpl Kenny Latham was the artist. It was something to get the team together.'

Even when relaxing it was not always possible to forget the effects of the war, as Mike Toft of XV Sqn testifies of Muharraq: 'You'd be out by the pool when the wind would change. The thick black smoke from the oilfields would come over, the sun was gone, the temperature dropped ten degrees and it was like nightime.'

Among the first to be given a firm date for departure were those at Tabuk. 'We were spending our days sunbathing,' says Mal Craghill of 16 Sqn. 'People kept coming and saying we'd be there for the foreseeable future. Then someone from the hierarchy told us they were going to start withdrawing some forces – and the good news was that they were starting from east to west, so Tabuk would go first.'

The following week and a half was spent 'panic tanning,' says Mike Warren. 'Everybody was concerned that they should be as bronzed as possible when they returned home. Others were very busy packing things up. People will say they were bored and couldn't wait to get home but I think it was good that we had that period at the end of the war before we left. It gave you a chance to settle yourself, wind down, relax a bit and get a few of the war stories out of your system.'

Flt Lt Malcolm Hammans of 27 Sqn suggests that the delay was equally important for the wives and families back home: 'I think my family had suddenly become exhausted. During the war my wife had kept herself very busy – every weekend she was going to see people or had people to stay – just to keep her mind occupied. And when she didn't have to do that and could relax it hit her. She didn't do anything for three weeks, so she was just about back to normal by the time I got home.'

Before departure there were farewell parties – formal receptions given by their hosts and rather more informal ones given by those who were leaving. In Dhahran 43 Sqn gave a party for the Saudis and Americans in a large hangar and then went back to their hotel to 'let our hair down. We threw our boss in the swimming pool fully clothed – and pulled people out who'd gone to bed for an early night, and threw them in. Our warrant officer who looks after the ground crew came in and we said, "Right, in the pool". He said, "Please, gentlemen, please. Let me take my clothes off first". He took them off carefully and went in the pool – somebody said, "Hang on, you've forgotten these" – and threw his clothes in after him. It was typical aircrew – rowdy and dishevelled.'

The lucky few flew themselves back – 'I did a barrel roll as I left Saudi territory' – while the rest were flown home either in the RAF's Hercules, Tristars and VC10s or in commercial airline jets from Kuwait or Saudi Arabia. Some returned within days of the signing of the peace accord, some in a few weeks, some had to stay on for an extra month or two. Connie Dale's departure from the Gulf was no more and no less typical than most: 'We found out 24 hours before we flew out. We had to flatten the site at Al Qaysumah when we left, so we were taking down tents, filling in the shelters, emptying sandbags. Our flight sergeant did his back in, so we took him down with us to Al Jubayl as a patient in the Chinook while the rest of the guys drove back in the Land Rovers. A lot of us were quite sad to leave Al Qaysumah – I was sad, because the squadron had been my family. But we were glad it was over and we were going home. We stopped overnight in Al Jubayl and flew out from Dhahran on a 747. We all thought we'd have a drink on the plane and celebrate – but it was alcohol-free, which was dreadful!'

Those flying from Tabuk were rather luckier. 'There was an enormous cheer as the aircraft got airborne,' remembers Mal Craghill. 'It was a six hour flight and the big surprise was that the Air Force presented everybody with a small bottle of red wine to drink with the meal. I thought I was dreaming . . .'

Chapter 13

FACE TO FACE WITH HISTORY

'How is it possible to be contented with anything else when one has come face to face with
History?'

General Charles De Gaulle,
War Memoirs vol III

There were few who weren't delighted to come home:
whether they returned by fastjets, commercial airliners
or troop transporters. 'I sat on the flight deck coming
back,' remembers Mark Robinson, 'and we saw the
lights of RAF Coningsby coming out of the mist. I
was just so excited. Everybody slates Coningsby for
being desperately horrible and I never thought I'd be
pleased to see this bloody place again – but I was. The
most frustrating bit was that some bigwig, the Deputy
Defence Secretary, was coming to welcome us, so we
had to fly around the airfield wasting time for half
an hour.'

Inevitably – and quite rightly – it was the aircrews
of the Tornado GR1s and GR1As, the Jaguars and the
Buccaneers who drew the most attention and made the
noisiest returns. 'We came into Bruggen rather low and
rather fast,' declares Flt Lt John Hogg. The Buccaneers
put on a show too as they returned to Lossiemouth: 'I
don't know what the others did,' says Keith Nugent, 'but

we did about 400 knots at 300ft over the top of the crowd because the Buccaneer looks nicer at that kind of speed and height. It was raining and it was beautiful.' Below they could see a two mile tailback of cars, queuing to get onto the base to join the already-waiting crowds. At Bruggen, too, the station and the local community had pulled out all the stops, as Jerry Witts discovered: 'We came back in dribs and drabs over a week, essentially in three four-ship formations, and about 14 others had come home about five days ahead of us. It was a beautiful day coming up across France with the Alps covered in snow, the green fields and all the lovely things that you don't see in the desert. We'd had a bit of a tip-off that there might be a reception for us but I didn't expect to be greeted by the RAF Germany band and half the station with flags. The Deputy Air Commander was there and it was all a bit over the top really. I remember standing up in the plane and saying to Adie [his navigator], "God, I'm embarrassed. What do I do now?" He told me I could try getting out.'

Mal Craghill's reception at Laarbruch was impressive too, although he'd been flown back in a VC10: 'Before I reached the bottom of the steps I had a bottle of champagne in one hand and a bottle of beer in the other. I was then faced with the problem of how to shake hands with the Chief of the Air Staff. Then it was over to the squadron for some beers and back to the mess for some more beers – and to have 12 hours of solid drinking, not having had a great deal to drink for three months, was a shock to the system.'

Alcohol also played a leading role in Shaun Hayward's return: 'Getting back to the booze was the biggest adjustment I had to make. We'd had three tinnies of Carlsberg Special Brew on the Hercules in which we'd hitched a lift, and there was a party laid on for us when we landed. We had three tinnies there, another three in the bus – I can only just remember arriving home and the house being all set up with ribbons.'

For Mike Trace the joy of returning to his Puma squadron's base at Gütersloh was all the greater for the sense of relief he felt: 'I remember briefing all the troops on the aircraft intercom before we got in. I said, "We'll do some work this week and then we're going to have a complete month off – and expect some sort of reception when we get down". When we got out, the C-in-C RAF Germany was at the bottom of the steps with the station commander, and my wife Mary in between the two of them – so it was salute, hug, salute! There was also a piper at the bottom of the steps and the local fire brigade volunteer band was doing "oompah" stuff in the background. Then Mary and I watched 250 boys come off – the moment they stepped out of that aircraft and down the steps they were floating on air. That was the moment I'd dreamed of from the start of the operation – the thought of getting off the aircraft here with all the guys I went out with – everybody except a cook who lost a finger in an accident in the kitchen. I'd cracked it and you can imagine what I felt!'

One wing commander who was determined to arrive in style – as well as to provide in-flight catering to a high standard – was Peter Bedford, officer commanding the Hercules detachment in Riyadh. He flew back with his deputy and his movements officer, Chris Hewat, up on the flight deck: 'Unknown to the crew Chris had bought 2lbs of bacon at the American PX, which you could buy but not eat in Saudi Arabia. As soon as we were airborne the bacon went into the tiny little oven we had on board – as soon as we left Saudi airspace we were eating the most delicious bacon sandwiches. We were really buoyed up and exhilarated. The 11 hours just flew by with banter, chat, jokes and repartee. I changed out of my flying suit – for the first time in 10 weeks – into my nicely-pressed desert fatigues and tried out my Arab head-dress. We'd found an old water-pipe in Riyadh which fitted perfectly for a flagpole, and I'd had a huge Union Jack sent out. We'd even planned how we'd come in. We flew south of Lyneham, put the aircraft in a left-hand turn, did a lowish fly-past and then a turn downwind to land. We stopped out of sight of everyone, took the roof escape hatch out, put the Union Jack up, our Arab head-dresses on and taxied in nice and slowly past all the families – with the Union Jack fluttering.'

It was a time of emotional reunions: 'I just couldn't get the grin off my face,' remembers Tornado pilot Sqn Ldr Paul Brown – while for VC10 tanker pilot Flt Lt Paul Smith it was 'like getting married again. There were banners and flags and I could see my wife. I remember feeling very nervous.' And there were tears on all sides, as Dave Pullen recalls: 'My wife sent the boys in front – they came running up to us. I'm not an emotional person. I keep my emotions to myself but I opened up, floodgates all the way. My wife stood back until the boys had finished and then that was it, she started. But I'd repeat it again, just for that emotional part of being together again like that. Being away has made my marriage more complete – to come back and relive everything with them.'

Nowhere were there more mixed emotions than at Marham, Bruggen and Laarbruch when the seven freed PoWs returned from Cyprus following medical treatment and debriefings. 'The psychologists were very good,' declares Robbie Stewart. 'The guy who debriefed us had been up at Lockerbie and had a lot of experience. I had no real problems mentally. Although I was beaten I wasn't really tortured.' The conditions of his imprisonment had not however allowed his broken leg to heal properly: 'There is that underlying worry, but people who've been much worse than me have got back to flying.'

David Waddington takes an equally robust view of his experiences in Iraq: 'People think it was such a horrendous ordeal but at the end of the day it was only six weeks. It wasn't anything that can be compared to what the prisoners-of-war of the Japanese went through or even the prisoners-of-war in Vietnam. I don't have nightmares or anything, and mentally I think my family and certainly my fiancée suffered far more, because they thought I was dead.'

Their experiences made both men identify closely with the families of those killed in air operations. Waddington and Stewart's return to the station closed the door on any lingering hopes that the aircrew of the other downed Tornado from Marham might still be alive. 'The hope had been that all four would reappear,' Padre Ian Lambert explains. 'The joy of these two chaps coming back was overshadowed by the knowledge that it confirmed the deaths of the other two.'

Not everybody was lucky enough to be met by banners, bands and cheering families, particularly those whose homecoming was delayed for one reason or another. 'There was no heroes' welcome for us,' declares Ian Tervit, who flew back to Odiham as one of a handful of passengers in a loaded-up Hercules, arriving late at night. 'But the station commander and the community relations officer met us and took us to a big hangar where there was a table with wine and beer. They rushed us through customs – it was a case of, "Have you got anything?" "No". "OK, on you go". I had a quick can of beer – then a two and a half hour drive up to Cottesmore.'

Gary Woods' return was similarly low-key, having discovered that his wife had a previous engagement: 'When we found we were coming back on the Friday

I jumped into the Land Rover and went into town. We were allowed ten minutes on the phone for free, so I phoned the wife and she said, "I hope it's not Friday that you're coming home". "Why?" "We've got the Queen visiting the unit and I've been invited". I said, "Well, aren't you going to come and meet me?" She said, "I want to meet the Queen!" So coming home was spoilt, because I didn't get home till four o'clock in the morning and I had to get the missus out of bed with the dog having a go at me and barking.'

Many brought mementos of war – which had been approved and passed as safe – back with them. Brian Aitken returned to Kinloss with 'Republican Guard helmets, berets, gas masks, empty shells, bullet heads' from Kuwait. One Hercules crew did rather better and brought back a four-barrelled anti-aircraft gun.

Others returned with less tangible souvenirs. 'When we got to the airport it was just, "Bye, see you",' remembers Cpl Julie Pugh. 'We'd all been very friendly. Everybody had looked after one another and it had been brilliant. I hate making friends and then losing them again, but that's part of the job in the Air Force. We're bound to all meet up again anyway.' The friendships that developed were the best part of the war, as far as Gary Woods was concerned: 'The comradeship was great. You got to know everybody and now that I'm back I miss my mates. That was the best thing, together with the cheap cigarettes.' Gary Morris, too, misses his comrades in arms: 'For a couple of weeks after I got back, I'd be waking up about half-past five every morning and I'd look around and think, "Where are the lads?" You'd got so used to being with other people around you. You'd hear them shouting, taking the mick out of each other, and it was weird to have spent all that time living with a bloke and then you get back and find he's not there. There were about four of us in the pub one night and we were sort of looking around and thinking, "Who the hell are this lot here? Where's all the boys?"'

Many felt the same way: 'The bonding was so strong it took me three or four weeks to get over not being with my people,' admits music director Rob Wiffin. 'It was difficult readjusting. You find now that people who were out there talk together in huddles and there's a divide between them and people who weren't there. There's no hostility. It's just a shared experience.'

Nursing officer Sqn Ldr Francis Shannon is also aware of this 'common bond. People who weren't involved feel left out in a way. This morning, for instance, I'd just finished a general list and the theatre tech who was running the floor hadn't been to the Gulf whereas the anaesthetist and myself had. He said, "Right, this is a Gulf-free zone this morning, you two!"'

Mal Craghill of 16 Sqn does however see a negative side to this Gulf bonding: 'It crops up in conversation and we talk about things that happened. But it's important now to forget about it and get the squadron back together again because some of the guys didn't come out with us. It's important to get them back into the squadron and to get the squadron back together as a unit.'

Some Gulf veterans found it harder to return to normal life than others. John Williams' experience was typical: 'We went straight on leave with the adrenalin still going and it took me about a week to calm down. I live in a little village in Lincolnshire and the people there don't run about. Everything's very slow, and when you go down to get sausages from the butcher it takes you half an hour while you hear about his granny's ingrowing toenails. My wife used the adrenalin to get things done – she had me doing all sorts of things like decorating and building! It was also a big anticlimax. We were told we'd feel like that and I tried not to let myself, but I couldn't help it.'

Restlessness and inability to relax were common indications, since, as Gary Morris puts it: 'You've been working sometimes 16 or 18 hours a day and then, bang, they send you home and say, "Right, you've got a month's leave. You can do what you want". Everyone asked me, "Are you glad to be back?" and I said, "No, I'm bored out of my head".'

The stress of what they'd been through showed itself in different ways. For Francis Shannon there was an almost compulsive need to communicate: 'My mouth went into autotrot. I just could not stop talking about it. Because it was such a different experience and such a lot had happened, I wanted to get it out. I could vent my feelings, purge my soul in a way.' Peter Bedford, too, felt 'the need to talk about what you've done' – but it was coupled in his case with the feeling that 'if I spoke about it and tried to portray what I felt they wouldn't understand really – that it would be cheapening what had happened. I felt almost like I was in a cocoon back in this country. I'd been plucked out of one existence and suddenly I was back in a totally different world where life was just carrying on totally normally – and that was strange.'

Paul Brown found an outlet at his local village school: 'The children used to write to me quite a lot and the week after I got back I went to give them a talk. I explained everything in as simple terms as I could – exactly what the war was all about, why we went to war and what happened – all from my point of view.'

For Andy Garton the problem was insecurity: 'The first thing they took off us was our rifles, which was a bit disconcerting. It was like taking your lifeline away. Everybody was walking round for a few days saying, "I'm missing something", because we'd been carrying them around for the last three months and it was like, "Where's my handbag?" When I got home, which was only a few miles down the road from Cottesmore, I couldn't bloody sleep because, although I knew where it was, it wasn't near enough for my liking.'

The war had also affected SAC Fred Reid: 'I still have dreams about it,' he admits. 'The dream I had last week was the other way round. It was us on the receiving end of that lot. There were Iraqis in the town. I woke up in a cold sweat. And instead of using up my aggression out there I've brought it back. If the slightest thing goes wrong I'm up there climbing the ceiling, so the wife and kids have suffered.'

Before going into combat, aircrews had been briefed by psychiatrists on the effects of battle stress and post-traumatic stress. Most coped remarkably well, but inevitably there were one or two 'RTUs' (returned to unit). Equally inevitable was the fact that some youngsters found themselves in situations that they couldn't handle, something that upset Kevin Traynor greatly at the time: 'They were so stretched for manpower that they were taking people from outside the movements trade at Brize Norton and a lot of younger lads were sent out there, 17- and 18-year olds. Just after the war a young lad had been mine-clearing and was blown up by a mine. There was no coffin and this young lad was in a bag and had to be picked up off a Land Rover and loaded onto the aircraft. The young lads wouldn't move the body. So me and this other sergeant picked him up and laid him in the aircraft and brought him back to Al Jubayl. They wouldn't pick him up because they were scared. They'd been thrown in at the deep end and they couldn't cope.'

There was also the less obvious effect of stress on wives, husbands and children. 'My second eldest girl was very worried about Saddam Hussein and kept mentioning him in her letters,' remembers Flt Lt Steve Norrie. 'At night the girls still say, "You'll never go away to fight another war with a bad man, will you?" They still worry about it, although on the whole they coped with it very well.'

While some marriages thrived – 'it was like a second honeymoon' – others withered. 'That length of separation is always difficult,' states Bruggen families officer Flt Lt Geoff Cheetham. 'It always takes about two or three months to get back together again. She's got into her own routine and when he comes back he's in the way. She's had use of the car, probably for the first time in light years, and suddenly he's coming back and saying, "Sorry dear, I'll drop you off if I need the car for work today". We've had several marriage breakups since then, where the guy has come back and the wife has realised that she's happy enough on her own.' However, Cheetham makes the point that 'with the couples I've spoken to who were separating, the problem was there before. All the Gulf did really was to exacerbate it.'

Not surprisingly, getting back to pre-war routines was not always easy: 'It's like Sleepy Hollow back here,' complains Cpl Mickey Gibson of RAF Uxbridge. 'I miss the aircraft and the adrenalin flowing.' And for Tornado pilot Flt Lt Colin Adair his sorties out of Bruggen airfield now seem 'naff. They're very Mickey Mouse.'

As well as radically changing the habits of those involved, the Gulf War also changed personalities and attitudes, not always for the better: 'When I came back my wife said I'd lost my sense of humour,' says SAC Tam McLure. 'Before I was always laughing, but I suppose I'd changed because you do get hardened. When you're just with lads for four months you change. I was swearing all the time and chain-smoking. My sense of humour was more vicious. Even at work – before I had a wee bit of respect for my corporals and sergeants, now every time they say something I snap at them.'

However, for most people the effects have been positive. MAMS officer Rachael Berry, Tornado navigator Mark Robinson and air mech Andy Garton each make the same point in different ways: 'You tend to take each day as it comes,' says Berry. 'I don't get bothered about things as much. I sit back and think, "What are you really worrying about?" and usually it's trivia. The amount of times I now say to myself, "What does it matter?"' Mark Robinson also finds it hard to 'take life seriously anymore. I do my job because every time I get airborne now, I know it could lead to something, and I'm acutely aware of that. But on the ground, all this walking around with a hat on to be saluted, well, I really can't be bothered with little things like that.' Andy Garton feels he no longer takes life for granted: 'Before, at seven o'clock on a Friday night you'd think, "Right, I'll go out and get pissed!" and you'd come in at five on Saturday morning spewing your guts up everywhere. Now, I sit and think and say, "No, I don't fancy this very much. I won't bother". You start to think more about life and the quality of life. And not to have a shower or proper toilets makes you really appreciate showers and porcelain toilets.'

Francis Shannon believes he has gained in maturity – 'I'm more tolerant now in some respects and I'm not frightened of some situations. You're always a bit wary of senior people but now I think, "What can they do? Shout at me? Somebody was trying to kill me a couple of months ago! It's an improvement!"' – while steward Nigel Phipps feels he has learned to accept responsibility: 'You learn to cope with yourself and to bring other people through as well, because there are times when some people around you can't cope. At first you think, "Just go away". Then you find you have to bring everyone together, you have to make it work. I'd never have thought I was that kind of person. I used to think that I should look after myself, but after a while I found I had to look after everyone around me as well.'

Many returned Gulf veterans share the satisfaction of having passed a test both as individuals – 'the tremendous feeling that you've been to war, that you didn't fall apart, coped with a difficult challenge' – and as part of a group – 'everybody behaved so professionally, from the lowest SAC right the way up to the base commander. Everybody worked for each other and got on with their jobs. That was terrific.'

And as well as self-respect gained, there was the bonus of the respect of others: 'Back at camp everyone respects you. It's all, "Well done", and they mean it. They've a good idea of what it must have been like and they respect and admire you probably that bit more.' Equally satisfying – as well as a 'huge booster' to morale – was the feeling that people in the UK supported them. Of the hundreds of letters that came his detachment's way Jerry Witts came across only one that was hostile: 'The writer objected to something one of my young officers was reported to have said. He was being questioned about civilian casualties and the punchline was that he'd said, "If you get killed, tough". What he'd meant was that if you happen to be sitting on a military target, and get hit by a bomb, that's pretty tough. But this chap was outraged and said he intended to write to the Ministry of Defence to demand the officer's dismissal or whatever. So I wrote him a polite letter saying that I disagreed with what he said – but that I would fight to the death for his right to say it.'

Widespread among those who went out to the Gulf was the conviction that this was a 'just war' – an assertion about which there were few dissenting voices. For some, like the Tornado GR1 pilot, the question of personal opinions was irrelevant because 'at the end of the day, you do what the taxpayer wants. And if the taxpayer wants to send people to the Gulf to fight, then that's it. You go and do it, whether you think it's right or wrong.' But for many more it was a war fought with conviction, tempered with regret: 'We came to fight a war,' says the Tornado F3 pilot. 'We fought the war, but at the back of my mind was the reason we were doing it, which was to get the Iraqis out of Kuwait. The ultimate result of war is devastation, and it should always be avoided if possible, but in this case it wasn't possible. I feel no satisfaction about it, but I'm relieved it was done in the way it was.'

'I can't remember having any conversations with people who said we shouldn't be there or that it wasn't our fight,' declares the director of music. 'I think we were all pleased that it was done the way it was, with a great show of force – that overwhelming force kept the casualties down. There was a lot in the press about this being all about oil, but when we were out there we didn't feel we were fighting to save oil. Nor did we feel any intense hatred towards the Iraqis, because we all felt very, very sorry for them. But after a while some Kuwaiti interpreters joined us in anticipation of prisoners-of-war coming down. Their stories of how families had been raped and murdered made you feel more resentful of the enemy.'

It is the belief of a detachment commander that 'we nipped it in the bud, that Saddam would have taken Kuwait, digested it, and moved on to Saudi and the Gulf states. We would undoubtedly have had a worse job if we'd left it any longer. The treatment he handed out to the Kurds would inevitably have been their fate and many of the other people around the Gulf who didn't see eye to eye with him.'

The air commander sees the conflict as 'a watershed' between the old Cold War power blocs and the new, more unstable world order of the 1990s; the Rapier squadron commander as 'an historic occasion' with the United Nations 'actually getting to work and doing something useful – with the US pushing it', and leaving 'the world a better place'.

At a lower level in the rank structure, the allies' role in the war seemed more personal, expressed in such terms as: 'He had to be stopped and that was that'; 'we couldn't let the guy get away with it'; 'the enemy, as far as I was concerned, was one person'; and 'we all had a tremendous feeling of incredulity that one man could cause so much heartache, so much pain'.

When it came to their own war leaders, however, there were few who did not feel they were very fortunate. General Schwarzkopf was admired because 'he was so unBritish and could get straight to the point' – and General Sir Peter de la Billière precisely because he was so British, as well as being, 'a real hard case. You just have to look in his eyes to realise that he was not a bloke to piss around.'

With hindsight, it could be argued President Bush's ceasefire call came 24 hours too soon. However, this was not the view at the time. 'The liberation of Kuwait was what we went out to attain, and that's what happened,' says the Buccaneer navigator. 'Once he [President Bush] said, "Right, that's it", everybody said, "Smashing". That was exactly what we'd set out to do, so everybody was happy not to go any further.' The GR1 pilot saw it as 'a quick clean job' that had to end when it did for political reasons: 'It's cynical to say this, but the ideal length of time for a media-orientated war appears to be something in the region of 40 days. Anything longer than that and people would have started losing interest.' The chief technician takes the view that 'had we carried on it would have caused more problems than it would have solved'. The mission planner emphasises the allies' common aim: 'The sovereign state of Kuwait should be returned to the Kuwaitis. We were doing what we ought, through the United Nations. It was really the belief of the whole world.'

Mistakes were made and lessons learned. From those who had the most to lose, because they had to 'put their lives on the line' as aircrew, come such thoughts and comments as 'My God, I hope we've learned now that air power is the decisive factor'; that 'we need to be as flexible as we can possibly be'; that 'you've got to have really good equipment from the word go so you can practise with it, rather than things arriving at the last minute'; that 'if snags had been spotted and reported in peacetime, we could have foreseen the problems'; that 'too much came from up top and a lot of the expertise we had at squadron and station level was ignored'; and, from a more personal point of view, that because 'it was a war we were always going to win, we took chances we didn't need to' and that 'my little pink body wasn't really cared about as much at high level as it was by me'.

There were some who had more cause for dissatisfaction than others – 'being a woman out there wasn't much fun. We wore clothes that didn't show any skin or any shape to keep the Arabs happy. As females we weren't allowed to go out unaccompanied or to drive. We couldn't eat in the same public restaurants as men without a screen, and we weren't allowed into the same shops as men. We tried to meet them halfway but we did feel like second class citizens' – while others' needs were more basic: 'The worst thing was the compo food. It looks different but it all tastes the same. You have cottage pie one day but it's steak and kidney, and the next day they've put a little crust on it but it's still steak and kidney. I used to like compo sausages before I went out there, but not any more.'

Despite these disadvantages, most look back with pride at their achievements. The first detachments who were rushed out in August served their purpose: 'If he'd attacked then, when we only had a couple of squadrons in, and we'd all died, the public would have said, "My God, get out there and take this guy out". Saddam knew that and I think we stopped him. We were then allowed the time to build up forces to go and beat him. That was brilliant. We didn't get any medals but I get a nice warm feeling about it.' From the very beginning, too, there was the 'non-glamour aspect of it' as all the supporting units on stations in the UK and Germany swung into action: 'Perhaps we'd like a pat on the back to say, "Yes, you did a good job", to all the people at Brize – where the volume of freight handled was greater than the Berlin airlift – or wherever, who worked harder than those in the Gulf, but were getting no recognition for it.'

There were also those at headquarters: 'The guys who were in the front line deserve every accolade, but the headquarters did their bit. It was a team effort, and the team worked, but it's the old adage that the reward is in the planning.' There were units that performed far beyond their highest expectations: 'The greatest achievement on the small scale was that we, as a tanker unit, flew every mission we were asked to fly and didn't fall down on one. We achieved 100% of what we were asked to do.' There were units that never expected to be required to go to war: 'If the hardest thing for me to take was the politics that got us out there in the first place, I'm proudest of our musicians and the way they took on such strange areas of responsibility when a war role was suddenly thrust on us.' There were units who had trained to go to war and found themselves more than up to the task: 'We were lucky. You can always pick and choose people but I think we were fortunate that at the time we had the right people in 29 Sqn. It's important when the chips are down that people know exactly what they've got to do – and all the guys here did it.' Drawing all these units together was 'this undercurrent of adrenalin that made you feel you were part of something that would go down in history', that expressed itself in team-spirit: 'We were really thrown together, we were working closely with each other and it was a superb team.'

Individuals gained in understanding – 'I've learned that I can go to war and that I can control the fear. I've learned a lot about human relationships. I now understand when I go down to the British Legion with my father on a Saturday night for a couple of pops. I understand now why they're still doing that 40 years on. I now understand that camaraderie'; and in fulfilment: 'I feel very privileged to have been there and feel very lucky that I went. It was a hell of an experience, but worth it just for those peaks of awareness. It was the best experience of my life, the most boring time of my life as well. You can come back and talk to people but they haven't experienced it and they don't really understand.'

As well as the insights gained, there are the memories: 'The memories do fade very quickly, along with the sun tans. I don't think we talk about it that much, but occasionally someone will mention a little event that took place – and as with all memories you tend to remember the good times rather than the bad.' One will remember the smell 'of almonds, because when we first put on our respirators they smelt of almonds and nobody had warned us, so there was a slight panic'; another the smell 'of fig trees and dusty sand'; a third the smell of 'stagnant water, because when it rained it

came down in buckets but it would never soak away';
and a fourth 'our own smell, because there was no time
to get away and have showers and it was so hot you
sweated buckets'.

There were also the sights as well as the memorable
moments: 'the single palm tree in the desert that was
miles from anywhere'; 'the aircraft sitting on the airfield that I strafed after we'd dropped our laser-guided
bombs – with the navigator in the back shouting out
the heights as we plummeted down'; 'seeing people
happy that they've got their country back, the tears
of joy on the women's faces – and sharing things with
the kids'; 'the entry in the aircrew's final log book in
green ink. Normally it's written in blue or black, but
on an operational mission the entry is in green. The
last occurrence of green writing would have been in the
Falklands War, prior to that Suez and Korea, and prior
to that the Second World War. That's something you
can show your grandchildren.'

Whatever future generations make of the Gulf War,
its epitaph comes from one who flew combat missions,
but who speaks for all who saw service with the RAF
during the conflict: 'It's something you wish had never,
ever happened, just as the situation itself should never
have arisen. But it did – you were there and you're glad
to be one of the ones who was there.'

GLOSSARY

A

AEDIT – Aircraft Engineering Installation Team
AEOps – Air Electronics Operator
AHQ – Air Headquarters
aircrew – RAF airman or airwoman, usually a commissioned officer, with a flying role
APC – armoured personnel carrier
APV – armoured personnel vehicle
AWACS – airborne warning and control system, thus AWACS aircraft

B

Baldrick Lines – tented accommodation at Al Jubayl, named after a character in the *Blackadder* TV series
berm – sand barrier
Blackadder Lines – tented accommodation at Al Jubayl, named after the *Blackadder* TV series
blanket stackers – RAF suppliers (slang)
blue on blue – an unintentional attack by a force on members of its own side

blueys – free air mail letters provided for HM forces (slang)
bondu – wasteland
bonedome – helmet (slang)
Bumrate – Thumrait, Oman (slang)
bund – embankment

C

CAP – combat air patrol
can-opener – Tornado GR1 (slang)
casevac – casualty evacuation
chaff – metallic streamers put out by aircraft to confuse radar
chalks – chalk marks indicating aircraft loads
CNN – Cable News Network
clicks – kilometres
colpro – collective protection
compo – composite rations
cross-hairs – aiming lines on bomb sights
C-in-C – commander-in-chief

D

daisy cutter – 15,000lb fuel-air bomb (slang)
Desert Shield – Pentagon code-name for the defensive phase of the deployment of allied troops in the Gulf
Desert Storm – Pentagon code-name for the offensive phase of the Gulf War
Dylan – Nimrod call sign

E
ESM – electronic support measures

F

Fat Albert – Hercules (slang)
flick-knife – Tornado F3 (slang)
FMA – forward maintenance area
fourship – a group of four aeroplanes
frag – fragment
full Lawrence – Arab robe and headdress (slang)

G

GAFA – Great Arabian F*** All, desert training area (slang)
G-Day – the day the ground war started (thus G+1 indicates second day of ground war)
GDT – ground defence training
Go bag – collection of items carried by aircrew on combat sorties
goolie chit – reward note carried by aircrew on combat sorties
GR1 – abbreviation applied to strike attack aircraft, most usually Tornado
GR1A – a version of the Tornado GR1 modified for reconnaissance
Granby – Ministry of Defence code-name for British military deployment in the Gulf
g-suit – gravity suit worn by fast-jet aircrew

H

HAS – hardened aircraft shelter
half-Lawrence – Arab headdress worn without robe
heads-down mode – when pilot/navigator has to look down at instruments

GLOSSARY

Hell's Highway – scene of mass destruction on the Basra
  road north of Kuwait
H-hour – start of air war
HUD – head-up display (in aircraft)

I

IFF – Interrogate Friend or Foe
ISO containers – large corrugated iron containers
interim NBC kit – modified suit providing a degree of
  protection from NBC attack for aircrew
in theatre – within area of deployment

J

JP233 – airfield 'denial' package of bombs and mines
  carried in a pod by Tornado GR1

K

KK International – King Khalid International Airport,
  Riyadh
KKMC – King Khalid Military City
killing road – see 'Hell's Highway'

L

liney – front line servicing aircraft tradesman/trades-
  woman (slang)
loadie – aircraft loadmaster (slang)

LSJ – life saving jacket

M

Mae West – life jacket (slang)
Magic Roundabout – codename for annual Nimrod deployment in Gulf of Oman
MAMS – Mobile Air Movements Squadron
MAWS – missile approach warning system
medevac – medical evacuation
MLRS – mobile launch rocket system
MMIF – Multi-national Maritime International Force
MSR – main supply route
MT – motor transport
mud mover – Tornado GR1

N

NAAFI – Navy, Army and Air Force Institution, which runs shops and canteens for forces members
NBC suit – nuclear, biological and chemical warfare protection suit
NCO – non-commissioned officer
NVG – night vision goggles
NIAD – nerve-agent immobilised-enzyme alarm detector
noddy suit – NBC suit (slang)

O

OC – officer commanding
OCU – operational conversion (training) unit
Ops – operations

P

pan – hardened surfaces of airfield (slang)
pillow tanks – pillow-shaped fuel tanks
PG – Persian Gulf
PI – practice intercept
picture clean – no enemy threats
PM – RAF nurse, from Princess Mary's RAF Nursing Service
pongo – infantry soldier (slang)
purple – joint armed forces (combined colours of Army, Navy and RAF)
PX – US military shop

Q

QRA – quick reaction alert

R

R and R – rest and recreation
recce – reconnaissance
Red Flag – combined allied anti-Soviet air exercises in Texas
REME – Royal Electrical and Mechanical Engineers
ROE – rules of engagement
RSAF – Royal Saudi Air Force
RTU – returned to unit
RWR – radar warning receiver

S

SAM – surface to air missile

Sandy House – British AHQ, Riyadh (after AVM Sandy Wilson) – aka 'White House'
sangar – defensive post made up of stones or sandbags
Scud – Russian ground-to-ground missile
SENGO – senior engineering officer
skyflash – air-to-air missile
snowdrops – RAF police (slang)
sootie – engineer tradesman/tradeswoman (slang)
SUCAP – surface combat air patrol
squippers – safety equipment fitters

T

TA – tactical area
TACC – tactical air control centre
tanking – air-to-air refuelling
TAP – target approach point
tasked – given orders
TOT – time on target
TRA – tactical refuelling of aircraft (mid-air refuelling)
triple A – anti-aircraft artillery
TSW – Tactical Supply Wing
TURD – towed radar decoy (TRD)

W

White House – see 'Sandy House'
Wild Weasels – USAF anti-radar aircraft
wingman – second aircraft in a pair

INDEX

INDEX